TECHNOLOGIES FOR WATER AND WASTEWATER MANAGEMENT

ENV BOOKS SERIES

TECHNOLOGIES FOR WATER AND WASTEWATER MANAGEMENT

Editors

Dr. Vijender Singh
Director
Green Consultancy and Research Pvt. Ltd.
3263, Urban Estate, Jind (Haryana)
(India)

&

Dr. Pawan Kumar 'Bharti'
Society for Environment, Health Awareness of
Nutrition & Toxicology (SEHAT)
B-225/5D, Top Floor, Subhash Gali, Road No. 7, Block B
Ashok Nagar, Shahdara, Delhi - 110 093
(India)

DPH

DISCOVERY PUBLISHING HOUSE PVT. LTD.
INDIA

Published by:
Namit Wasan

DISCOVERY PUBLISHING HOUSE PVT. LTD.
4383/4B, Ansari Road, Darya Ganj
New Delhi-110 002 (India)
Phone : +91-11-23279245; 23253475; 43596065
E-mail : discoverybooksindia@gmail.com
discoverypublishinghouse@gmail.com
namitwasan9@gmail.com
web : www.discoverypublishinggroup.com

First Edition: **2020**

ISBN: 978-93-88854-53-5

Technologies for Water and Wastewater Management

Printed at:
Infinity Imaging Systems
Delhi

PREFACE

The life support system on this planet consists of air, water, land, flora and fauna. Normally these are mutually interconnected and also interdependent. The activities of man constitute one single factor, which often disrupt the intricate balance among the foregoing constituents of the life support system. In his eagerness to urbanize and industrialize, man has not only destroyed plant cover built up meticulously by nature over millions of years, but also polluted air, water and land, so much so that development has become synonymous with deforestation and desertification and progressed with pollution.

Water is one of the most important substances on earth. All plants and animals must have water to survive. If there was no water there would be no life on earth. Fresh water resources have faced a crisis worldwide for the last five decades. The crisis is growing rapidly. This is manifested in numerous challenges showing the various elements of the problem. These challenges include, increasing scarcity of fresh water, lack of accessibility to adequate clean drinking water and sanitation, deterioration of water quality, fragmentation of water management, nationally and globally, threat to world peace and security and a continuing lack of awareness of the magnitude of the problem by the decision makers and the public at large.

The present book updates the subject content of Water Resources on Earth; Water Crisis Management; watershed development; ground water movement, and modeling; effluent for crop farming; Arsenic Removal by Saw Dust; Effect of Wastewater on Trees.

Thanks are due to publisher and contributors from various institutions and universities.

The book will be helpful for the researchers, academia working in the field of Water Resources on Earth; Water Crisis Management; Water scarcity in agriculture; watershed development, water use efficiency challenges and policy; ground water movement, and modeling; Utilization of treated water effluent for crop farming; Arsenic Removal by Saw Dust; Effect of Wastewater on Growth of Trees.

Editors
(envbooks@gmail.com)

CONTENTS

Preface

1. Water Resources on Earth 1

   Pawan Kumar 'Bharti'

2. Water Crisis Management and Policy Interventions 16

   Anitha G. and Esakkimuthu M.

3. Hydrogeological Setting and Status of Water Table in Bonai Area of Sundargarh District, Odisha, India 38

   Pramod Chandra Sahu

4. Water Scarcity in Agriculture: *Watershed Development, Water Use Efficiency Challenges and Policy* 63

   Anitha G. and Esakkimuthu M.

5. Basic Concept of Ground Water Movement, Monitoring and Modeling 91

   Pawan Kumar 'Bharti'

6. Utilization of Treated Water Effluent for Crop Farming 97

   Anitha G. and Esakkimuthu M.

7. Thermodynamics, Kinetics Study and Statistical Approach of Arsenic Removal in Waste Water Utilizing Activated Carbon from Saw Dust in Different Impregnation Ratio 123

   Swapnila Roy, Ashok Kumar Shaw

8. Effect of Urban Wastewater on Growth and Development of Multipurpose Tree Species 145

   Alok Kumar Patra, Ambraprava Mishra and Ranjan Kumar Kar

Index 169

Technologies for Water and Wastewater Management Pages 1-15
Edited by: Dr. Vijender Singh & Dr. Pawan Kumar 'Bharti'
ISBN: 978-93-88854-53-5
Edition: 2020
Published by: Discovery Publishing House Pvt. Ltd., New Delhi (India)

1

Water Resources on Earth

Pawan Kumar 'Bharti'

World's available freshwater supply is not distributed uniformly around the globe throughout the seasons or from year to year. Nearly three quarters of the worlds annual rainfall comes down in areas inhabited by less than one third of the world's population, while two third of the world's population lived in areas receiving only one quarter of the world's annual rainfall. A water crisis, which has come about because rain as a source of water has been ignored. The potential of rain to meet water demand is tremendous. Theoretically, the average rainfall of 100 mm of rain falling on one hectare of land in arid regions like Jaisalmer can yield up to one million liters of water.

Despite several initiatives taken by Government & public bodies, in 1995 some 20% of the world's population of 5.7 billion people still lacked safe, fresh and reliable water supply, while more than 50% were without adequate sanitation system. Today, thirty-one countries having nearly 8% of the total population face water shortages, affecting more than 2.8 billion people, which is more than one third of the world's projected population.

1. Water on Earth

The amount of freshwater available on Earth today is no more than that was available 2,000 years ago when the Earth's population was less than 3% of its current size. Rising demands of water in agriculture, domestic (municipal) consumption and industry are forcing stiff competition over the distribution of scare water resource, both amongst different regions and types of use. Water is likely to play the same role in world economy in the 21st century that oil played in the 20th century and will be source of conflicts world over to pose a major threat to human security if proper preventive measures are not taken globally. Growing water scarcity has become a very real obstacle to sustainable development.

Water is not only essential for life but predominant inorganic constituent of living matter forming in general nearly three quarters of the weight of living cells. It makes some 5 percent of the body weight of an adult human and can forms as 98% of the mass of certain jellyfish. Organisms that contain relatively small amounts of water are generally in dormant state or show very slow development; seeds and certain invertebrates that live in arid environments are examples. On the other hand high rainfall over a landmass in variably means a large biomass per unit area.

India is a rich country in natural resources. One has to realize the need and importance of water conservation. Conservation and management of water resources was advocated even in ancient times when there was not much pressure on this resource. This is evident from this verse as quoted from the Atharva Veda:

आपो यद् वस्तपस्तेन तं प्रतितपत यो।
स्मान द्वेष्टि यं वयं द्विष्मः।।
-अथर्व0 2: 23: 1

i.e. water of river, well, pond etc, if used and managed efficiently will reduced the intensity of drought and water scarcity. Some such strategies of water conservation/management are described in his pamphlet. Water is used in everything people do; for irrigation, for industry, for power generation, for navigation, drinking, cooling, waste disposal and recreation.

Water conservation basically aims at matching demand and supply. The strategies for water conservation may be either demand oriented or supply oriented. The strategies may vary depending upon the field of water use domestic, irrigation or industrial. Some of the supply oriented strategies such as creation of storage; long distance transfer and control of water loss through evaporation are generally common to all the fields of water use, whereas the others may be applicable only to specific field.

Storage of water by construction of various water resources projects has been one of the measures of water conservation. A reference from Vrahat Sanhita (550 A.D.) as quoted below describes utility of ponds for effective storage of water.

पाली प्रागणरायताम्बु सुचिरं धात्ते न याम्योन्तरा।
क्ल्लौलैख दारमेति मरूता सा प्रयष्ठाः प्रेरितैः।।
तां चेदिच्छति सारदारूमिरपा सम्पातमावांरयेत,
पाज़ाणदिभिरेव वा प्रतिचयं क्षुज़्णं द्विपा वादिभि।
वृहत संहिता- 54: 118

i.e. a pond laid East to West remains water for a long time while one from North to South is spoilt invariably by the waves raised by the winds. To render it stable the walls have to be lined with timber or with stone and the adjoining soil strengthened by stamping and tramping of elephants, horses etc.

For centuries, streams and rivers have provided a convenient place to dump wastes. Today, water pollution comes from many different sources.

These include untreated sewage, industrial discharge, leakage from oil storage tanks, mine drainage and mine drainage and pesticides. Water pollution varies in severity in one region to the next depending on the density of urban development, agricultural and industrial practices and the presence or absence of system for collecting and treating the wastewater. The large industrial cities of the world produce huge amount of sewage, both from households and industries, causing problems not only for human health but also for ecosystems.

Industry is also highly water-intensive. For example, making one tonne of steel can consume as much as 300 tonnes of water. Driven by stiffer regulations and the need to cut costs, such water-intensive industries as chemicals, iron and steel, and pulp and paper have made impressive strides in reducing the amount of water in current production processes. Some of these industries have also redesigned production processes, which require less water per unit of production.

Conserving water for personal use in cities (including use by households and municipalities) requires managing both the supply of and demand for water. Much of the municipal water supply is lost before it can reach consumers, leaking out of water mains, pipes, and faucets, or disappearing through illegal tapes. Moreover, when they have convenient access to running water, consumers often use much, more water than they actually need. In India over 40% of the total municipal water supply is lost in transit, before it reaches the consumers. In most cities, nothing more than tightening the joints in the water pipes and fixing leaky community standpipes and household connections could save more than one third of the water that is currently wasted. Many cities could manage the water supply better if they could eliminate illegal water taps. Beside, treated wastewater can be used for purposes where the quality standard requirements are not very high, for example, flushing toilets, washing cars, cleaning floors, gardening, etc.

Since agriculture accounts for nearly 70% of all water withdrawn from rivers, lakes and underground aquifers for human use, large potential for conservation lies with increasing irrigation, efficiencies. Typically, only about 45% of water withdrawn for irrigated agriculture ever reaches the crops. Even when sufficient irrigation water reaches agriculture fields, it can spoil much of the land unless drained properly. Also, poorly drained irrigation water can raise the groundwater table until it reaches the root zone, thereby water logging and drowning crops. Globally some 80 million hectares of farmland have been degraded by a combination of salinization and waterlogging. Efficient irrigation techniques not only save water but also protect the land. Drip irrigation is one such technique. It consists of a network of perforated piping, usually installed on the surface or just below ground, which delivers water directly to the root zone of crops. This technique keeps evaporation losses low, at an efficiency rate of 95%. Drip irrigation systems can cut water use by an estimated 50% compared with gravity systems.

Another promising conservation technique–low-energy precision application (LEPA) – offers substantial improvements over conventional sprinkler systems that spray water in to air. Instead the low-energy precision application method delivers water to the crops from drop tubes that extend from the sprinkler's arm. When applied together with appropriate water-saving farming techniques, this method also can achieve efficiencies as high as 95%. Since this method operates at low pressure, it results in 20% to 50% energy savings as compared to conventional systems.

Apart from leakage and pilferage, another major reason for large-scale wastage of municipal water in cities is the nominal cost or no cost charged for it. Water should be treated as a commodity and sold to consumers at rates that reflect its value in order to encourage conservation. With higher cost recovery, utilities in developing countries could improve the quality and availability of water even in low-income areas. Water supply projects require huge capital investments, yet cities are faced with diminishing funds for urban water supply to provide for the burgeoning urban populations.

According to a recent analysis of a World Bank financed project, in developing countries, consumers play only about 35% of the costs of supplying water. Recovering a greater percentage of these costs could provide city managers with funds to expand coverage to new areas or to maintain and improve existing facilities. Other measures that could reduce municipal demand include: building codes that require installation of low flush toilets, low water use landscaping – known as xeriscaping – in arid and semi arid areas. Such measures could be adopted in both developed and developing countries.

2. Distribution of Water

About 30% of the area of the continents (except Antarctica) is underlain by relatively homogeneous aquifers containing important groundwater reserves. About 19% is endowed with groundwater, some of which is extensive, in geologically complex regions. Half of the continental area contains generally minor occurrences of groundwater that are restricted to near-surface unconsolidated gravels, sands, and rock debris; but these groundwater resources are still sufficient to sustain small to medium-sized population centres. Fifteen percent of the world's land area receives less than 200 mm average annual precipitation (c. 200 litres per square metre). In these low rainfall regions there is normally very little groundwater recharge, so groundwater used will not generally be replaced for hundreds - perhaps thousands of years. Extraction in these areas must therefore be considered as "mining" a limited resource, rather than tapping a continuous supply. The geological conditions and hydro-geological characteristics of the rocks are critical controls on groundwater quantity, quality and flow regime. According to the UN, Planet Earth's mean annual renewable volume of water is 43,000 cubic kilometres. This is about half of all the fresh water contained in all the Earth's natural lakes and about ten times the volume of all man-made reservoirs. Groundwater recharge accounts for about 10,000 cubic kilometres annually, (c. 0.1% of all groundwater resources). Thus, only a tiny proportion of the total volume of groundwater reserves is recharged each year, compared to the large volume in stock (www.yearofplanetearth.org).

Some groundwater systems are non-renewable under current climatic conditions because they formed under much wetter climates that prevailed perhaps 1000 or 10,000 years ago. These groundwater reservoirs are being increasingly "mined" in the arid zones of the world. For example, in the north-eastern Sahara, the Nubian Sandstone Aquifer System underlies an area of more than two million square kilometres in Chad, Egypt, Libya and Sudan, and contains huge amounts of fresh groundwater. It is thought to contain about a hundred times the present annual global water consumption. Giant groundwater deposits of comparable size and limited recharge are thought to exist on nearly all continents, but the amount of groundwater that can be pumped out is unknown. Information about the age, travel times and flow of the water underground, and other features such as chemical characteristics and processes are needed.

Water covers nearly 70% of the globe, but most of it is salt water that fills the oceans. By volume, less than 3% of all the water on earth is freshwater, most of which lies frozen in Antarctica and Greenland in Polar ice and is unavailable to humanity. Less than 1% of the all water on earth is easily accessible in the form of surface freshwater, found in lakes, rivers and underground in shallow aquifers. This amount of water is regularly renewed by precipitation in the form of rain and snowfall or by melt by glaciers in the mountains and supplemented by dew and fog drip in some locations.

Atmospheric water is about % of the total estimated distribution of world's water resources taking part in the hydrological cycle. It is also estimated that the freshwater resources is about 3%, 77.2% of this is in cold storage, frozen in the ice caps and glaciers. Most of the remaining supply of freshwater i.e. 22.4% is groundwater and soil moisture. This leaves only a very small amount of fresh surface water i.e. 0.35% contained in lakes and swamps and less than 0.01% in rivers and streams. The freshwater resources with their estimated volumes in km^3 with average residence time in the earth environment are:

Atmospheric water	-	113,000 (8 to 10 days)
Oceans and open seas	-	1,370,000,000 (4000 + years)
Freshwater lakes and reservoirs	-	125,000 (from days to years)

Saline lakes and inland seas	-	104,000
River channels	-	1,700 (2 weeks)
Swamps and marshes	-	3,600 (years)
Biological waters	-	65,000 (1 week- used by plants)
Moisture in soil & unsaturated zone	-	65,000 (2 week to 1 year- zones of aeration
Groundwater	-	4,000,000 to 60,000,000 (10 days to thousands of years
Frozen water (Glaciers & ice caps)	-	30,000,000 (10 days to thousands of years)

The total quantity of water on our planet is fixed and its distribution is highly uneven. Almost 95% of the total water present on the earth is chemically bound in to rocks and does not cycle. Of the remainder, about 97.3% is in the ocean, about 2.15 exists as ice in the polar caps and permanent glaciers and the rest is freshwater present in the form of atmospheric water vapour, ground water, and inland surface water. Thus, less than one percent of the total freshwater precipitates in the hydrological cycle.

Table 1.11: Total Estimated Water Resources on Earth.

S. No.	Reserves	Volume Km^3	Percentage
1.	Oceans	1,32,20,00,000	92.200
2.	Ice caps & Glaciers	2,92,00,000	2.150
3.	Underground	41,70,000	0.625
4.	Freshwater Lakes	1,25,000	0.009
5.	Saline Lakes & Inland Seas	1,04,000	0.008
6.	Soil Moisture	67,000	0.005
7.	Atmosphere	13,000	0.001
8.	Rivers	1,250	0.001
	Total	**1,35,56,80,250 Km^3**	**100%**

3. Water Demand & Crisis

A water crisis that has come about, because rain, as a source of water has been ignored. The potential of rain to meet water demand is tremendous. Theoretically, the average rainfall of 100 mm of rain falling on one hectare of land in arid regions like Jaisalmer can yield up to one million litres of water.

The demand for water is continually growing globally at an accelerated pace. The demand for water in various sectors including domestic use, irrigation, energy and industry etc, during year 1990 and projections four years 2000 & 2025 are given in Table 1.1. The total quantum for water available on the average may be enough to meet all our demands put together. But its availability is highly irregular. It is not available in places where we want it, at times when we want it and in which we want it – hence the need for conservation.

Table 1.2: Demands for Various Sectors.

Purpose	Demand (km³) - in the year		
	1900	2000	2025
Domestic use	25	33	52
Irrigation	460	630	770
Energy	19	27	71
Industrial use	15	30	120
Others	33	30	37
Total	552	750	1050
Surface water	362	500	700
Ground water	190	250	350

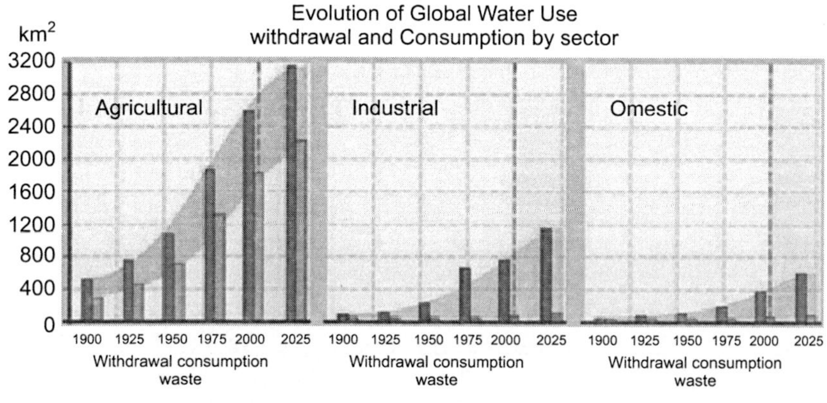

Fig. 1.1: Water requirement for various sectors (source: www.yearofplanetearth.org)

Conservation is defined as preservation against loss of waste. Technically conservation of water implies the same meaning in a much wider perspective. Briefly stated it means putting the water resources of the country for the best beneficial use with all the technologies at our command. In other words, surface water running down to sea should be stored to the maximum extant, evaporation and other losses minimized and benefits spread with the sole criteria of maximum benefit to maximum number having due regard to the properties like drinking, irrigation, industrial use, navigation etc.

World's available freshwater supply is not distributed uniformly around the globe throughout the seasons or from year to year. Nearly three quarters of the worlds annual rainfall comes down in areas inhabited by less than one third of the world's population, while two third of the world's population lived in areas receiving only one quarter of the world's annual rainfall.

Despite several initiatives taken by Government & public bodies, in 1995 some 20% of the world's population of 5.7 billion people still lacked safe and reliable water supply, while more than 50% were without adequate sanitation system. Today, thirty-one countries having nearly 8% of the total population face water shortages, affecting more than 2.8 billion people, which is more than one third of the world's projected population.

Among the country likely to run short of water in the next 25 years are India, Ethiopia, Kenya, Nigeria, Peru, China, Bangladesh. Now more than 25 countries already facing chronic water problems. Groundwater, which now accounts for 80% of rural and 60% of the urban water supply in India, is depleting at an alarming rate. In fact, today 19 major cities of India already face chronic water shortage.

Many rivers are already dead or dying. All the 13 great river systems in India are endangered. They are fought over and dammed in discriminately by states to provide water for irrigation and industrial use. A typical example of dying river is the Yamuna in Delhi. Because of overuse, there is no original water left in the Yamuna at Delhi. Instead it carries only narrow streams of urban and industrial wastewater. The result of tests conducted by a reputed institute of Delhi on Yamuna water is alarming. For example, the biochemical oxygen demand (BOD), which is a measure of the burden of organic waste from industries and sewage, was found to have a value between 4-75 mg/l in Yamuna water at different sites in Delhi. The permissible level of BOD is 3 mg/l or less for human consumption. Similarly dissolved oxygen, which is essential for aquatic life and measures the amount of oxygen dissolved in water, was found to be much below the required level of 5 mg/l in Yamuna water at most test sites in Delhi. This indicates that no aquatic life can survive in the Yamuna along its entire stretch in Delhi. The only exception being the water at the Wazirabad barrage, the point where Yamuna enters Delhi.

The public sector has often failed to deliver sustainable water supply and adequate sewage treatment systems. Although officially 70% of Delhi's sewage is treated, in realty, due to the malfunctioning of ill-maintained sewage treatment plants, half that volume comes out as raw sewage. The polluted water, improper sewage disposal, and poor water management combined together cause serious public health problems. The coliform count, which is an indicator of contamination by bacteria coming mainly through domestic sewage, is found to be between 23,000 and 1,40,000 in most of the Yamuna water in Delhi. The upper level of safe level of coliform count is 500. Once again, Yamuna water only at Wazirabad is found to be safe in terms of coliform count, with a value of only 28.

The world is now facing water crisis of dimensions that no earlier generation has had to face. It may already be late for some water scare countries with rapid population growth to avoid a water crisis unless they take immediate and drastic steps for sustainable management of urban water resources. But a water crisis in the near future can be avoided if appropriate policies and strategies are formulated and acted upon quickly. In this regard, water conservation and its better management are the effective strategies for consideration. To avoid a catastrophe over the long term, it is also important to act to reduce the demand of freshwater by slowing the population growth. Urgent and decisive action must begin now if regional water crisis are to be avoided during the next century. There is an imperative need to change people's attitudes towards water. Water must be an environmental issue at the top of the agenda of Governments, institutions and individuals alike. Because knowledge of water resources and availability is the key to development, access to reliable water data needs to be given high priority by governments. At local level, everyone must use water more efficiently without wasting it. At the national level, especially in water scare-regions with dense population, adopting a watershed or river basin management perspective or harvesting of rainwater is required as an alternative to uncoordinated water-management policies. At the international level, countries that share river basins can design workable policies to manage water resources more equitably.

Ancient techniques of water harvesting, like digging of deep underground chambers for storing rainwater from the wet season for use during the dry season, or placing of long lines of stones along the contours of gently sloping ground to slow runoff and spread the water across a wider area, are prevalent in some societies. These practices when applied together have been known to increase crop production by as much as 50%. Treated urban wastewater from towns and cities, often referred to as 'brown water', may be channeled onto nearby farms for growing vegetables and fruits. In Calcutta, much of the raw sewage is channeled into a system of natural lagoons, where fish are raised. The city's hectares of lagoons produce about 6,000 metric tons of fish a year for urban consumers. However, there is a need to be cautions as unless urban wastewater receives some pre-treatment, either from natural wetlands or sewage treatment plants, it can transfer disease organisms to vegetables and fruits or fish and endanger human health.

Watershed management, which refers to managing an entire land area served by all the rivers and aquifers that drain into a particular body of water, such as a semi-enclosed bay, has assumed great importance as a water conservation measure. A river or a lake must be seen along with its entire watershed and all its physical, chemical, and biological elements, as part of a complex, integrated system. People living in most of these watersheds have radically altered the natural drainage systems around them. Tempering with watershed has proved ruinous for many developing countries, where hillsides, denuded of vegetation, empty tonnes of soil into watercourses every year, causing floods during the wet seasons and suffocating aquatic life during the dry seasons. Deforestation has ruined land and altered climates, causing less rain in some areas. In others, rainwater runs off so fast that little can be collected for use later. Watershed management is generally complicated and can be contentious because watershed boundaries do not coincide with those of political or administrative jurisdictions. It involves many levels of Government and many different communities, each with its own constituencies and concerns. Balancing the multitude of interests involved which is time consuming and troublesome, is the key to the success of watershed management. But if we carried out properly, watershed or river basin management pays multiple benefits.

Every year India gets an estimated rain and snowfall spread over 400 million hectares of land. Even if rain is captured from just one to two percent of India's land area, it can provide a population of one billion as much as 100 litres of water per person per day. Harvesting rainwater is one of the most effective ways of tackling water crisis. The basic principle is to collect the rainwater where it falls, us it and let it seep into the ground. In fact, India has had a long tradition of water harvesting. Aizawl in Mizoram meets most of its water needs through rooftop harvesting. In 1994 a law was promulgated for the residents of Chennai making it mandatory for new buildings to harvest rainwater if they wanted municipal water connection. This has also resulted into a few business ventures devoted exclusively to artificial recharge. As a result of rainwater harvesting, the coastal aquifers in Tamilnadu are healthy again after several years.

Check dams can be built to store monsoon flows and recharge aquifers. Rainwater can also be stored in wells by channeling it through pipes from the rooftop terrace. Further, percolation tanks may be built to allow slow percolation and collection of rainwater into the ground. It is efficient both for soft and hard ground. Recharge wells or injection wells are just like tube wells but have the provision for pumping in water from the surface after treatment.

According to some projections, the city of Delhi can actually retrieve around 720 million liters of water every year by artificial recharge. Installing a rooftop harvesting system can cost nearly ₹ 100,000 to ₹ 150,000 for a suitably sized apartment. A rooftop recharge can provide nearly 300 litres a minute at the time of good rain. Delhi's master plan for the year 2001 projects per capita need of 400 litres of water every day and this demand can be met by adopting these new ways of harvesting water. Rainwater can not only provide much needed drinking and irrigation water but can also increase groundwater discharge, reduce urban floods and overloading of sewage treatment plants and sea water ingress in coastal areas.

One solution proposed and already being adopted around the world is to set a price of water to cover its 'real costs'; a price which would take into consideration all of the associated services such as treatment, infrastructure, distribution. Placing a price of water might attract big companies to invest in remote areas where their profit margin – because of a high consumption potential – could be high. It would also 'make it possible to reduce the burden of expenditures which up until now were met by public funds.' But what happens when people simply cannot pay? Or when they live in small, poor communities, which don't interest the big water companies? In such cases, voluntary agencies and NGOs can pay a key role. In Cambodia, for example, NGOs have helped create local drilling teams and encouraged self-management of water projects.

Nowadays, due to water crisis, state/ centre dispute occur on water requirement like Kavery river in between Tamilnadu and Karnataka; Yamuna - Satluj in between Haryana, Punjab & Delhi; Sharda river in between Nepal and India; Brahmaputra river in between Bangladesh & India.

4. Global Supply and Demand for Water

Total water supply

Water supply depends on several factors in the water cycle, including the rates of rainfall, evaporation, the use of water by plants (transpiration), and river and groundwater flows. It is estimated[3] that less than 1% of all fresh water is available for people to use (the remainder is locked up in ice sheets and glaciers). Globally, around 12,500 cubic kilometres (km^3) of water are considered available for human use on an annual basis. This amounts to about 6,600 m^3 per person/year[4].

Total water demand

Today, the quantity of water used for all purposes exceeds 3,700 km^3 per year. Agriculture is the largest user, consuming almost two-thirds of all water drawn from rivers, lakes and groundwater. While irrigation has undoubtedly contributed significantly to world agricultural production, it is extremely water intensive. Since 1960, water use for crop irrigation has risen by 60-70%. Industry uses about 20% of available water, and the municipal sector uses about 10%. Population growth, urbanization and industrialization have increased the use of water in these sectors.

Access to water

The previous section examined the gross supply of and demand for water on a global basis. However, the world's available freshwater supply is not distributed evenly around the globe, throughout the seasons, or from year to year. About three-quarters of annual rainfall occurs in areas containing less than one-third of the world's population, whereas two-thirds of the world's population live in the areas receiving only one-quarter of the world's annual rainfall. For instance, about 20% of the global average runoff each year is accounted for by the Amazon Basin, a vast region with fewer than 10 million people. Similarly, the Congo River and its tributaries account for about 30% of the entire African continent's annual runoff, but the basin contains only 10% of Africa's population. Throughout much of the developing world freshwater supply comes in the form of seasonal rains, such as the monsoons in Asia. Such rains often run off too quickly for efficient use. India, for instance, gets 90% of its rainfall during the summer monsoon season – at other times rainfall over much of the country is very low. Because of the seasonal nature of the water supply (without storage), many developing countries can use no more than 20% of their potentially available freshwater resources.

Water supplies can also vary from year to year, depending on variations in the weather. For example, monsoons may fail in some years. Also natural phenomena such as the El Nino Southern Oscillation can lead to significant differences in rainfall in the southern Pacific Ocean, affecting south-east Asia and south and Central America. (www.parliament.uk/).

5. Possible Solutions

It is estimate that more than more than one billion people drink unsafe water and 2.4 billion, that is, 40% of the human race does not have access to adequate sanitation, and 3.4 million people, mostly children, die every year of water-related diseases (more than one million from malaria alone), the majority of them unnecessarily (Prakash and Prakash, 2001).

But the picture is neither gloomy nor hopeless, says the World Health Organization (WHO) in a report on water and sanitation. "Clearly, a problem of this magnitude cannot be solved overnight, but simple, inexpensive measures, both individual and collective, are available that will provide clean water for millions and millions of people in developing countries – now, not in 10 or 20 years," said Dr. Gro Harlem Brundtland, Director-General of WHO. "We do not have the luxury of waiting around for large infrastructure investments to provide water supplies and basic sanitation services for all who need them. It makes no sense, and it is not acceptable, to ignore the immediate priorities of the most needy."

Optimistic but realistic, the WHO report, entitled *Water for Health – Taking Charge,* strongly urges several basic measures, including purifying water and improving hygiene, as immediate means of improving people's water supply in developing countries. Chlorination, for example, is, "a proven means of ridding water of disease causing microorganisms in piped water," according to the report. Moreover, research carried out at the Centers for Disease Control and Prevention in Atlanta, Georgia, and by the Pan American Health

Organisation, supports chlorination in households without piped water, even through the prevailing wisdom is that chlorination should follow and not precede the creation of water and sanitation services. Even in conditions of very poor sanitation and hygiene, where people collect whatever water is available to use for their household water supply, if the water is chlorinated, the water quality is improved microbiologically, and there are statistically significant decreases in diarrhoel diseases.

A good example of successful chlorination can be found in the Maltheves where a national control programme used it in wells. Rainwater was also collected for drinking. Twenty years after the programme started, the entire populations of the Maltheves islands have their own community rainwater collection tanks, and deaths from diarrhea are virtually unknown.

Another easy, small-scale, and cost-effective technique for providing safe water, individually or collectively, is still little known but highly effective solar thermal technique. It is called SODIS and was promoted by the Swiss Federal Institute for Environmental Science and Technology near Zurich. SODIS, an acronym for Solar water Disinfection, is a nearly cost free system because sunlight costs nothing, and the only other elements are throw-away transparent plastic soft-drink bottles or used mineral water bottles and a black surface. The transparent bottles are filled with water and placed horizontally on a flat surface for about five hours. The disease-causing microorganisms (pathogens) in the polluted water succumb to the killing effect of the ultraviolet light in solar radiation. The process is enhanced when the solar water disinfection is combined with a 'solar thermal water treatment' which makes use of the fact that black colour absorbs light and heat more efficiently. This is accomplished by painting the bottom half of the bottle black or placing it on black-painted corrugated iron or plastic sheets. Field studies in Bolivia, Burkina Fasco, China, Colombia, Indonesia, Thailand and Togo show that the process works.

A third recommendation of the report calls for 'changing behaviour'. Studies of diarrhea show that the simple act of washing hands with soap and water reduces incidence of the disease by 35%. Elsewhere, good water management has almost eradicated guinea worm, a disfiguring, disabling disease which afflicted 50 million people in Africa and Asia in the mid-1900s. By 1999 that number had fallen to below 10,000. But poor irrigation water management, in sharp contrast, had let to a huge spread of schistosomiasis (snail fever) to areas of the world where it never existed before. An estimated 200 million people are infected today with schistosomiasis, according to WHO.

What should be done differently to prevent water-related diseases and to ensure that everyone access to at least some safe water and sanitation? For one thing, says the WHO report, the health sector must get fully involved in water management. It can no longer be left to water management authorities or to environment ministries. Just as major development projects always have environment impact assessment, they should also require health impact assessments. Those involved in water management should be made responsible for its effects on people's health.

During the past 50 years there has been a strong emphasis on medical interventions including, for example, drug therapy, to tackle water-borne and sanitation related diseases and this has tended to reduce the attention and priority given to safe water supply and adequate sanitation. With the increasing resistance to antibiotics, insecticides and standard drugs, health authorities now understand the limitations of a strictly medical approach. That makes safe water and sanitation more important than ever before.

Interlinking of Rivers

A familiar phenomenon in human history is the fight to secure natural resources. This essay shall examine how one country, India, is seeking to solve its water problems via the interlinking of all its rivers. River interlinking is a project that is both visionary and controversial in claiming to cure all of the country's water problems. The goal of the project is to interlink all the country's rivers together. This, allegedly, will provide water to all by diverting water from areas that have a 'surplus' to those that don't and "by preventing the unnecessary spillage of water into the sea." Furthermore, such water transfers would also be aimed at flood control during the erratic monsoon season, where floodwaters could simply be diverted away. However, Interlinking at the same time has the potential to become another grand, large-scale project of the sort that creates more problems than it proposes to solve. To assess the risk of this fate, the author provides comparisons with other countries that have undertaken similar projects. These comparisons will show that such large-scale projects typically tend to run into difficulty and usually fail. The goal of this essay is to evaluate why, in spite of these historical precedents against large projects, governments nonetheless tend to follow through with them. Two possible answers come to mind. The first is that governments believe that these are genuinely beneficial projects based on some explicit or implicit calculation of costs and benefits. The second is that government officials are acting self-interestedly, prompted by the influence of special interest groups. The author believes that the answer lies in examining the nature of the benefits and costs involved, and the distribution of these benefits in relation to political power and government self interest. Therefore, in this essay begins with an examination of the cost-benefit procedure, and then examines Interlinking using a qualitative cost-benefit analysis. It follows with possible reasons behind the motivation of Interlinking based on the distribution of costs and benefits and the interests of government leaders, and ends with questioning whether such a project would pass through the legislature regardless (Dev Goel, 2005).

Negative Impacts of River linking

The Ken-Betwa river linking project which includes a dam on the river Ken and a 231 km. canal linking it to the Betwa will submerge significant forest areas including parts of the Panna Tiger Reserve. The feasibility report of the project says that the project will submerge some 100 sq. km. in Panna, Chatarpur and Damoh districts – including 19 villages and about 37.5 sq. km. of forestland as well as 30 km. stretch of the Gangau-Shahpura road in Madhya Pradesh. (PAU, 2005). Leading scientists of India have a doubt that the interlinking of rivers may affect the local weather, monsoon cycle and contribute to Climate change.

REFERENCE

Dev Goel, (2005): "A Political-economic Analysis of India's River Interlinking Project" (August 30, 2005) *Florida State University D-Scholarship Repository,* Article #132. (http://dscholarship.lib.fsu.edu/undergrad/132)

http://www.yearofplanetearth.org

Prakash, G. and Prakash, J. (2001): Water-present, Past and Future, *Science Reporter*-Cover Story, July, pp. 10-14 & 62-63.

PAU (2005): Ken Betwa River Link to Submerge Parts of Panna TR. In: Protected Area Update, October, 2005, (No. 57) Vol-XI, No-5, pp. 10.

Technologies for Water and Wastewater Management **Pages 16-37**
Edited by: Dr. Vijender Singh & Dr. Pawan Kumar 'Bharti'
ISBN: 978-93-88854-53-5
Edition: 2020
Published by: Discovery Publishing House Pvt. Ltd., New Delhi (India)

2 Water Crisis Management and Policy Interventions

Anitha G.[1] and Esakkimuthu M.[2]

Introduction

People living in third world countries are suffering from a water crisis that has become a major global health issue. Water is essential for life not only for the body's physical needs but also for domestic use. The lack of available clean water contributes to numerous waterborne and water washed diseases, causing the death of millions of people annually and hindering the development of communities. Across the planet, in many countries, there are thousands of poor people with no access to clean water and no adequate sanitation facilities. Their continuing plight and the terrible suffering they endure in disease and early death has to reflect on all of us as a failure of collective will to resolve the global water crisis. This paper will explore the problems due to water and present solutions at individual and community levels that can help solve the water crisis in third world countries.

Water is absolutely essential for the existence, development and preservation of all human life, making it an essential commodity in the world. However, nearly 1 billion people in the world lack access to potable water, mainly those living in third world countries (*Sekler et.al*, 2003). A water crisis has gripped these regions, threatening the quality of life of those in the developing world. According to the United Nations Human Development Report, the water and sanitation crisis claims more lives through disease than any war claims through weapons (*Water Facts*, 2012). Every year, approximately 1.4 million children die from unavailable, clean drinking water; and 3.6 million people die each year from water-related diseases. Of that large number, 84% are children and 98% are living in the developing world. Clearly this is a major health issue in the world today that must be addressed to save the lives of the millions of people that are dying from preventable ailments.

[1] Assistant Professor (Soil Science and Agricultural Chemistry), S. Thangapazham Agricultural College, Vasudevanallur, Tamil Nadu, India

[2] Assistant Professor (Agricultural Extension), Regional Agricultural Research Station, Pilicode, Kerala, India

All life on earth depends on water. Man uses water for many purposes drinking, irrigation, fisheries, industrial purposes, transportation, and waste disposal. The origin of water on the earth is not clear so far. However, the current presumption is that the primordial earth had no oceans, and perhaps very little atmosphere. It is believed that the volatile constituents bound in the earth's crust, oozing to the surface through volcanoes, rock movements, and hot springs, condensed to from the ocean and the atmosphere. This way, perhaps this remarkable combination of hydrogen and oxygen-called water-came into being and eventually became an indispensable component of the earth's environment.

Water found on the surface of the earth in lakes, rivers and oceans is called surface water. It is polluted by various means like biological, physical, chemical, aesthetic and radioactive substances. Therefore it is essential to manage water resources from pollution (*Aaron et al.* 2006)Local and community based water management seems to be an old idea whose time has come again. For too many years, the role of local people has been, if not totally ignored, at least downplayed. Not that the developing world suffered from any failure to see water as a problem, or from the absence of water projects intended to alleviate water scarcity. Only in the last decade the efforts have been made to improve water quality.

Water: A Valuable Resource

Water (from the Anglo-Saxon and Low German word, water) is a colourless, tasteless, and odourless substance that is essential to all forms of life that we know of. Water is remarkable. It is only one thing on earth that can exist naturally as a solid, a liquid and a gas. Liquid water is found in river, lakes and ocean. Solid water is water that is frozen, like snow and ice. Water is a gas when it is in the air of our atmosphere as vapour or steam.

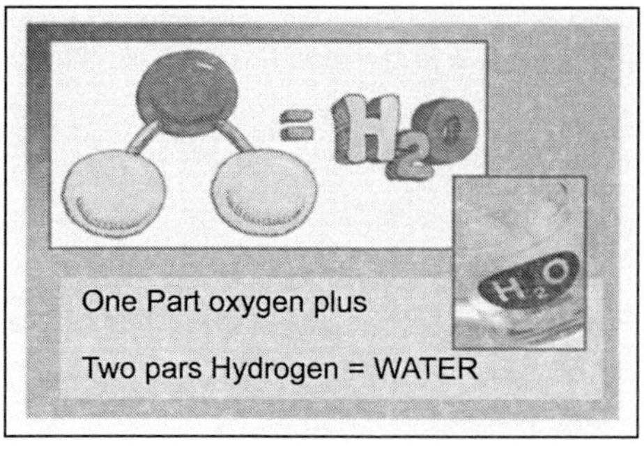

Fig. 2.1: Structure and Chemical formula of water

Water is known in science as H_2O. That means the smallest possible amount of water, one molecule, is made from two hydrogen atoms that attach to one oxygen atom. The hydrogen atoms have a positive electrical charge and the oxygen atom has a negative charge. Because opposite charges attract, the charges on either end of the water molecule attract other water molecules and group together, forming water drops. The charges act like magnets. That is how water sticks together in raindrops, rivers, oceans, and ponds.

Earth is a watery place, unlike most other planets in our solar system. Water covers over 70% of the earth's surface, but also underground and in the atmosphere. Out of all the water like oceans. That means only 3% percent of all the water on earth is fresh water. Of the 3% fresh water, 2% is solid-frozen in icecaps and glaciers. Out of all the water on earth, only 1% is drinkable, and half of this drinkable water is found below the earth's surface. So even through earth is a watery planet, the amount of water we can use is limited.

Water found on the surface of the earth in lakes, rivers and oceans is called surface water. The ground soaks up water like a sponge. The soaked-up water is called ground water. It fills the spaces around sand, gravel and rock below the earth's surface. Sometimes, it moves slowly, and some of it has been underground for thousands of years. These underground streams are created when precipitation such as rain and melted snow seeps into the earth. Ground water can come to the surface in rives or natural springs. Because of the underground water supply, some rivers, streams, ponds and lakes can remain full even when it doesn't rain or snow.

However, in spite of enormous quantity of the substance that exists, only a small proportion of it is actually usable by human beings. Humans use water in the home, in industry, in agriculture, and for recreation. These applications differ widely in the quantities and quality of the water require. In one way or the other we use all available sources- inland water, ground water, and even ocean water. We pollute it, re-purify it, and re use it over and over again.

Masses and Relative Proportions of the Various Forms of Water in the Hydrosphere

Form	Mass	Relative proportion (%)
Oceans	1348000	97.39
Polar ice	27820	2.01
Underground water, soil moisture	8062	6.58
Lakes and rivers	225	0.02
Atmospheric water vapour	13	0.001
Total hydrosphere	1384120	100
Of which, fresh water is	36020	2.6

Source: Water and Environment Pollution (U. Kumar, 2006)

Distribution of Fresh Water in the Hydrosphere (%)

Particulars	Amount (%)
Polar ice, glaciers, etc.	77.23
Underground water (800 m)	9.86
Underground water (between 800 m and 4 km)	12.35
Soil moisture	0.17
Fresh – water lakes	0.3
Rivers and other waterways	0.003
Hydrated minerals	0.001
Biomass	0.04
Total	**100.00**

Source: Water and Environment Pollution (U. Kumar, 2006)

Importance of Water

Water takes many different shapes on the earth: water vapour and clouds in the sky, waves and icebergs in the sea, glaciers in the mountain, and aquifers in the ground. Though evaporation, precipitation and runoff, water is continuously flowing from one from to another, in what is called the water cycle or Hydrological cycle.

The hydrological cycle involves the continuous circulation of water in the Earth-Atmosphere system. At its core, the water cycle is the motion of the water from the ground to the atmosphere and back again. Of the many processes involved in the hydrologic cycle, the most important are...

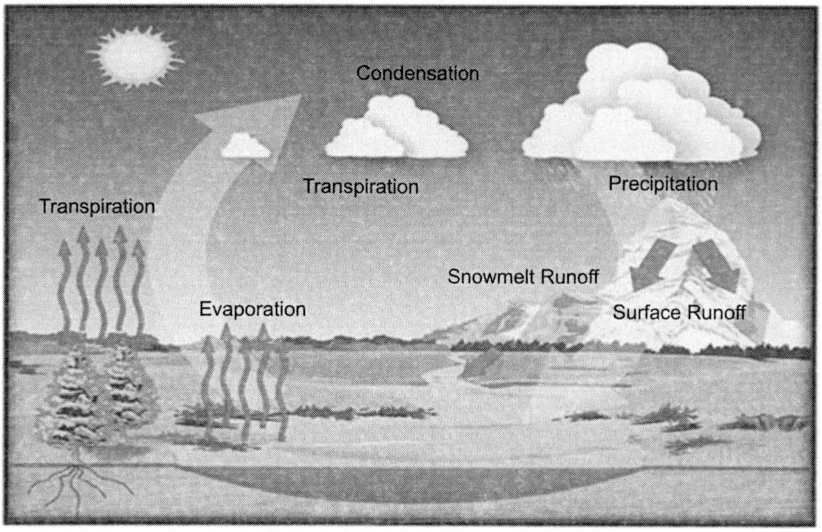

Fig. 2.2: The Hydrological Cycle

- Evaporation
- Transpiration
- Condensation
- Precipitation
- Runoff

Evaporation

Evaporation is the change of state in a substance from a liquid to a gas. In meteorology, the substance we are concerned about the most is water. For evaporation to take place, energy is required. The energy can come from any source: the sun, the atmosphere, the earth, or objects on the earth such as humans.

Transpiration

Transpiration is the evaporation of water from plants through stomata. Stomata are small openings found on the underside of leaves that are connected to vascular plant tissues. In most plants, transpiration is a passive process largely controlled by the humidity of the atmosphere and the moisture content of the soil. Of the transpired water passing through a plant only 1% is used in the growth process of the plant. The remaining 99% is passed into the atmosphere.

Condensation

Condensation is the process whereby water vapour in the atmosphere is changed into a liquid state. In the atmosphere condensation may appear as clouds or dew.

Condensation is not a matter of one particular temperature but of a difference between two temperatures; the air temperature and the dew point temperature. At its basic meaning, the dew point is the temperature where dew can form. Actually, it is the temperature that, if the air is cool to that level, the air becomes saturated. Any additional cooling causes water vapour to condense. Foggy conditions often occur when air temperature and dew point are equal. Condensation is the opposite of evaporation. Since water vapour has a higher energy level than that of liquid water, when condensation occurs, the excess energy in the form of heat energy is released. This release of heat aids in the formation of hurricanes.

Precipitation

Precipitation is the result when the tiny condensation particles grow too large, through collision and coalesce, for the rising air to support, and thus fall to the earth. Precipitation can be in the form of rain, hail, snow or sleet. Precipitation is the primary way we receive fresh water in earth. On average, the world receives about 38½" (980 mm) each year over both the oceans and land masses.

Runoff

Runoff occurs when there is excessive precipitation and the ground is saturated (cannot absorb any more water). Rivers and lakes are results of runoff. There is some evaporation from runoff into the atmosphere but for the most part water in rivers and lakes return to the oceans.

If runoff water flows into the lake only (with no outlet for water to flow out of the lake), then evaporation is the only means for water to return to the atmosphere. With evaporation only pure water evaporated, and therefore any contaminates and salts are left behind. The result is the lake becomes salty as in the case of the Great Salt Lake in Utah or Dead Sea in Israel.

Evaporation of this runoff into the atmosphere begins the hydrologic cycle over again. Some of the water percolates into the soil and into the ground water only to be drawn into plants again for transpiration to take place.

Sources of Water

Water can be divided into four marked classes;

Atmospheric water

Rain water and water formed by snow grouped under atmospheric water. As the rain and snowfall, they wash the dusty atmosphere and bring down the dust, soot and other suspended particles to the earth. Along with these non-living particles atmospheric water also carries air borne bacteria to the earth surface.

Surface water

As soon as rain drops and snowflakes reach to surface of the earth, they quickly become contaminated with soil microflora of the area. Such water are a few microorganisms but as it flows from higher region to lower regions, it contains large amount of organic matter, the population of microorganisms increases considerably. Such water facilitates the growth of saprophytic species and protozoa. River water shows their highest count during rainy season.

Stored water

Water which is present in ponds, reservoirs, lakes or ocean for considerable period is called stored water. The microbial population increases greatly in such water.

Ground water

When rain falls on the earth, two forces act on it. One is the earth gravity which pulls the water downward through any open path. The second force is the electrical attraction between water and other materials to which water tends to stick. The movement of water upward through small holes is called capillary action.

When rain drops fall on the dry soil they will wet the soil particles. As the rain continues after all the land surface will wet, gravity will pull the excess of water down through the holes in the rock, sand, or gravel below. The larger the underground spaces, the faster the water will flow down. Finally, the downward flow of water will be stopped when the water meets rock that has no porosity. Since water can go no further, it blocks up, filling all the pores in rock above the barrier. This causes saturation of water in the soil and zone is called saturation zone. The upper boundary of the zone of saturation is called the water table. Below the water table the rock is saturated; above it the rock may be moist but is not saturated.

Soil water

Soil water is normally surrounded by a thin film of water. It is from these films that plant roots take up all the water they need. This water can be in a chemically combined or uncombined form. In the former, it exists as water of crystallization of mineral grains and water of hydration of clay mineral particles. Both of these kind of combined water are not at all available to the living organisms. Uncombined water is not chemically combined with the soil particles and is held in soil adhesion and cohesion. Soil water sources are of four types:

1. Gravitational water
2. Capillary water
3. Hygroscopic water
4. Water vapour

In soils, water is supplied to plants through the roots, it lubricates the soil allowing root penetration, it is necessary for microbial mobility and action, it allows nutrient mobility, in dry portion of soil, water uptake stops, nutrient absorption essentially ceases, and the root growth practically stops. A typical wetted loam soil will contain water in about 25 per cent of its volume, with only about half of that water being available to plants.

The properties of soil water are usually most favourable in the medium textured soil. Water entry into soil is too fast in sands and too slow in clay for optimum crop production. Inadequate air exchange will occur in small and water filled pores in clayey soil. Sandy soils hold low plant available amounts of water following wetting. Thus soil will require frequent rain or irrigation to supply adequate water. Clayey soils will have slow drainage of excess water; sandy soil will be well drained, if drainage is possible.

Soil Water Classification for Water Management

The most useful classification of water are those relating water plants can use and to water which they cannot use. Terms include gravitational water, plant available water, field capacity and permanent wilting point.

Ecological Classification of Soil Water

Plant available water is the portion of stored soil water that can be absorbed fast enough by plant roots to sustain life. It is defined as weight percentage of total soil water held with water potential between -33 and -1500 kpa .The water held within these potential makes up most of storage water used by the plants. The wilting point is the percentage of soil water held with water potential less than -1500 kpa; it is held so strongly that plants are not able to absorb it fast enough for their needs.

Field Capacity

Field capacity is the percentage of soil water that is held with water potential less than -33 kpa and is a measure of greatest amount of water that a soil can hold, or store, under conditions of complete wetting followed by a free drainage. Field capacity values are used to determine the amount of irrigation water needed and the amount of stored soil water available to plants. Plants-available water is equal to the difference of water percentage at field capacity and at permanent wilting point.

Hygroscopic Water

The tension varies from 31- 10,000 atmospheres. It held mostly by soil colloids. It is mostly non liquid and therefore biological inactive and moves mostly in vapour form. The film thickness not more than 15-20 layers of water molecules and maximum thickness of 4-5 mμ. It is related to texture and organic matter content of soil.

Capillary Water

Capillary water moves through the soil pores because of a water potential gradient. Water potential gradient is difference in total water potential between two locations in the soil. The saturation percentage is the water content of soil when all pores are filled with water. It is approximately double the field capacity value. The saturation percentage is approximately by the water in a soil.

Capillary water held at hygroscopic coefficient. The tension varies from 31-10,000 atmospheres. It holds mostly by soil colloids and non- liquid therefore, biologically inactive. It moves mostly in vapour form. The film thickness not more than 15-20 layers of water molecules and maximum thickness of 4-5 mμ. It is related to texture and organic matter content of soil.

Gravitational Water

Such water held by a negative tension of 0.3 atm. Or, loosely held between less than 0.1-0.3 atm. It is free water which drains out, also called drainage water and usually present in, macro pores. It is undesirable and nutrient leaching takes place. The downward movement of water due to gravitational force.

Biological Classification of Soil Water

Superfluous water

1. Moisture tension < 1/3 atm. (Less than or equal to).
2. Such water held at field capacity but not beneficial for higher plants
3. Harmful for crops if too much
4. Also called gravitational water

Available water

Portion of capillary water lying between field capacity 1/3 atm and wilting coefficient. Availability of moisture depends upon crops when wilting coefficient is measured at 15 atm pressure; it is a measure of soil condition and that of plant because ability to adsorb soil moisture differs according to plant types.

Unavailable water

Water held at the permanent wilting point. It includes hygroscopic water which is removed too slowly by plants to prevent wilting. Optimum growth of plants occurs when soil moisture content near field capacity with a moisture tension of 1 bar or less.

Field capacity

When macro pores drain their water and are filled by air but micro pores or capillary pores are still filled with water then soil is called at field capacity. The matric tension is around 0.1 -0.3 .The Pf range of capillary moisture is 6.0- 4.2 .the pF range of available moisture is 2.5-4.2. Moisture with about pF 2.54 is very favourable for plant growth.

Permanent wilting percentage

Concept by Briggs and Shantz. although plants not dead , but they are not in permanent wilting condition and will die if water is not added .The tension is atm for the crops the water remaining in the soil is found the smallest of the micro pores and individual soil particles the pF at 15 atm is about 4.2.

Hygroscopic coefficient

After the removal of liquid water completely from micro pores, the remaining water is associated with the surface of the soil particles. The tension is above 31 atm. pF is about 6. The moisture held at this point is called hygroscopic coefficient.

Moisture equivalent

The weight percentage of water retained by a previously saturated sample of soil 1 cm in thickness after it has been subjected to a centrifugal force a thousand times gravity for 30 minutes. Moisture equivalent was introduced by Briggs and Mc.Lane (1907), Briggs and Shantz (1912) used the moisture equivalent as an indirect of measure of wilting point.

However, this factor i.e 1.84 cannot be used for all soils. Moisture equivalent is assumed to represent moisture held under field conditions or the field capacity. The pF at moisture equivalent (1/3) is above 2.54.

1. Maximum capillary capacity (MCC).
2. MCC = water holding capacity – hygroscopic coefficient.

Soil Water Reservoirs

Water in soil is held as films on particle surface and in small pores. Large pores (as in sands and in between large aggregates) allow water to drain by gravitational flow. Small pores (clays) retain water by capillary pores. Generally , the more clayey the soil and the higher the humus content, the large the amount of water the soil can store not only does the quantity of water retain in clay soils remains large, but much of it is tightly held the large to the clay surface area. This means that the clay soil will hold a large amount of water to the water to the permanent wilting point percentage.

Water Availability in the World

Today's water crisis is not always an issue of scarcity, but mainly of portability. The majority of the earth is covered in water, yet only a small percentage of that amount is available for use as clean water. In the United States and other modernized countries, water availability is not very problematic. Even though the majority of people in these countries do not receive a sufficient intake of water, there is still a significant amount of uncontaminated drinking water available. However, this is not the case in developing countries across the world. Currently, 12% of the earth's population, mainly those living in third world countries, is using 85% of the world's available water (*Shah*, 2010). So the primary issue at hand is not a water shortage crisis, but a water management crisis.

World Over Water Crisis Takes Many Shapes

Around a billion people today, that is one in every seven people on earth; don't have access to safe drinking water. According to the UN, in the past century, water use has grown at over twice the rate of population increase. By 2025, an estimated 1.8 billion people will be living in areas hit by water scarcity. And, two in every three persons on this planet will be living in regions classified as 'water-stressed.'

The crisis is particularly severe in the more populated regions of Asia and Africa. This could have a direct bearing on regional and global security. A 2012 report, by the US intelligence community, warned that water overuse in countries like India could become a source of conflict. And, the Pacific Institute, which is into studying issues of global security and water crisis, has noted that violent confrontations over water have quadrupled in 10 years.

Iran

Iran faces multiple challenges as far as its water management is concerned. Iranians use 66 gallons of water daily, on an average. But lack of fresh water and over consumption of water has made it the world's 24th most 'water-stressed' country, as per the 2013 report of the World Resources Institute. As of 2014, and according to Iran's Ministry of Energy, the country is making use of 70 percent of the total renewed freshwater, which is far beyond the suggested limit of 40 percent.

A glaring example of the water crisis is Lake Urmia, once a mighty salt lake, but now has shrunk to a shocking five percent of its earlier volume in just 20 years. The Zayandeh river, which stands for "life-giving river", and was once the largest river that flowed through the heartland of Iran is now mostly dry after being used for several purposes.

Alarming rise in population, over exploitation of groundwater, and rampant wastage of water, especially in cities, are among the reasons for the situation of water crisis that Iran finds itself in.

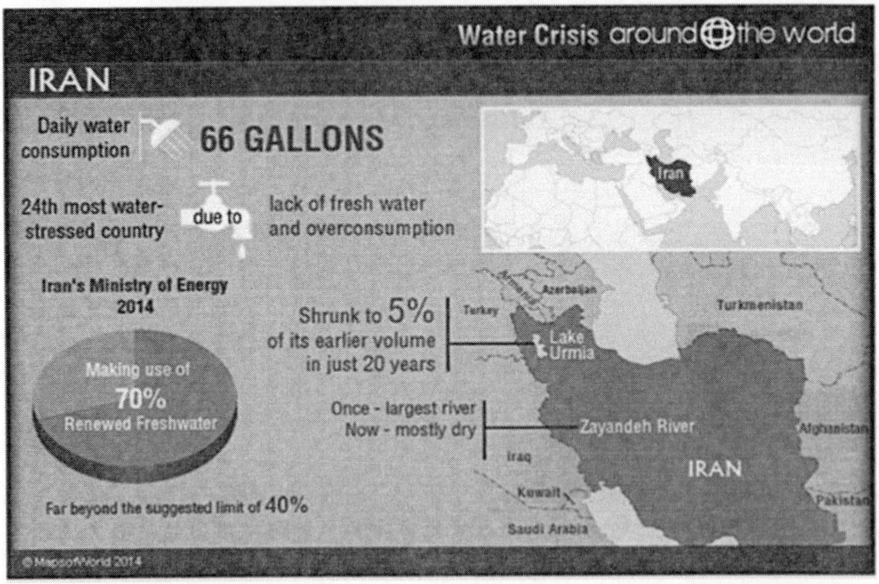

Fig. 2.3: Water crisis - Iran

Egypt

In the 1960s, people in Egypt had a water share per capita of 2,800 cubic meters. In 2013, it stood at 660 cubic meters, significantly lower than the international standard - 'water poverty' mark of 1,000 cubic meters. The future looks bleak.

As the country's current supply of water could clog by 2025 given the situations of poor water management, impacts of climate change, and already existing water scarcity. Egypt will then require 20% more water with the pressure on the mighty Nile river, which gives Egypt 95 percent of its fresh water. Unfortunately, in such a situation, Egypt's desiccated neighbour's like Burundi and Ethiopia may have to avoid depending on Nile river.

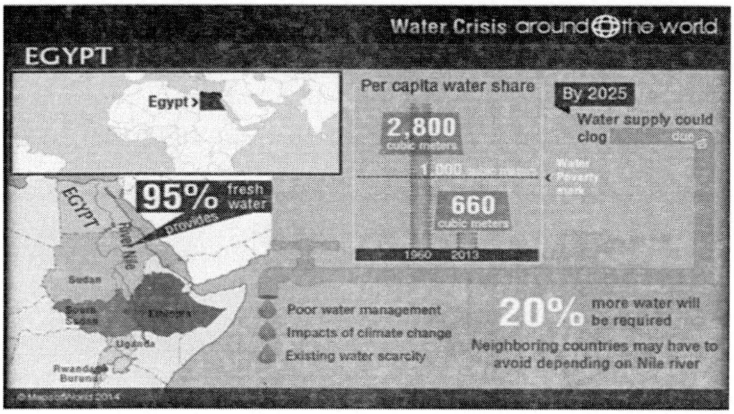

Fig. 2.4: Water crisis - Egypt

Ethiopia

The hard, cold numbers reflect the enormity of the water crisis that Ethiopia faces. Around 44 million people -that's nearly half of the country's population have no access to safe drinking water. More than 70 million three in every four Ethiopians lack access to proper sanitation. Unsafe water and inadequate sanitation take a huge toll on this poor African nation, with more than 33,000 children dying every year from diarrhoea.

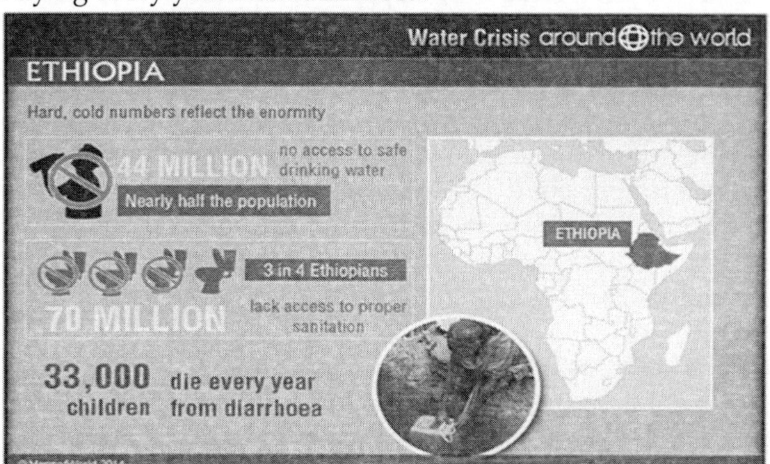

Fig. 2.5: Water crisis - Ethiopia

South Africa

According to estimates, by 2020, the country may face serious water shortages, and its total water requirements will double in the next three decades. Current challenges to secure water resources, include acid mine drainage in Johannesburg, large-scale pollution of the Vaal River Barrage and Hartebeespoort Dam, and contamination of the Umgeni River.

However, the situation of water crisis does not end here. At several places of Africa violent confrontations, protests, dissents sparked due to water scarcity that led to the killings of innocent people. In Nkandala, hundreds of families go without a regular supply of water. People are often seen carrying filthy water buckets from the river.

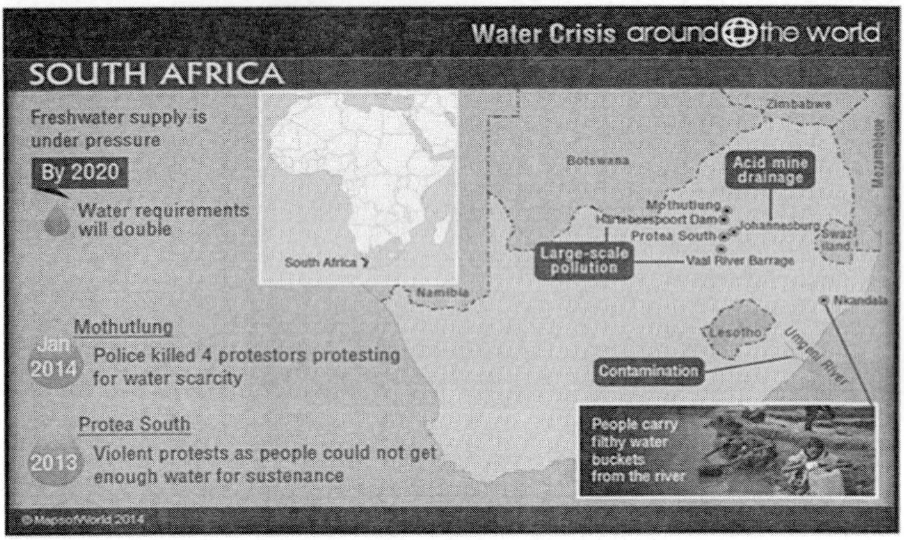

Fig. 2.6: Water crisis - South Africa

Australia

In the dry state of Western Australia, because of climate change, dams now get one-sixth of the water from rain than they used to 15 years ago. It seems like a full-blown water crisis. For the state's capital Perth, a city of two million, the solution has been an expensive and energy-guzzling one: desalination. Another novel experiment that's being currently implanted is treating wastewater, which is then injected into aquifers that are 1,000 meters underground. The realization that water is a scarce commodity has also made residents of Western Australia more conscious of not wasting it.

Also, according to the latest studies, Australia is on the verge of drying due to the shortage in annual rainfall and emissions of carbon and greenhouse gases. So far, the danger of facing the worse water crisis prevails over perth, as it may have to depend upon other water resources in near future.

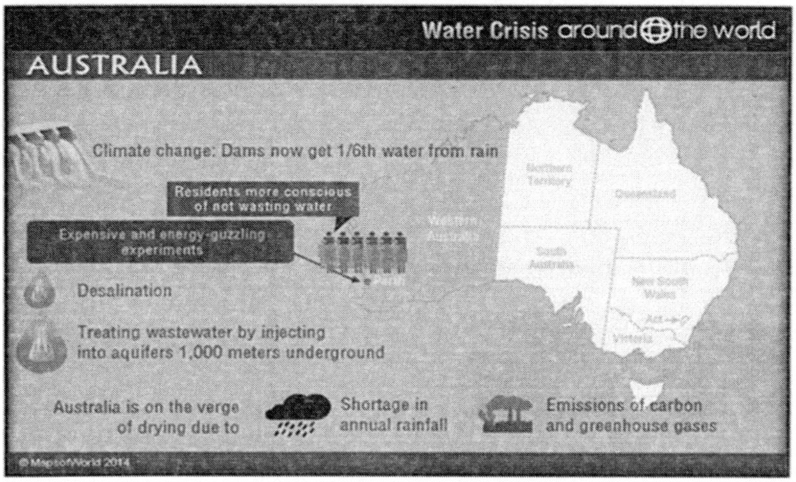

Fig. 2.7: Water crisis - Australia

Niger

About 8.2 million population of Niger has little access to clean water and more than 15 million people lack access to adequate sanitation. Some 12,000 children are known to die every year from diseases like diarrhoea and typhoid caused due to unclean water and poor sanitation in this West African nation. Years of internal conflicts and the situation of severe drought in 2005 that gave rise to food and water paucity have only added to the problem.

However, in the last couple of years, with levels of violence down, some steps are being taken to address the water crisis. The World Bank has initiated a program, wherein nearly 100 wells and pumps will be installed every year to meet the demands of an extra 25,000 people.

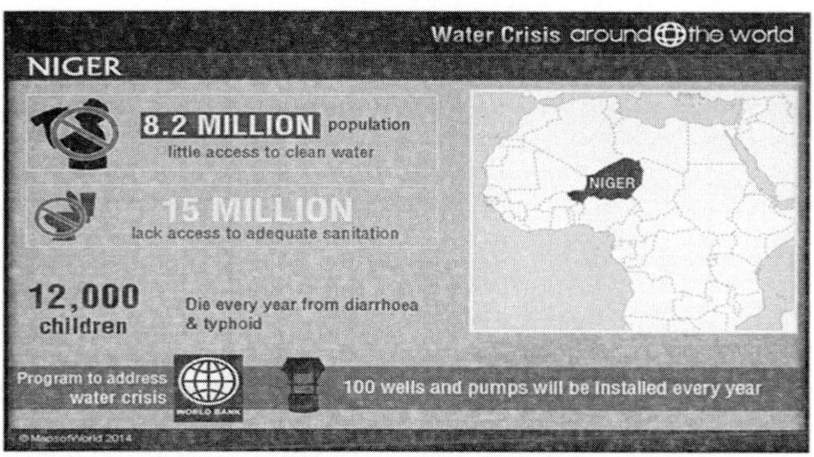

Fig. 2.8: Water crisis - Niger

Turkmenistan

According to some experts, Turkmenistan will confront serious water shortage by 2020 unless urgent steps are taken. Water has been historically scarce in this part of the world. More than half the country is desert. One study in 2010 stated that Turkmenistan is ranked ninth among the 10 most 'water insecure' nations in the world.

One of the steps this central Asian nation is taking to bolster its water resources is building an artificial lake at Garashor, which will collect and purify drainage water and sewage for re-use. Attempts are also being made to collect water from mud flows along the foothills of the Kopet Dag mountain range.

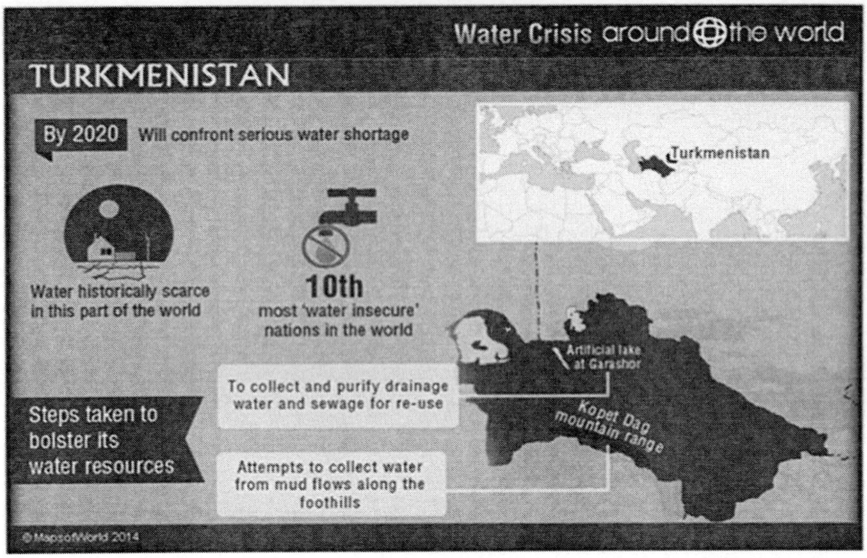

Fig. 2.9: Water crisis - Turkmenistan

Pakistan

According to a July 2013 report by the Asian Development Bank, Pakistan is one of the most "water-stressed countries in the world." The amount of water this country of over 185 million people has on reserve for emergency use will only last 30 days. The recommended number of days for a country with similar climate is 1,000. With lesser water flowing into the Indus River and a rapidly increasing population, Pakistan is sitting on another ticking time bomb.

Here are some glaring facts on the current situation in this country: The level of underground water has gone down to 1,020 feet from 80-110 feet and is termed a worse scenario. For main crops, water requirement is 99 million acres feet (MAF), however, often only 78 MAF water is made available. Also, since partition per capita availability of water in a year has dropped drastically to about 1,500 cubic meters from 5,000 cubic meters.

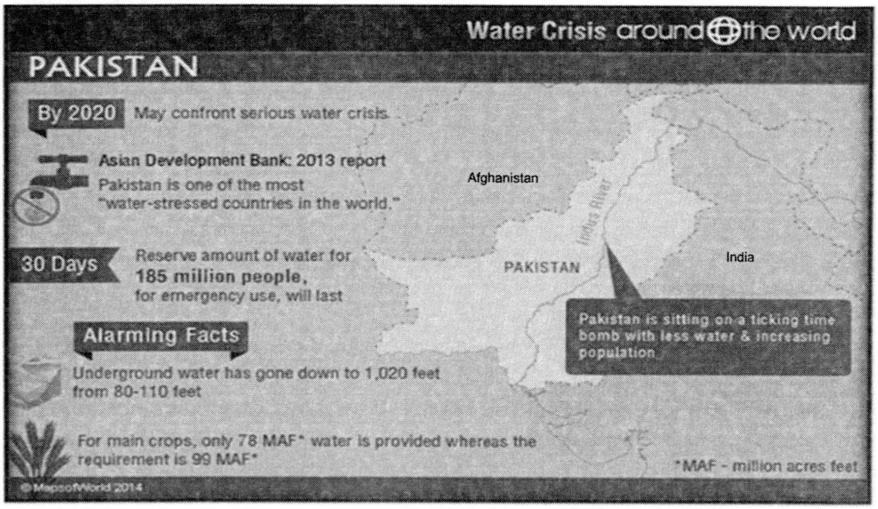

Fig. 2.10: Water crisis - Pakistan

Morocco

Morocco has limited renewable water resources. Agriculture is a major activity here that accounts for 80 percent of water consumption in the country. But climate change and drought cycles have had a major impact on water supply. Besides, the quality of water is deteriorating. The reasons for this include the silting of dams and untreated waste mixing with water. According to estimates, 35 percent of water is lost because of the poor condition of water pipes in urban areas.

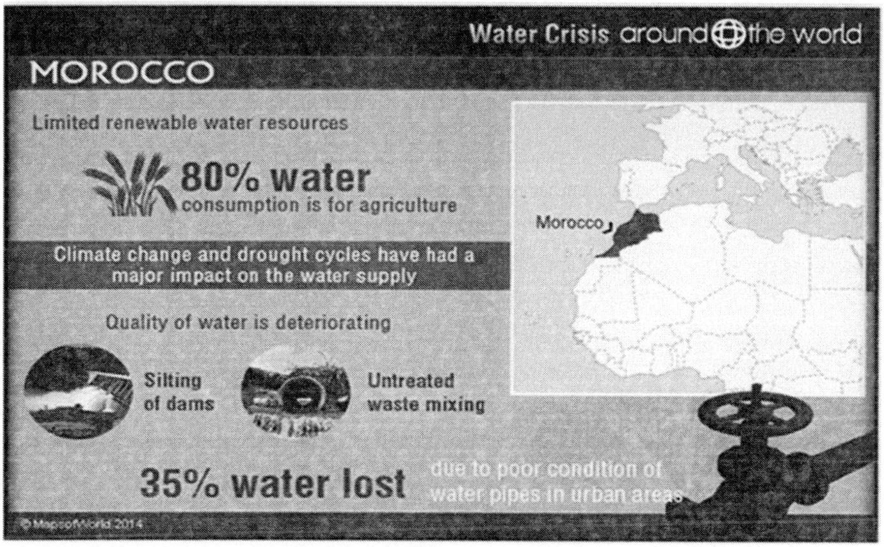

Fig. 2.11: Water crisis - Morocco

India

India faces a water crisis that's been building for decades, and may soon reach a flash point. While India's population increased from 1.03 billion in 2001 to 1.21 billion in 2011, the yearly average per capita availability of water went down from 1,816 cubic meters to 1,545 cubic meters in the same period. This makes India officially 'water-stressed' that is, per capita availability is below 1,700 cubic meters. India's water crisis is set to get worse: by 2025 the per capita availability is projected to be 1,340 cubic meters.

Severe depletion of groundwater is another serious concern, with 60 percent of agriculture in north India dependent on groundwater. In another two decades, according to the World Bank, India's underground aquifers will reach a "critical condition."

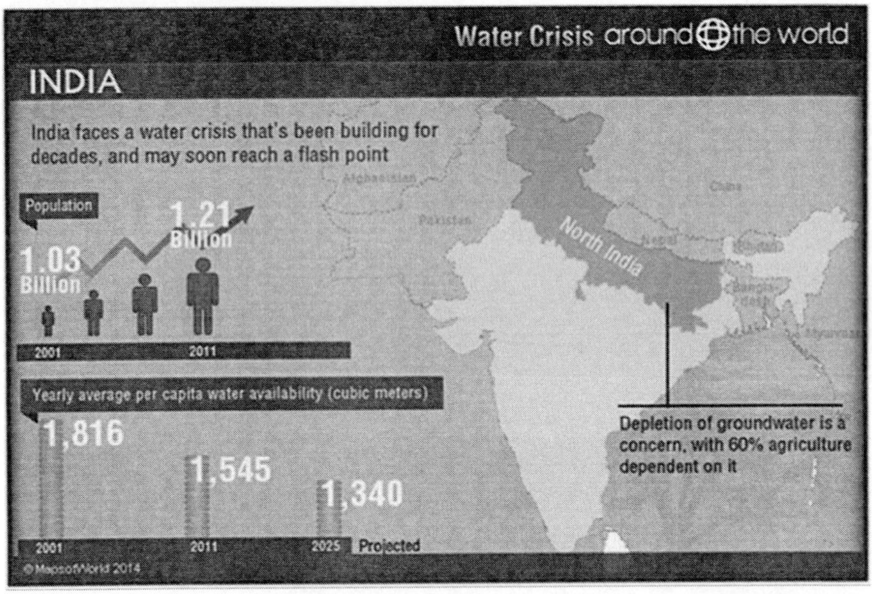

Fig. 2.12: Water crisis - India

China

Along with its spectacular economic growth over the last two decades, China faces huge ecological challenges. One of them is the looming water crisis. Indeed, if India and China can get their acts together, a significant dent would be made in the global water crisis. Incredibly, more than half of China's 50,000 rivers that existed at the beginning of the 20th century have disappeared.

Jiao Yong, the country's vice-minister of water resources, was quoted as saying in 2014: "China has more than 400 cities with a shortfall of water, some 110 of which are facing serious scarcity."

More bad news: Over 70 percent of the country's lakes and rivers are polluted and this according to government reports with nearly half suspected to contain water unfit for human contact or consumption. Though China has over 20 percent of the world population, but contains only seven percent of its fresh water.

This implies that the current water situation has reached to an awful stage globally and it's high time when nations must come together and take unified, concrete, and definitive measures to combat this critical situation.

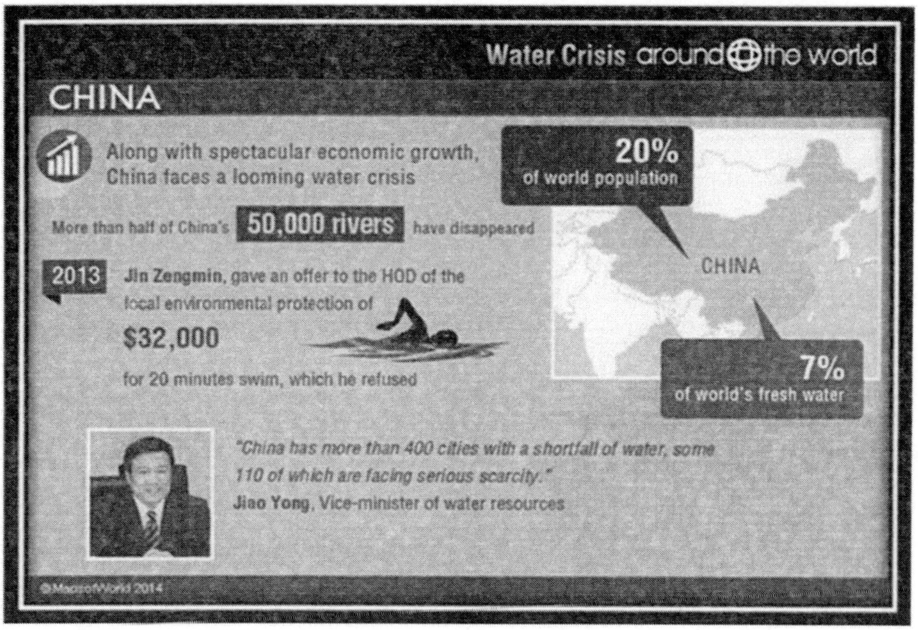

Fig. 2.13: Water crisis – China

Key Policy Interventions Needed

1. Water conservation through development of watersheds and river basins,
    - increase in storage capacity and linking of rivers;
2. Effective water use through improved irrigation systems, water efficient crops and recycling of waste water;
3. Prevention of water pollution by banning the discharge of untreated sewage and effluent in river, judicious use of agro-chemicals and regulation on over-exploitation of ground water;
4. Water resources management and distribution through metered water supply, pricing of water for sustainability;
5. Awareness and orientation of water users for conservation of water and change in lifestyle.

How to Conserve Water

A shortage is caused by too much demand, or not enough supply. Therefore, there is an urgent need to conserve fresh water through household conservation. The following measures may be implemented:

1. Limit the time you spend watering the lawn, showering, running the garbage disposal, and the running faucets.
2. Fix leaky faucets. One drip a second can waste 2,000 gallons a year.
3. Buy water-efficient plumbing fixtures. If all plumbing fixtures in United States were replaced with water conserving fixtures, we could save 3.4 to 8.4 billion gallons of water a day.
4. Use moderate amounts of low phosphate cleaners and detergents. Eliminate the use of drain cleaners. Use recycled products.
5. Wash your car on the lawn instead of the driveway. Water that lands on an impermeable surface, such as pavement, flows through the watershed to the nearest body of water and deposits its contamination. Your lawn, on the other hand, can trap and break down most foreign agents.
6. Limit the use of lawn fertilizers, and be sure to use only phosphorus-free lawn fertilizers. Most lawns already have sufficient phosphorous, and when more is added it runs through the watershed and causes algae growth in surrounding lakes.

There is a Need to Learn

1. Realize that many human activities affect water quality. Wetlands, groundwater, and waterways are destroyed by construction, polluted runoff, and spills. Population growth only intensifies these impacts.
2. Become an educated consumer; buy recycled and environmentally friendly products.
3. Learn to recognize and become knowledgeable about aquatic nuisance species. Exotic invaders (such as Eurasian water milfoil, zebra mussels, and thousands more) cause habitat destruction, decrease biological diversity, and cause millions of dollars of damage in United States each year.

Change Your Daily Habits

1. Rethink your daily habits and help reduce water pollution and water use. Bike, walk, or carpool to reduce the production toxic air pollutants that acid rain.
2. Turn down the water heater temperature and the home thermostat to reduce your energy usage and help curb pollutants that cause acid rain.
3. Finally, share your knowledge with others. Try to remember that our actions have a widespread impact on the lasting quality of freshwater resources. We can and must make a difference.

Conclusion

India is not a water deficit country, but due to severe neglect and lack of monitoring of water resources development projects, several regions in the country experience water stress from time to time. Further neglect in this sector will lead to water scarcity during the next 1-2 decades. It is therefore necessary to prevent this crisis by making best use of the available technologies and resources to conserve the existing water resources, convert them into utilisable form and make efficient use of them for agriculture, industrial production and human consumption. Imposing regulatory measures to prevent the misuse of water and introducing rewards and punishment to encourage judicious use of water, will be helpful to conserve water. Finally, awareness and orientation of all the water users to change their lifestyle to conserve water can help the country to tide over the water crisis in the future. The challenge is manageable provided we have favourable policies and mechanisms to persuade our people to change their lifestyle.

REFERENCES

Aaron, T. and Wolf, A. K. (2006). Water Can Be a Pathway to Peace, Not War, *Environmental Change and Security Program*, 1-6.

Amarasinghe, U. A., Shah, T., Turral, H. and Anand, B.K. (2007). India's Water Future to 2025-2050: Business as Usual Scenario and Deviations. Research Report 123, IWMI.

Camilleri, F. (2003). The World's Water Crisis: Present Developments and Future Conditions. *Division for Industry, Research, Energy, Environment and STOA* , 1-39.

Christopher, M. (2013). Water Wars: The Brahmaputra River and Sino-Indian Relations. *Center on Irregular Warfare & Armed Groups* , 1-39.

Cooley, J. K. (2008). World War for Water. *Foreign Policy* . 54, 3-26.

George williamsherk, P.W.(2012). Water Wars in the Near Future? Reconciling Competing Claims for the Worlds Diminishing Fresh Water Resources-The Challenge of the Next Millennium. *The Centre for Energy, Petroleum and Mineral Law and Policy*, 1-8.

Govt. of India. 2009. Background Note for Consultation Meeting with Policy Makers on Review of National Water Policy. Ministry of Water Resources. 50.

Hofwegen, P.V and Svendsen, M.(2000). A Vision for Water for Food and Rural Development. The 2nd World Water Forum, 1-73.

HRH Rijsberman, F.R. (2000). Summary Report of the 2nd World Water Forum: Water Policy 2(2000):387-395.

Hull, J. W. (2000). The War Over Water. *Regional Resource of Strategic Management*, 1-12.

IUCN (2000). Vision for Water and Nature: A World Strategy for Conservation and Sustainable Management of Water Resources in the 21st Century, 1-34.

IWMI (2000). World Water Supply and Demand in 2025. World Water Scenario Analyses.

Kijne J.W., Barker, R. and Molden, D.J. (2003). Water Productivity in Agriculture: Limits and Opportunities for Improvement, 1-31.

Keller,J., Keller,A. and Davids,G.(1998). River Basin Development Phases and Implications of Closure. *Journal of Applied Irrigation Science*. 33(2):145-164.

Kumar, S. (2013). The Looming Threat of Water Scarcity. *World watch institute*, 1-7.

Lemly, A.D., Kingsford, R.T. and Thompson, J.R. (2000). Irrigated Agriculture and Wildlife Conservation: Conflict on a Global Scale. *Environmental Management* 25(5):485-512.

Meigh, J.R., McKenzie, A., Austin, B.N., Bradford, R.B., and Reynard,N.S. (1998). Assessment of Global water Resources – Phase II. Estimates of Present and Future Water Availability in Eastern and Southern Africa, 1-17.

Mehta, P. (2012). Impending Water Crisis in India and Comparing Clean Water. *Archives of Applied Science Research*, 4 (1): 497-507.

Narayanamoorthy, A. (2004). Drip Irrigation in India: Can it Solve the Water Crisis? Water Policy 6(2):117-130.

Postel, S. (1998). Water for Food Production: Will there be Enough in 2025. *Bio Science* 48(8): 629-637.

Postel, S. (2001). Safeguarding Our Water - Growing More Food with Less Water. *Scientific American Journal*, 40-45.

Pruss, A, Day K, Fewtrell, L and Bartram, J. (2002). Estimating the Global Burden of Disease from Water, Sanitation and Hygiene at a Global Level. *Environmental Health Perspectives*, 110, 537-542.

Raskin, P., Gleick, P., Kirshen, P., Pontius, G. and Strzepek K. (1997) Water Futures: Assessment of Long Range Patterns and Prospects, 1-19.

Renault, D. and Wallender,W.W. (2000) Nutritional Water Productivity and Diets. *Agricultural Water Management* 45, 275-296.

Richard,A., Lane, M. L. (2010) The Water Crisis in Third World Countries. *Monterey Starkey*, 1-30.

Rijsberman, F.R. and Molden D.J. (2001) Balancing Water Uses: Water for Food and Water for Nature. *International Conference on Freshwater*, 43-56.

Rijsberman, F. R. (2004). Water Scarcity: Fact or Fiction? *International Water Management Institute*, 1-14.

Rijsberman, F.R. (2004). The Water Challenge. *Global Crises, Global Solutions*, 1-15

Rijsberman, F.R. (2002). Troubled Waters, Water Troubles: Overcoming an Important Constraint to Food Security. Sustainable Food Security for all by 2020: *Proceedings of an International Conference*, 141-144.

Rijsberman, F.R and Mohamed, A. (2003). Water, Food and Environment: Conflict or Dialogue? *Water Science and Technology* 47, 53-62.

Robb, J. (2012). World War III: War for Water? *The Omega Letter Christian Intelligence* 1-3.

Rosegrant, M.W., Cai, X. and Clire, S.A. 2002. Global Water Outlook to 2025: Averting an Impending Crisis. *Food Policy Report, IWMI*. 36.

ShamaPerveen, R. S. (2012). India's Deepening Water Crisis. *Water Risks for Indian Industries*, 1-19.

Seckler, D., Molden, D.J. and Sakhtivadivel, R. (2003). The concept of Efficiency in Water Resources Management and Policy, 1-9.

Seckler, D., Amarasinghe, Molden, U .D.J,de Silva, R., Barker, R. (1998). World Water Demand and Supply, 1990 to 2025: *Scenarios and Issues*. IWMI Research Report 19.

Selby, J. (2005). The Geopolitics of Water in the Middle East: Fantasies and Realities. *Third World Quarterly* , 1-21.

Shiklomanov, I.A. (1998). World Water Resources: An Appraisal for the 21st Century. IHP Report, 1-23.

Smakthin, V., Revenga, C.and Doll, P. (2004). Environmental Water Requirements in Global-scale Water Resources Assessments. Comprehensive Assessment of Water Management in Agriculture Research Report, 445-471.

UNWWDR (United Nations World Water Development Report) (2003). Water for People, Water for Life, 1-25.

Wallace, J.S. and Gregory, P.J (2002). Water Resources and their Use in Food Production. *Aquatic Sciences* 64, 363-375.

Wallace, J.S. (2000). Increasing Agricultural Water Efficiency to Meet Future Food Production. *Agriculture, Ecosystems and Environment* 82, 105-119.

Wathab,A. (2009). water and war. *ICRC Response, Ecosystem and Environment,* 1-24.

Yang, H, P., Reichert, K., Abbaspour and Zehnder, A.J.B. (2012) A Water Resources Threshold and its Implications for Food Security. *Environmental Science and Technology* 37, 3048-3054.

Technologies for Water and Wastewater Management **Pages 38-62**
Edited by: Dr. Vijender Singh & Dr. Pawan Kumar 'Bharti'
ISBN: 978-93-88854-53-5
Edition: 2020
Published by: Discovery Publishing House Pvt. Ltd., New Delhi (India)

3

Hydrogeological Setting and Status of Water Table in Bonai Area of Sundargarh District, Odisha

Pramod Chandra Sahu

ABSTRACT

Hydrogeolocial setting of an area is described with respect to the nature and disposition of subsurface geological features followed by the type of aquifer system and occurrence of groundwater. Systematic well inventory studies and its significance in the evaluation of water table configuration, groundwater flow direction and also water table fluctuation from pre-monsoon to post-monsoon periods have been dealt with. Depending upon water bearing and water yielding properties, the rock formations in the study area are broadly divided into following two units. 1. Consolidated formations. 2. Unconsolidated formations. The aquifer thickness is maximum in Bonaigarh area whereas its thickness is minimum in K-Balang area. Occurrences of potential saturated fractures are more frequent in granitic rocks than other hard rocks in the study area. Granitic rocks exhibit up to 3 sets of saturated fractures within a depth of 60m in Bonai and Lahunipada blocks. The numbers of sets of fractures decreases downward. The yield potential of wells in granitic rocks ranges from 3 lps to 20 lps. The water level in the pre and post-monsoon periods in the study area shows the following trends. 1. Falling trends in both the periods. 2. Falling trends in pre-monsoon and no change in post-monsoon period. 3. No change in both the periods.

Keywords: *Hydrogeology, Water table, Crystalline, Fracture, Trend*

Introduction

Groundwater is one of the most valuable natural resources, which supports human health, economic development and ecological diversity. Because of its several inherent qualities (consistent temperature, widespread and continuous availability, excellent natural quality, limited vulnerability, low development cost, drought reliability etc.), it has become an immensely important and dependable source of water supplies in all climatic regions including both urban and rural areas of developed and developing countries. The occurrence, origin and movement of groundwater depend mainly on the geologic

P.G. Department of Geology, M.P.C. Autonomous College,Takhatpur, Baripada, Dist: Mayurbhanj, Odisha, India. Pin-757003 framework, i.e. lithology, thickness, structures and permeability of aquifers. Groundwater in hard rock aquifers is essentially confined to fractured and/ or weathered horizons. Therefore, extensive hydrogeological investigations are often requisite to systematically understand groundwater conditions. The typical objectives of any exploratory groundwater investigations are to locate, delineate and evaluate new sources of groundwater. Hydrogeolocial setting of an area is described with respect to the nature and disposition of subsurface geological features followed by the type of aquifer system and occurrence of groundwater. Besides this, systematic well inventory studies and its significance in the evaluation of water table configuration, groundwater flow direction and also water table fluctuation from pre-monsoon to post-monsoon periods have been dealt with. In the study area, groundwater is exploited through dug wells and bore wells to meet the domestic and irrigation requirements tapping mostly the shallow depth aquifers.

The study area occupies the eastern part of the Sundargarh district, lying towards the northern extremity of Orissa. It is bounded by the north latitudes 21° 35′ - 22° 10′ and east longitudes 84° 30′ - 85° 25′ and falls in the Survey of India Toposheet Nos. 73B/12, 73B/16, 73C/9, 73C/10, 73C/13, 73C/14, 73F/4, 73G/1, 73G/2 and 73G/5. It is delimited by the state of Jharkhand in the northeast, Keonjhar district of Orissa in the east, Deogarh and Angul districts in the south,Sambalpur district in the west and Panposh subdivision of Sundargarh district in the north. In ancient time i.e. during Samudragupta's era, the present district of Sundargarh was a part of the territory of south Kosala and later on it was a part of the Gangpur Estate. The total geographical area of the study area is around 2200 sq.km. The Bonai subdivision is divided into 4 administrative blocks namely Bonai, Gurundia, Koira and Lahunipada.

The literature available on groundwater resources related studies was reviewed in detail. Choudhury et. al. 2010, Deepika et. al. 2013; Dinesh et al. 2007; Jaiswal et. al. 2003; Jesiya et. al. 2015; Magesh et. al. 2012; Reddy et. al.2003; Saud 2010; Shaban et al. 2006; Sharma & Ray2015; Suja Rose & Krishna(2009 and Serelathan, P. (2007). GEC (1997), P.C. Sahu (2018) and Tweed et al. 2007 have emphasized on utilization of remotely sensed data in conjunction with co-lateral data in GIS platform in delineation of groundwater potential zones. The literature available on ground water evaluation, development and management was reviewed in detail. Sikdar et al. (2007), Sankar and Venkatram (2002), Chauhan (2000) Rokade et al. (2007), Mahapatra et al. (2000), Patnaik (2003), Reddy et al. (2003), Sahu and Sahoo (2006) and Sahu (2008) in their study relating to ground water exploration and targeting potential ground water zone, have emphasized that integrated geological, geophysical, remote sensing and GIS techniques should be adopted for targeting potential ground water zones in hard rock areas.

Methodology

1. Geologic methods, involving interpretation of geologic data and field reconnaissance represent the first important step in any groundwater investigation. Published geologic data concerning to an area supplemented by field reconnaissance provide much information regarding groundwater occurrence of the area.
2. A preliminary evaluation with regards to groundwater occurrence and yield prospects has been drawn from the geological studies of the area. A detailed geological study with special reference to lithology, landform and structure was undertaken to understand the groundwater regime better and visualise the gross aquifer conditions like the nature of aquifer materials, types of aquifer, the type of wells suitable, their depth range, yield range, success rate, sustainability etc. in each unit.
3. Lithologs of different locations in the area by CGWB and some state government organisation were collected and compiled to get a clear picture of the subsurface formations and to draw meaningful inferences regarding the depth of soil/ overburden, weathered zone, fractured zone and bedrock.
4. This was again strengthened by Vertical Electrical Sounding (VES) at 44 locations employing Schlumberger electrode configurations.
5. Systematic hydro geological data have been collected both for pre and post monsoon periods during well inventory from 85 dug wells. The data comprises of location, depth to water table, total depth of wells and well diameter. From these data, different types of water level maps were prepared and the water level data are statistically analysed.
6. To understand the nature of the deep and medium aquifer systems data relating to the deep bore wells & tube wells respectively drilled by CGWB and Rural Water Supply and Sanitation (RWSS) in different localities of the area have been collected and a comparative study was made for deep, medium and shallow aquifers.

Results & Discussion

Lithostratigraphy

The study area forms the eastern part of the Sundargarh district. The rocks of Iron Ore Group and Darjing Group are exposed in the eastern and western parts of the study area respectively. The middle part of the area is underlain by Bonai Granite. The Precambrian rocks of the Deogarh Group are exposed along the southern margin of the study area. The various lithostratigraphic units of the study area which have been shown in the Fig. 3.1 are discussed below.

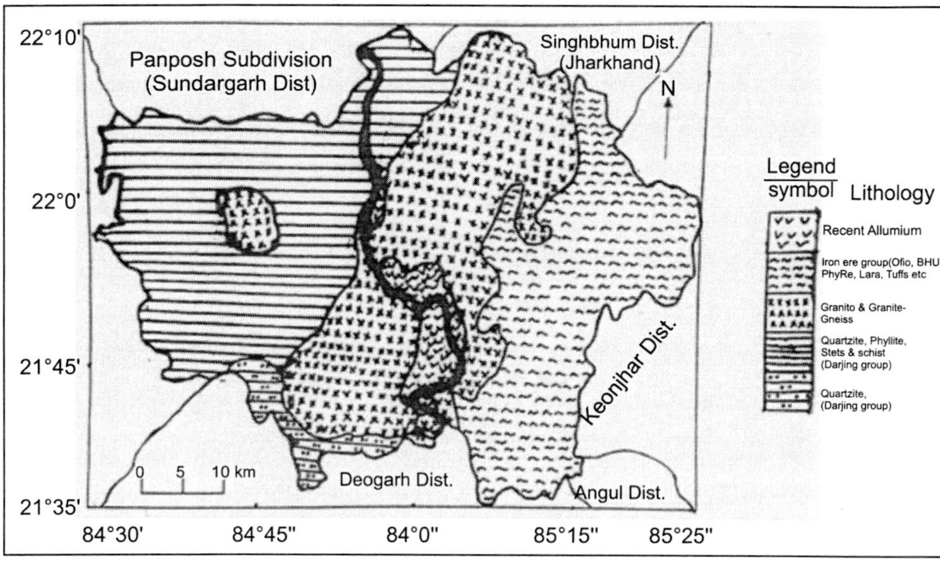

Fig. 3.1: Lithological map of the study area

Iron Ore Group: The Iron Ore Group (IOG) of rocks are exposed in the eastern part of the study area (Koira & Lahunipada block). The stratigraphic succession of IOG begins with a locally developed basal orthoquartzite and conglomerate. The basal beds are successively overlain by lower lava formation, lower phyliite, Banded Iron Formation (BIF) and upper phyliite and upper lava formation. The BIF crops out in ridges arranged in sharply bent horse-shoe pattern. The manganese ores are restricted to upper phyliite formation found in the valley region. Occasionally phyllites have been bauxitised. In the rocks of Iron Ore Group, groundwater occurs in the secondary porosity developed during tectonic disturbances. The hydrogeology of this terrain is controlled by the thickness of the weathered zone, degree and extent of fracturing, slope of hills and infilling materials of the intermontane valleys. However, at some places the intrusive act as barriers preventing the groundwater flow.

Darjing Group: These rocks are exposed in the western part of the study area lying between Bonai Granite and Gangpur Group . The lithoassemblage is characterisedbyarepetitivesequenceofmetamorphosedrudaceous,arenaceous, carbonaceous and argillaceous sediments having basic and ultrabasic dykes. The dominant lithounits are feldspathic quartzite,carbonaceous phyliite, slate, staurolite schist, mica schist etc. These rocks have undergone deformation in several phases during Satpura cycle (c.a. 1200 my) with a typical E-W to ENE-WSW tectonic trend. They show features of shearing and faulting probably related to Singhbhum Thrust. The Tamporkela Granite, a small granite body is intrusive into the Darjing Group of rocks. Groundwater movement and storage in this group of rocks occurs within weathered residuum, joints/ fractures and other secondary porosity like foliation plane.

Deogarh Group: The rocks of this group occupy the southern margin of the study area. The important rock type is Quartzite, a member of Clastic Formation of the Deogarh Group). Two types of quartzite are noticed in the study area, i.e. (*a*) micaceous quartzite, (*b*) massive quartzite. The micaceous quartzite mainly consists of quartz, sericite and muscovite along with few grains of orthoclase. This quartzite forms linear hills trending E-W in the southern margin of the study area.

Bonai Granite: The Bonai Granite occupies a triangular area covering over 700 sq. km. in the central part of the study area. It is bordered on the east by Iron Ore Group. Within the granite body there are numerous enclaves of amphibolite and quartzite-quartz schist. The major component of the Bonai Granite is a porphyritic granite which encloses small patches of a migmatitic tonalite. Mineralogically, the porphyritic granite consists of megacrysts of plagioclase and K-feldspars (Orthoclase and Microcline) in a finer quartz-biotite groundmass. The Bonai Granite itself is intruded by dolerite dykes and ultramafic bodies. Most of the dykes are quartz dolerite which are slightly metamorphosed and consists of saussuritised plagioclase, clino-l Pyroxenei with varying degree of alteration to chloritic and actinolitic amphibolite . Apart from the quartz dolerite, other rocks found in the dyke suite are peridotite. The prominent trends of dykes in granite body are NE-SW, NW-SE and NEE-SSW. In the rocks of Bonai Granite, groundwater occurs in the secondary porosity. The hydrogeology of the area is controlled by the thickness of the weathered zone, degree and extent of fracturing. However, at some places fractured and weathered dykes act as potential groundwater zone (Juniani and Kantasara).

Laterite: Both ferruginous and manganiferous laterites are developed as small discontinuous patches in Koira, Lahunipada and Bonai blocks of the study area which act as a potential source of groundwater, forming shallow aquifers.

Alluvium: Alluvium of recent origin has limited occurrence along the banks of the stream and rivers which are comparatively more fertile and also have good groundwater potential.

Structure

The principal lithostratigraphic units of the study area are Iron Ore Group, Darjing Group, Deogarh Group and Bonai Granite with intrusives. The important structural features observed in this area are described below.

1. The BIF has been folded into a major synclinorium i.e. the horse-shoe synclinorium. It is a low north to north-easterly plunging structure with inverted western limb.

2. The Darjing Group of rocks have been affected by major fold movements giving rise to ENE-WSW trending major folds. This fold structure has been interpreted as a synclinorium. Several faults and shear zones have been developed in the rocks of BIF and in the metasediments of Darjing Group. These are represented by occurrence of quartz veins, fault brecccia etc.
3. Several regional axial plane faults are associated with the horse-shoe synclinorium.
4. Very prominent fracture system occupied by the dolerite dykes are noticeable in Bonai Granite. The prominent trends are NW-SE, NE-SW and NNE-SSW.
5. The area is traversed by a number of lineaments which are traces of major fractures. In the study area, the lineament density is more in the eastern and western parts of the study area than in the central part.

Subsurface Geology

Study of subsurface formations is essential for locating potential water bearing zones in an area. Suitable structures for groundwater occurrence depend primarily on geology and geomorphologic set-up of an area. Since the present area is characterised by a variety of rock types, it is quite natural that the groundwater potential also vary widely. For hydro geological study, the area can be broadly divided into two hydro geologic units namely- (*a*) Consolidated formations (*b*) Unconsolidated formations. In the hard rock terrain the occurrence of groundwater depends on the presence of weathered layer, fractures and fissures while in the unconsolidated formations it depends on porosity and permeability of the formations. To meet the rapidly increasing demand of water for domestic and irrigational use with assured supply throughout the year, identification of water bearing zone is essential. Borehole lithology study is the direct method for obtaining true information about subsurface strata along with the nature, composition, thickness and potentialities of the aquifer(s).

In the study area, exploratory drilling operations have been undertaken by different central and state government organisations like CGWB, DWR and RWSS Sundargarh etc. The exploratory drilling data is presented in Table 3.1.

Table 3.1: Exploratory Drilling Data of the Study Area

Sl. No.	Location	Block	Geo-logical Forma-tion	Depth drilled in m.	Length of casing (m bgl.)	SWL (mbgl)	Dis-charge (lps)	Draw down	Type of well
1.	Bonaigarh (E)	Bonai	Bonai Granite	139.90	35,3	10.24	8.50	31.90	E/W

2.	Bonaigarh (W)	Bonai	Bonai Granite	166.70	32.6	9.38	8.51	31.40	O/W
3.	Jamkei (N)	Bonai	Bonai Granite	178.50	28.5	12.17	10.00	21.13	E/W
4.	Jamkei(S)	Bonai	Bonai Granite	166.70	31.5	12.74	8.50	10.25	O/W
5.	Kantasara	Bonai	Bonai Granite	189.30	41.6	11.55	9.68	20.42	E/W
6.	K.Bolang (Ei)	Koira	Bonai Granite	172.80	21.2	8.05	10.00	8.77	E/W
7.	KBolang (Ej)	Koira	Bonai Granite	148.40	18.2	8.61	10.15	6.33	O/W
8.	K.Bolang (Wi)	Koira	Bonai Granite &Basic Intrusive	19.30	18.5	8.24	1.00	2.32	O/W
9.	K. Bolang (W2)	Koira	Bonai Granite Basic Intrusive	16.20	15.5	8.10	—	—	O/W
10.	Lahunipada (N)	Lahuni-pada	Bonai Granite	143.70	26.4	3.18	4.80	32.85	E/W
11.	Lahunipada (S)	Lahuni-pada	Bonai Granite	166.70	27.2	3.52	3.50	15.65	O/W
12.	Rajamunda (N)	La-hunip-ara	Bonai Granite	104.70	37.2	3.30	8.00	16.25	E/W
13.	Rajamunda (S)	La-hunip-ara	Bonai Granite	105.45	37.0	3.16	10.00	23.77	O/W
14.	Banki	Gurun-dia	Darjing roup (Mica Schist)	191.10	21.0	8.64	1,50	22.60	E/W
15.	Chandiposh	Gurun-dia	Darjing Group (Mica Schist)	175.40	24.5	7.85	1.95	28.42	O/W

During the present study the borehole data available from different areas have been analysed in detail to understand the subsurface configuration of the study area (Table 3.2). The lithologs derived from the borehole data and lithologs prepared from resistivity data of selected places have been compared (Fig. 3.2). It is quite evident from the comparative study that the observed resistivity values closely tally with the lithologs obtained from boreholes in the study area. Hence, the resistivity data is found to be reliable to infer the subsurface geology of the present area. From the fence diagram (Fig. 3.3) it is evident that the thickness of the aquifers is not same in all the places. The aquifer thickness is maximum in Bonaigarh area whereas its thickness is minimum in K-Balang area. The fence diagram gives a clear picture about the spatial variation in thickness of aquifers of the study area.

Table 3.2: Borehole Data of the Study Area

Sl. No.	Location	Block	Depth drilled (in m)	SWL (mbgl)	Dis-charge (lps)	Aquifer Mate-rials	Weath-ered zone tapped in m bgl.	Depth of frac-ture zone
1.	Bonaigarh (E)	Bonai	139.90	10.24	8.50	Weathered & fractured Granite	4.0-39.6	34, 68, 74
2.	Bonaigarh (W)	Bonai	166.70	9.38	8.51	Weathered & fractured Granite	3.2-33.6	76, 82, 91, 196
3.	Jamkei (N)	Bonai	178.50	12.17	10.0	Weathered & fractured Granite	5.0-41.9	28, 76, 85, 95, 130
4.	Jamkei (S)	Bonai	166.70	12.74	8.50	Weathered & fractured Granite	2.4-35.6	28, 74, 86, 90, 132
5.	Kantasara	Bonai	189.30	11.55	9.68	Weathered Granite and Basic Intrusive	3.0-37.0	25, 75, 110
6.	K.Bolang (E1)	Koira	172.80	8.05	10.00	Weathered Granite Gneiss with fractured Basic Intrusive	4.0-42.0	26, 31, 88, 122

7.	KLBolang (E2)	Koira	148.40	8.61	10.15	Weathered Granite Gneiss with fractured Basic Intrusive	5.9-33.0	26, 30.4, 76, 94, 131
8.	K.Bolang (Wi)	Koira	19.30	8.24	1.00	Weathered Granite	3.0-17.2	10.3, 16.5, 31.0
9,	K. Bolang (W_2)	Koira	16.20	8.10	—	Weathered Granite	2.8-15.0	7.3, 13.5
10.	Lahuni-pada (N)	Lahuni-pada	143.70	3.18	4.80	Weathered & fractured Granite	6.8-45.8	37, 59, 70, 75
11.	Lahuni-pada (S)	Lahuni-pada	166.70	3.52	3.50	Weathered & fractured Granite	5.4-40.0	84.3, 136.2, 152
12.	Rajamun-da (N)	Lahuni-pada	104.70	3.30	8.00	Weathered & fractured Granite Gneiss	3.9-37.7	54, 79.3, 96
13.	Rajamun-da (S)	Lahuni-pada	105.45	3.16	10.00	Weathered Granite Gneiss	2.8-41.5	68, 88, 103,
14.	Banki	Gurun-dia	191.10	8.64	1.50	Weathered Mica Schist	5.0-37.2	8.2, 48.2, 71.8
15.	Chandip-osh	Gurun-dia	175.40	7.85	1.95	Weathered Mica Schist and Phyllite	3.9-40.8	18, 45, 89.6

Hydrogeological Units

The study area comes under the Precambrian crystalline groundwater province of Orissa. A wide variety of rock types occur in the study area. Granite, granite gneiss, mica schist, phyllite, slate, BIF, basic intrusive and metavolcanics (meta-basalt and amphibolite) are common rock types in this shield area commonly referred to as hard rock terrain. Subjected to polyphase deformation, the rocks are intensely folded, faulted and fractured. The hydrogeological conditions in different parts of the study area show wide variation. Depending upon water bearing and water yielding properties, the rock formations in the study area are broadly divided into following two units.

1. Consolidated formations.
2. Unconsolidated formations

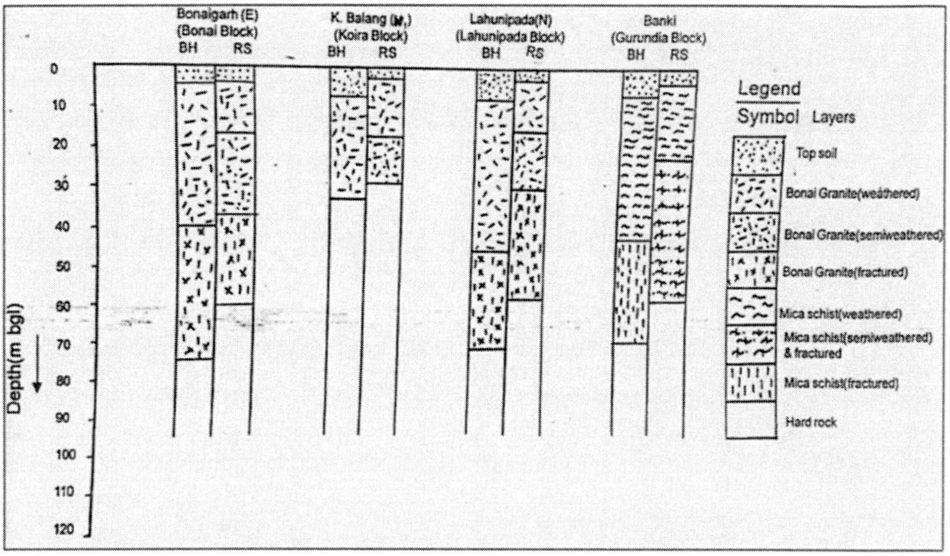

Fig. 3.2: Comparison of lithologs derived from the borehole data and resistivity

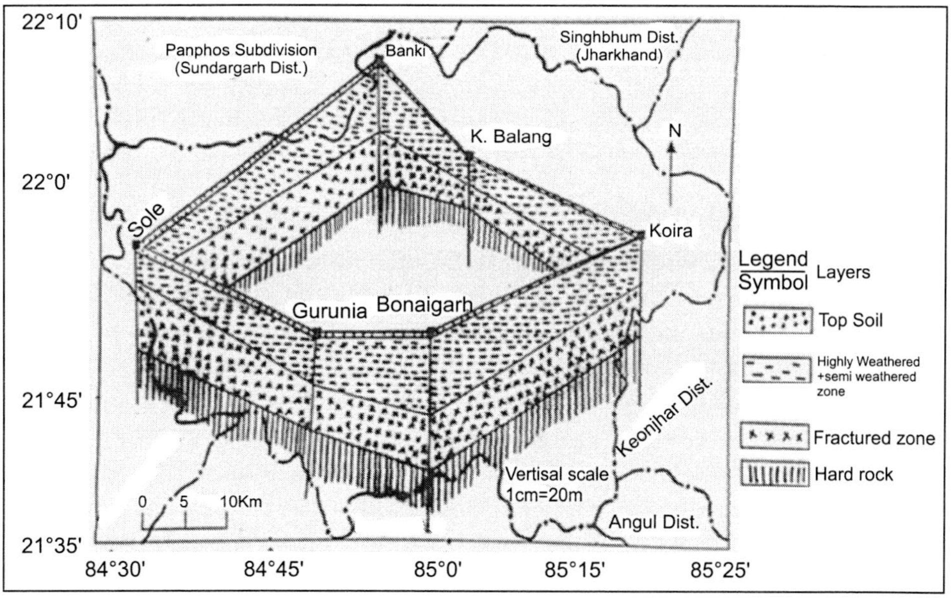

Fig. 3.3: Fence diagram of the study area

Consolidated formations: In the study area, nearly 98% of the total area is underlain by consolidated formations comprising of the Precambrian metasediments such as mica schist, phyllite, quartzite of Darjing Group and BIF, phyllite etc. of IOG and Bonai Granite. These rocks are devoid of primary porosity. The occurrence and movement of groundwater in these hard rocks are controlled by secondary porosity developed through weathering and fracturing. Groundwater occurs in weathered residuum under unconfined condition and circulates through fractures and fissures below. The water bearing and water yielding capacity of these rocks depend upon the degree of weathering and extent of fracturing and fissuring. Hydraulic troughs in morphological depressions and fracture lineaments provide favourable locales for groundwater reserves.

The weathered residuum is the product of in-situ disintegration and decomposition of the parent rocks. The thickness of weathered residuum depends upon topography, vegetative cover, texture and mineralogy of the host rocks. The weathered residuum is generally thicker in topographic lows than in upland areas. Under favourable circumstances, the weathered residuum is a good repository of groundwater. Granite and granite gneiss when weathered produce quartzitic residuum with kaolin and clayey materials leached out whereas slate and phyllite yield clayey products. Granite and granite gneiss are susceptible to deep weathering and form a weathered mantle which is good aquifers. Due to their inherent rheologic properties, the regoliths developed on slate, phyllite and mica schist are clayey and poor water yielders. Quartzite is generally resistant to weathering and form uplands.

Intensely weathered and fractured granite form most productive aquifers in the study area. The yield potential ranges from 3 to 10 Ips (CGWB). The yield potential in slate, phyllite and mica schist ranges from 1 to 5 Ips. Tensile fractures within a depth of 100m form potential conduits for groundwater movement. Generally, the fracture system consists of two or more sets of syntectonic fractures which together form one hydraulic system in the rocks.

Unconsolidated Formations: Laterite and alluvium of sub-recent to recent origin constitute the unconsolidated formations. Laterite and lateritic soils occur in patches as capping over Bonai Granite and Iron Ore Group in Bonai, Koira and Lahunipada blocks. This formation is usually porous and permeable in nature and form very good shallow aquifers, developed through open wells. Alluvium occurs as small discontinuous patches along the course of the Brahmani River. The average thickness of the alluvium is 15m. Alluvium forms very good shallow aquifer to be developed through dug wells. The coarse grained sands and gravels form the main repository of groundwater. The yield of dug well is generally 5 to 6 Ips, though higher yield of 10 Lps is encountered at few places (Kantasara, Tendra and Bargogua).

Aquifer Systems: Groundwater in the study area occurs primarily in four different aquifer systems: (*a*) weathered mantle (*b*) saprolitic zone (*c*) fractured zone (*d*) alluvial zone.

Weathered mantle: The weathered mantle has a thin layer of top soil underlain by weathered rocks. The thickness of the weathered mantle varies from place to place and reaches maximum to a depth of 20 m bgl. Groundwater occurs under water table condition and it is mostly developed by dug wells, the most common groundwater structure of the study area. Depending upon the topography and geological set-up, the productivity of the aquifer varies from place to place. In general, groundwater fluctuation is high in this zone and in peak summer some of the dug wells go dry.

Saprolitic zone: This zone is sandwiched between the weathered mantle and fresh rock mass. It is a partly weathered zone but retaining its original features like joints, fractures etc. It represents a kind of transitional character between fresh rock and weathered mantle. In general , the depth of occurrence of this zone varies from 15 to 35 m bgl. Normally, deep and prolonged process of weathering (hydrolysis) facilitates formation of thick saprolitic zone. Groundwater occurs under semi confined condition and yield of this aquifer sometimes go up to 3 Ips which is nearly 40% of the total yield of a successful bore well in this area.

Fracture zone: Rainwater directly or indirectly percolates down into the fracture zones of underlying rocks through interconnected joints, fissures, foliation planes and other weak planes in the Precambrian terrain. The movement and storage of groundwater in the fractures depends upon continuity of fractures, their interconnection, openness, degree of penetration, inclination and closeness to fault planes and shear zone etc. The study of borehole data reveals some relevant information regarding types of fractures encountered during drilling, distribution of saturated fractures at depth and yield from fractures vis-a-vis rock types. The principal types of fractures encountered below weathered zone are Saturated and unsaturated fractures. The unsaturated fractures are of two types - one is completely dry and the other is non-productive. The dry fractures are identified by the presence of quartz veins. The non-productive fractures are those in which fractured rock particle bears the marks of passage of water and air (oxidation mark) but the zone has no recoverable discharge. Besides this, another type of fracture, through rare in occurrence, was encountered during drilling which indicated isolated, more or less perched type of situation. When such fractured zone was encountered, the yield is only for a short initial period after which its yield reduced considerably. The occurrence of potential saturated fractures is mostly restricted down to 60m depth and further below. The litho logical characteristics, age of rock mass and their structural features have significant control on the nature of saturated aquifers. The saturated fractures within the litho logical units most commonly occur in the form of (*i*) fractured and saturated quartz and pegmatite veins and also as basic intrusive (dykes) (*ii*) fractured country rock not having any secondary intrusion or deposits. The contact zone of two lithological units (including intrusive bodies) very often forms aquifer zones in the study area. The contact zone of two hard rock formations generally forms better water yielding situation than the contact zone between hard and soft formations.

The saturated fractures of hard rock terrain of the study area are divided into 2 groups: (1) fractures in Bonai Granite and (2) fractures in metasediments. Saturated fractures in Bonai Granitic terrain which occur below saprolitic zone can be grouped into 3 groups depending upon the depth of occurrence.

(*a*) **Very shallow fractures** - saturated fractures occurring within the semi weathered zone (commonly formed by basic intrusive bodies) or just below the semi weathered zone normally restricted within 20 to 25m depth.

(*b*) **Shallow fractures** - Saturated fractures occurring within the depth range of 25 m to 60 m.

(*c*) **Deep fractures** - saturated fractures occurring below 60m and extend downward up to a depth of 150 to 250m.

It has been studied from the exploratory wells that the above types of fractures exhibit following characteristics in general with respect to yield, drawdown etc.

(*a*) **Very shallow fractures** - (*i*) An increase in discharge, sometimes as high as two to three times than recorded during drilling (*ii*) Drawdown of pumping water level is less and recovery of water level is much faster than that of shallow & deep fractures.

(*b*) **Shallow fractures** - (*i*) A little increase in discharge than that recorded during drilling, discharge remaining more or less same during regular pumping (*ii*) Drawdown of pumping water level is high but less than that of deep fractures. Similarly, though the rate of recovery of water level is slow it is faster than deep fractures.

(*c*) **Deep fractures** - (*i*) yield lower discharge during regular pumping than that recorded during drilling. (*ii*) Records high drawdown of pumping water level and very slow rate of recuperation of water level (*iii*) shows slow rate of drawdown in the initial few minutes of pumping, with higher rate of drawdown afterwards.

Saturated fractures and yield vis-a-vis lithological unit: The yield potential and depth persistence of saturated fractures in different lithological units of the study area have been shown in Table 3 which is summarised below.

1. Occurrences of potential saturated fractures are more frequent in granitic rocks than other hard rocks in the study area. Granitic rocks exhibit up to 3 sets of saturated fractures within a depth of 60m in Bonai and Lahunipada blocks. The numbers of sets of fractures decreases downward. The yield potential of wells in granitic rocks ranges from 3lps to 20 Ips. In general yield potential of saturated fractures in granitic rocks of later age is better than that of the earlier age. The maximum concentration of saturated fractures generally restricted within a depth

of 100m and highly potential saturated fractures are common within a depth of 60m.

2. The schistose rocks of Gurundia block form very low yielding aquifers but presence of substantial amount of non-flaky minerals such as quartz, feldspars etc. facilitate creation of better yielding aquifers in schistose rocks.
3. Phyllite, carbonaceous phyllite and slate, though in general form very low yielding aquifer, hard and brittle variety often forms moderately potential aquifers.
4. The metabasic rocks (metabasalt and amphibolite) form moderately good aquifers, restricted within 100m depth.

Table 3.3: Yield Potential and Depth Persistence of Saturated Fractures in Different Litho-units of the Study Area.

Sl. No.	Litho-units	Depth range of saturated fracture (mbgl)	No. of saturated fractures occurring at different depth ranges				Yield (lps)	
			Up to 60m depth	60-100m depth	100-150m depth	150-200m depth	Range	Avg.
1.	Granitic rocks	11-200.0	1 to 3 sets, very common	Mostly 1 set very common	Mostly 1 set less common	1 set, -only in one well	Negligible -20	3-10
2.	Mica schist	3.2-178.9	1 to 4 sets very common	1 set less frequent	1 set less frequent	—	Negligible -11	1-2
3.	Phyllite	18- 99.5	1 to 4 sets very common	1 set very rare	—	—	Negligible -8	1-2
4.	Basic meta-volcanics	19-87	1 to 4 sets common	1 to 2 sets	—		2-12	3-5

5. Alluvial zone - Alluvium occurs along the bank of the Brahmani river. The average thickness of alluvium is 15 m. It forms good shallow aquifer where groundwater occurs in unconfined conditions. Groundwater from this zone can be extracted through dug wells . The yield potential is high, may be upto 10 Ips.

Well Yields

Pumping tests have been conducted by Central Ground Water Board (CGWB) in a number of open wells tapping different lithounits for assessing the hydraulic characteristics of the formations. The results show that discharge of such wells varies from 2.15 to 9 Ips. It is observed that granite and granite gneiss have better water yielding capacity than schist and phyllite. Pumping tests have been carried out in Exploratory Well (EW) and Observation Well (OW) in the study area by CGWB, whose maximum depths are 200 m bgl. The main objectives of such exploratory drilling is to delineate the occurrence and distribution of potential deeper water bearing fractures in different lithounits and also to assess the development potential within such a great depth. Some of the important results of the exploratory drilling and pumping tests by CGWB are shown. The depth range of saturated fractures varies from 7.3 to 196 m bgl. In general, the productive fractures are restricted within 60 to 70m of depth, though in rare cases, deeper fracture produces high yields as at Rajamunda, Lahunipada etc. In Bonai Granite, the yield ranges from 1 Ips to 10.15 Ips. The highest yield is at K. Bolang (E2) i.e. 10.15 Ips . The depth ranges and numbers of saturated fractures encountered during explotory drilling by CGWB are given.

Well Inventory

During the hydro geological investigation in any area, well inventory studies are most essential and forms an integral part of the study which enable us to understand the nature of the aquifer and to find out characteristics of groundwater in the study area. The various data collected from dug wells during the well inventory includes - location, diameter and depth of wells, depth to water table during pre-monsoon and post-monsoon and use of groundwater etc.

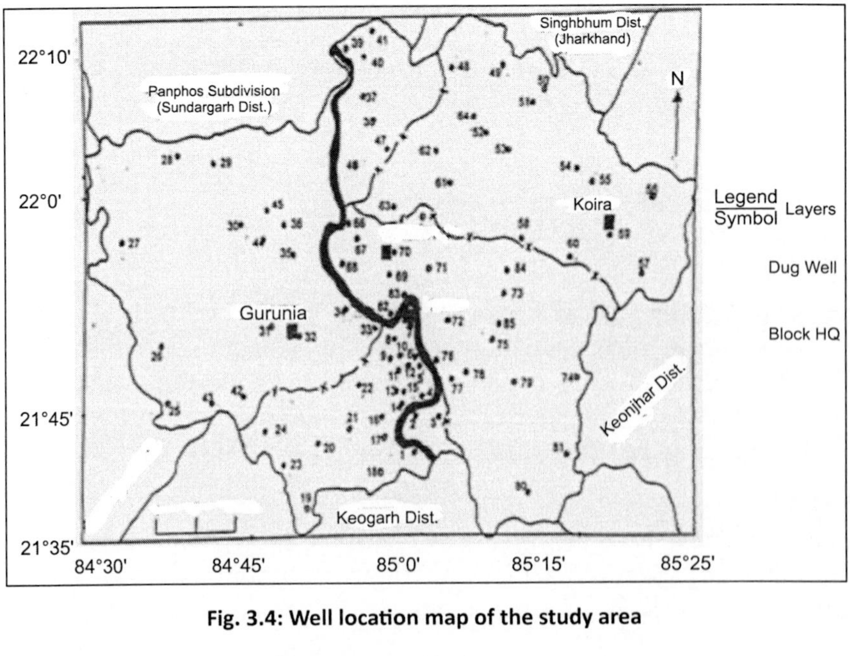

Fig. 3.4: Well location map of the study area

In course of the present study, 85 dug wells at different locations have been observed (Fig. 3.4) and their details are presented in Table 3.4. Water levels were recorded during pre-monsoon (April-May) and post-monsoon (September) periods in 2017 and 2018. The depth to water table (both pre and post-monsoon) and the annual fluctuation of water table have been assessed between two successive years. It is found in the study area that the wells are constructed with cement rings and bricks to prevent the collapse of the structure. These wells are with diameters varying from 1,6m to 3.9m but most of wells have diameter within the range of 2 m to 3m. All the wells are used mostly for domestic and drinking purposes. Depth of dug wells varies from 6.5 to 13.5 m bgl with most of the wells falling in the range of 8 to10m bgl. Depth to water table during pre-monsoon period varies from 5 to 11.4 m bgl in 2017 and 4.2 to 11.8 m bgl in 2018.

Similarly post-monsoon levels were 1.3 to 5.4 m bgl in 2018 and 1.05 to 5.10 m bgl in 2017. The seasonal fluctuation of water level calculated block wise tells that in 2017 Bonai and Lahunipada blocks had the minimum fluctuation, whereas Gurundia block had the maximum. The same trend is found in the year 2018 also. It is found that where the water is in deeper levels, fluctuation is more and it is due to its higher topographic elevation.

Table 3.4: Well Inventory Data of the Study Area.

Sl. No	Name of the Location	Total depth of the well (m)	Diam-eter of the well (m)	Depth to water table in m bgl(2000)		Water table Fluctuation (m) during 2000	Depth to water table in mbgl(2018)		Water table Fluctuation (m) during 2001	Utility
				Pre mon-soon	Post mon-soon		Pre-monsoon	Post mo-nsoon		
1	Tendra	9.45	2.10	6.64	1.85	4.79	6.90	1.65	5.25	Domestic
2.	Ruguda	10.00	3.15	7.25	2.86	4.39	7.15	2.75	4.40	Domestic
3.	Deoposh	11.15	2.75	7.15	2.50	4.65	7.28	2.60	4.68	Drinking
4	Bargogua	10.45	1.95	7.05	2.90	4.15	7.40	3.00	4.40	Drinking
5	Jakeikela	8.25	2.85	6.70	1.55	5.15	6.90	2.00	4.90	Drinking
6	Jarnkei	8.00	2.30	6.75	1.90	4.85	7.00	2.15	4.85	Drinking
7	Bonaigarh	10.05	3.15	6.25	1.75	4.50	6.50	2.00	4.50	Drinking
8	Kendrikela	8.25	3.75	6.00	1.65	4.35	6.45	1.85	4.60	Drinking
9	Pandurisila	9.00	2.30	6.15	2.00	4.15	6.54	2.00	4.54	Drinking
10	Daraikela	7.80	2.45	6.70	2.45	4.25	6.90	2.30	4.60	Drinking
11	Dharani-dharpali	10.25	2.25	7.00	2.45	4.55	7.00	2.35	4.65	Domestic
12	Talita	7.50	2.45	6.45	1.45	5.00	6.65	2.10	4.55	Domestic
13	Kenaveta	8.10	2.10	6.80	2.89	3.91	7.00	2.95	4.05	Domestic

14	Kantasara	9.15	1.95	7.30	2.70	4.70	6.95	2.7	4.25	Domestic
15	Telidihi	9.25	2.85	7.15	2.48	4.67	7.55	2.56	4.99	Drinking
16	Kantapali	10.25	2.40	7.00	2.61	4.39	7.15	2.60	4.55	Domestic
17	Tikayatpaii	7.25	2.65	6.15	2.19	3.96	6.85	2.25	4.60	Domestic
18	Kasada	8.00	2.50	5.60	1.95	3.65	5.85	2.05	3.80	Domestic
19	Dalki	11.00	2.95	7.85	3.25	4.60	7.95	3.15	4.80	Domestic
20	S.Balang	8.25	2.90	6.15	1.95	4.20	6.25	1.86	4.39	Domestic
21	Chandra-pur	7.50	3.15	5.60	1.85	3.75	6.00	1.80	4.20	Domestic
22	Patrapali	7.90	3.00	6.50	2.04	4.46	6.90	2.25	4.65	Domestic
23	Kulkutta	13.00	3.96	10.85	4.05	6.80	10.05	4.00	6.05	Domestic
24	Barghat	12.50	3.90	11.80	5.10	6.70	10.95	4.10	6.85	Domestic
25	Jarda	10.45	3.85	9.45	2.75	6.70	9.65	2.80	6.85	Domestic
26	Kello	10.50	3.65	9.30	4.00	5.30	9.45	4.15	5.29	Drinking
27	Sole	13.00	3.80	9.25	4.15	5.10	9.98	4.36	5.62	Drinking
28	Joda	9.95	3.90	9.40	2.45	6.95	9.50	2.60	6.90	Drinking
29	Pankdihi	9.90	3.85	8.35	3.00	5,35	8.45	3.25	5.20	Drinking
30	Jamudara	10.25	3.50	8.00	2.40	5.60	8.65	2.45	6.20	Domestic
31	Madhapur	10.50	3.60	7.95	2.50	5.45	8.06	2.55	5.51	Domestic
32	Gurundia	9.50	3.65	8.50	3.00	5.50	8.60	3.28	5.32	Domestic
33	Narendra	7.00	2.45	6.45	2.00	4.45	6.33	1.95	4.38	Domestic
34	Satkuta	7.50	2.40	6.38	1.96	4.42	6.77	2.17	4.60	Domestic
35	Kantapah	8.50	2.65	7.15	2.45	4.70	7.30	2.50	4.80	Domestic
36	Bonaikela	9.75	2.95	7.75	2.95	4.80	8.25	3.00	5.25	Domestic
37	Champa-jhara	10.25	3.00	8.75	3.25	5.50	9.05	3.16	5.89	Domestic
38	Chandip-osh	9.80	3.25	6.80	2.00	4.80	7.15	2.30	4.85	Domestic
39	Banki	8.75	2.85	6.75	1.80	4.95	7.05	1.95	5.10	Domestic
40	Kucheita	8.50	2.75	6.50	1.75	4.75	6.90	2.00	4.90	Domestic
41	Ergeda	8.90	2.95	7.15	2.15	5.00	7.35	2.30	5.05	Domestic
42	Kundhei-diha	10.25	3.00	8.25	3.06	5.19	8.50	3.15	5.35	Domestic
43	Kansar	9.50	3.15	7.15	1.34	5.81	7.30	1.85	5.45	Domestic
44	Sagdungri	9.00	3.10	7.16	2.25	4.91	7.50	2.50	5.00	Domestic
45	Bareaon	8.80	2.90	7.45	2.50	4.95	7.45	2.65	4.80	Domestic
46	Sulgura	12,55	3.50	11.45	4.06	7.39	10.95	4.15	6.80	Drinking
47	Tumbai	12.10	3.15	11.80	5.50	6.30	11.40	5.40	6.00	Domestic
48	Jharbeda	7.45	2.15	7.95	3.30	4.15	8.05	3.45	4.60	Domestic

49	Banko	8.30	2.15	8.05	3.85	4.20	8.15	3.63	4.52	Domestic
50	Badbali-jore	9.45	3.00	7.80	3.30	4.50	7.70	3.15	4.55	Domestic
51	Soyamba	9.50	2.65	8.45	3.45	5.00	7.98	3.18	4.80	Domestic
52	Roxy	10.50	2.85	9.45	4.00	5.45	9.15	3.95	5.25	Domestic
53	Jamudihi	11.00	2.15	8.15	.2.65	5.50	8.05	2.50	5.55	Domestic
54	Kalta	13.00	2.50	7.15	2.00	5.15	7.75	2.35	5.40	Domestic
55	Kusumdihi	12.45	3.00	9.65	3.95	5.70	8.77	2.95	.5.82	Domestic
56	Malda	12.00	3.15	10.25	4.00	6.25	10.90	3.90	7.00	Domestic
57	Pota-munda	11.50	3.25	9.90	3.84	6.06	9.95	3.88	6.15	Domestic
58	Barsua	13.50	3.20	8.45	3.00	5.45	8.36	3.40	4.96	Domestic
59	Koira	12.00	2.80	9.90	3.15	6.75	9.76	3.10	6.66	Domestic
60	Dengula	10.50	3.15	10.05	3.25	6.80	10.00	3.55	6.45	Domestic
61	Biralagarh	9.90	2.65	7.05	2.00	5.05	7.18	2.95	4.23	Domestic
62	K.balang	8.75	2.15	7.25	2.35	4.90	7.35	2.50	4.85	Domestic
63	Gopna	7.50	2.30	5.85	1.09	4.76	7.05	2.25	4.80	Domestic
64	Bakhara-tola	8.25	3.00	8.00	2.65	5.35	7.70	2.50	5.20	Domestic
65	Sankha-posh	7.55	1.85	7.15	2.50	4.65	7.00	2.48	4.52	Domestic
66	Darjeeing	8.50	3.00	7.05	2.45	4.60	7.15	2.38	4.77	Domestic
67	Juniani	8.00	2.15	7.75	2.95	4.80	7.95	2.85	5.10	Domestic
68	Kapanda	7.75	1.90	6.95	2.05	4.90	6.75	2.00	4.75	Domestic
69	Raja-munda	7.00	1.75	7.35	2.90	4.45	7.75	2.80	4.95	Domestic
70	Lahuni-pada	6.50	2.00	6.00	1.90	4.10	6.25	1.75	4.50	Domestic
71	Kaleiposh	6.50	1.85	6.45	1.75	4.70	6.75	1.80	4.95	Domestic
72	Kurda	8.50	1.95	6.80	2.35	4.45	7.00	2.30	4.70	Domestic
73	Randa	11.00	2.80	9.95	3.25	6.70	10.00	3.45	6.55	Domestic
74	Telkuda	10.50	3.00	8.90	3.35	5.35	9.40	3.30	6.10	Domestic
75	Talbahali	7.00	1.75	4.90	1.35	3.55	5.15	1.30	3.85	Domestic
76	Poigaon	9.90	2.35	8.80	3.22	5.58	8.95	3.00	5.95	Domestic
77	Khunt-agaon	8.50	2.00	6.00	2.39	3.61	6.25	2.30	3.95	Domestic
78	Dhuddi	7.50	1.60	7.00	2.90	4.10	7.15	2.80	4.35	Domestic
79	Phulijhar	7.55	1.95	7.85	3.30	4.55	7.45	3.06	4.39	Domestic
80	Mahul-pada	8.50	2.80	8.00	3.45	4.55	8.15	3.90	4.25	Domestic

81	Trizanga	9.90	3.00	9.80	4.15	5.65	9.20	4.05	5.15	Domestic
82	Gamlei	8.50	2.00	8.20	3.25	4.95	8.25	3.23	5.02	Domestic
83	Tumkela	9.00	2.70	8.10	3.30	4.80	8.30	3.35	4.95	Domestic
84	Saskella	10.25	2.85	8.90	3.45	5.45	8.05	2.64	5.41	Domestic
85	Khandhar	7.00	2.45	4.20	1.05	3.15	5.00	1.32	3.68	Domestic

Status of water table: From the well inventory data of the study area, it is clearly evident that the depth to water table both in pre and post-monsoon periods as well as the seasonal water table fluctuation vary greatly from place to place and formation to formation. Therefore, basing on the above data, depth to water table maps for pre and post-monsoon periods (2018), water table fluctuation map (2018) and water table contour map for the pre-monsoon (2018) have been prepared for the detail understanding of the water table configuration.

Depth to Water Table Map: The depth to water table map (Fig. 3.5*)* of the study area shows that during pre-monsoon period of 2018, the depth to water table values are 6 to 8 m bgl in 50% to 60% of the area and 8 to 10 m bgl in 20% to 25% of the area. There are very small pockets having depth to water table value more than 10 m bgl and less than 6 m bgl From the map it is clear that the deepest water level (11.40 m bgl) during pre-monsoon, 2018 was recorded around Tumbai (Gurundia block). The shallowest water level (5.00 m bgl) during pre-monsoon 2018 was recorded around Khandadhar (Lahunipada Block). The depth to water table of post-monsoon, 2018 (Fig. 3.6) of the study area reveals that the depth to water table varies from 1.30 m bgl to 5.40 m bgi. Depth to water table between 2 to 3 m bgl is observed in 60% of the area,

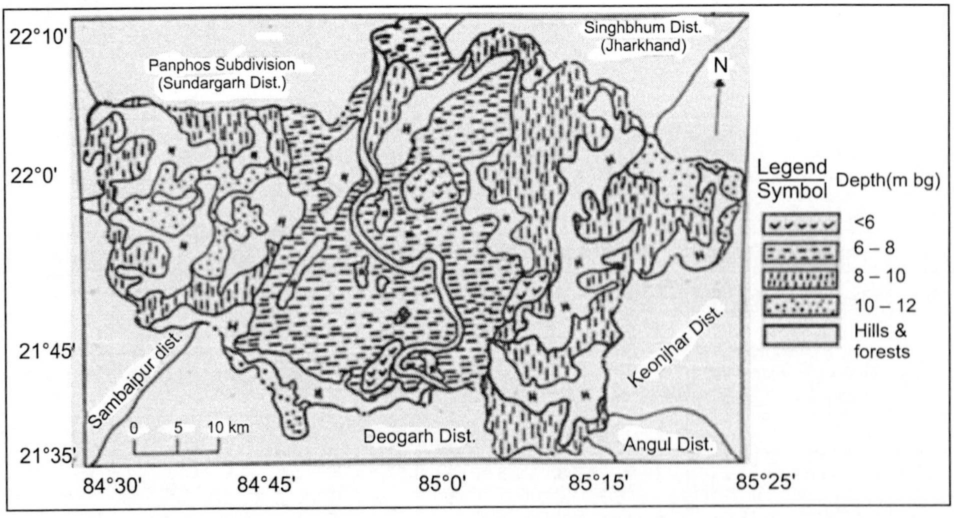

Fig. 3.5: Depth to water table map of the study area(pre-monsoon 2018)

between 3 to 4 m bgl in 25% area and greater than 4 m bgl in 10% area. There are also very small pockets in Bonai and Lahunipada block where the depth to water table is between 1 to 2 m bgl. The deepest water level during this period was recorded at the same place(i.e.Tumbai) but the shallowest water table has been shifted from Khandadhar to Talbahali which is located 2 km west of Khandadhar. The water table is recorded at 1.30 m bgl at Talbahali.

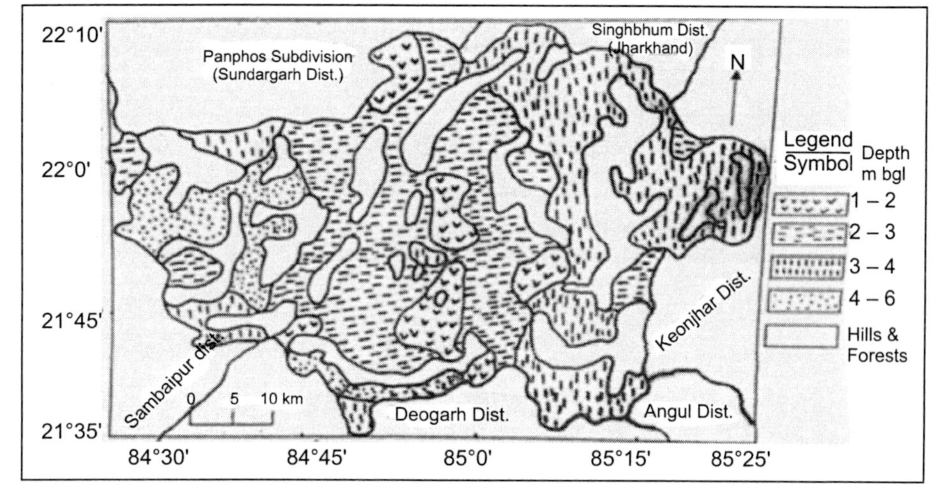

Fig. 3.6: Depth to water table map of the study area (post-monsoon 2018)

Water Table Fluctuation Map: Water table fluctuation is a natural phenomenon owing to recharge and discharge conditions. The water table fluctuation generally follows a fairly rhythmic seasonal pattern. High water level occurs during the month of September and low level during the month of June. The water table fluctuation map (Fig. 3.7) of the study area is prepared based on the measured water levels in the pre and post-monsoon periods of 2018. The values of seasonal water level fluctuation (2018) ranges from 3.68 to 6.90 m. Most of the areas show fluctuation between 4 to 6m. Higher fluctuations (> 6m) are observed in some parts of Gurundia and Koira blocks. Fluctuation of less than 4m is very limited and occurs as pockets, mostly near the river course of Bonai and Lahunipada blocks and near Khandadhar waterfall. The groundwater level fluctuation reflects the net change of storage resulting from the interaction of two components (recharge and discharge). The study and interpretation of water level fluctuation thus forms an integral part of the study of groundwater storage. Water level changes can be classified into the following two types.

1. Changes due to change in groundwater storage.
2. Changes due to other influences i.e. change in atmospheric pressure, deformation of aquifers, disturbance within the well etc.

The area of recharge and discharge can be detected from the water table fluctuation map. Areas characterised by higher fluctuation in water table are usually recharge areas. They generally represent topographically high lands. Areas with less change in water table are usually discharge areas. They generally represent low-lying lands and topographical depressions adjacent to high lands.

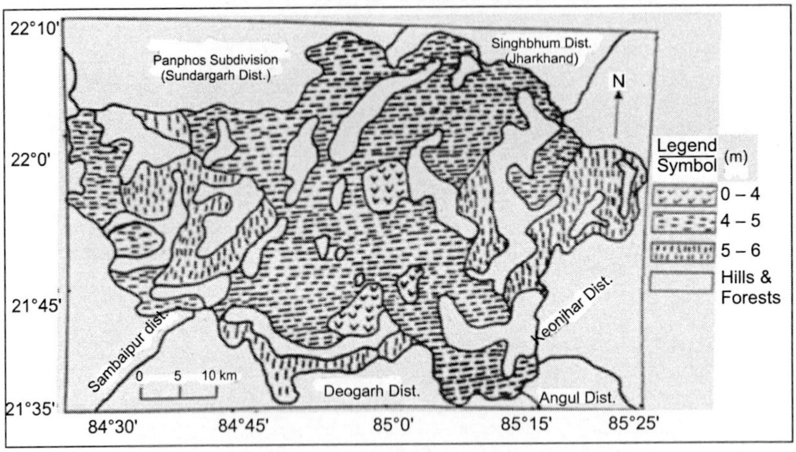

Fig. 3.7: Water table fluctuation map of the study area

Water Table Contour Map: It has generally been accepted that the water level in a well represents fairly the level of water table in the surrounding aquifer. The water table contour map of the study area has been prepared based on the water level data of the observation wells with respect to mean sea level (Fig. 3.8).

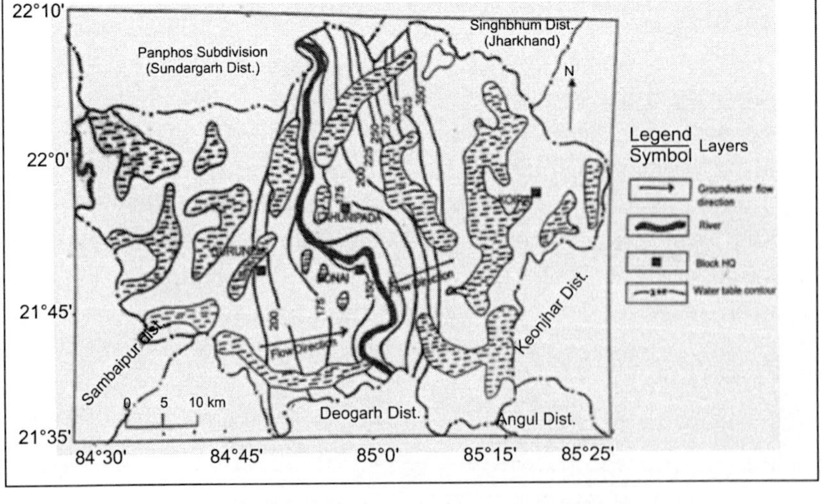

Fig. 3.8: Water table contour map of the study area

The highest water level is found in Koira block where prominent topographic features are structural hills and intermontane valleys. The lowest water level is around southern part of the Bonai block near Brahmani river course. The water table contour map indicates that in the central part of the study area, the slope of water table is towards Brahmani river. Flow lines perpendicular to the water table contours show direction of movement of groundwater. Such contour map of water table along with the flow lines are useful for locating new wells, with better yields and better permeability of the aquifers. The contour map indicates that in the flow direction the spacing of the contour lines is wide in Bonai and part of the Lahunipada blocks which means low hydraulic gradient. This indicates high hydraulic conductivity of the water transmitting materials.The narrow contour spacing in the flow direction (i.e. greater hydraulic gradient) indicates lower hydraulic conductivity of the material. Major parts of Koira and Gurundia blocks are characterised by hills and valleys. The flow direction and shape of water table contours do not show any definite trend but is highly influenced by topographic setting. Major parts of Bonai and Lahunipada blocks are gently sloping surface. The shape of contour lines is roughly parallel to the Brahmani river course. In general, the flow direction / water table slope of the study area is towards Brahmani river which runs from north to south in central part of the area.

Short term water level trends: Short term trends of water level for the periods from 2000 to 2018 in the study area have been studied for assessing the change in storage of groundwater in response to rainfall, evaporation, pumpage, surface irrigation, deforestation etc. The water level in the pre and post-monsoon periods in the study area shows the following trends.

1. Falling trends in both the periods.
2. Falling trends in pre-monsoon and no change in post-monsoon period.
3. No change in both the periods.

1. **Falling trend in both the periods:** Gurundia and Koira show such falling trends of water level during pre and post-monsoon periods. The falling trend during post-monsoon on these blocks indicates low recharge mainly due to deforestation and mining activities. The falling trend during pre-monsoon is due to low recharge during post-monsoon and greater groundwater withdrawal in successive years. The aquifer is probably being depleted gradually. So groundwater withdrawal should be carefully planned and recharge measures should be undertaken.
2. **Falling trend in pre-monsoon & no change in post-monsoon:** Only Bonai block shows such trend of water table. This indicates that the aquifer is probably being depleted due to greater groundwater withdrawal in successive years. So measures should be taken to enhance the groundwater recharge and cares must be taken for withdrawal in order to avoid overdraft.

3. **No Change in both the Periods:** Only Lahunipada block shows such trend of water level indicating that both recharge and discharge are balanced.

Conclusions

Hydrogeolocial setting of an area is described with respect to the nature and disposition of subsurface geological features followed by the type of aquifer system and occurrence of groundwater. Besides this, systematic well inventory studies and its significance in the evaluation of water table configuration, groundwater flow direction and also water table fluctuation from pre-monsoon to post-monsoon periods have been dealt with. In the study area, groundwater is exploited through dug wells and bore wells to meet the domestic and irrigation requirements tapping mostly the shallow depth aquifers.

Depending upon water bearing and water yielding properties, the rock formations in the study area are broadly divided into following two units. 1. Consolidated formations. 2. Unconsolidated formations. The aquifer thickness is maximum in Bonaigarh area whereas its thickness is minimum in K-Balang area. Occurrence of potential saturated fractures is more frequent in granitic rocks than other hard rocks in the study area. Granitic rocks exhibit upto 3 sets of saturated fractures within a depth of 60m in Bonai and Lahunipada blocks. The numbers of sets of fractures decreases downward. The yield potential of wells in granitic rocks ranges from 3 lps to 20 Ips.

The saturated fractures within the litho logical units most commonly occur in the form of (*i*) fractured and saturated quartz and pegmatite veins and also as basic intrusive (dykes) (*ii*) fractured country rock not having any secondary intrusion or deposits. The contact zone of two lithological units (including intrusive bodies) very often forms aquifer zones in the study area. The contact zone of two hard rock formations generally forms better water yielding situation than the contact zone between hard and soft formations. The saturated fractures of hard rock terrain of the study area are divided into 2 groups: (1) fractures in Bonai Granite and (2) fractures in metasediments.

The highest water level is found in Koira block where prominent topographic features are structural hills and intermontane valleys. The lowest water level is around southern part of the Bonai block near Brahmani river course. The water table contour map indicates that in the central part of the study area, the slope of water table is towards Brahmani river. Flow lines perpendicular to the water table contours show direction of movement of groundwater. Such contour map of water table along with the flow lines are useful for locating new wells, with better yields and better permeability of the aquifers. The contour map indicates that in the flow direction the spacing of the contour lines is wide in Bonai and part of the Lahunipada blocks which means low hydraulic gradient. This indicates high hydraulic conductivity of the water transmitting materials.

The water level in the pre and post-monsoon periods in the study area shows the following trends. 1. Falling trends in both the periods. 2. Falling trends in pre-monsoon and no change in post-monsoon period. 3. No change in both the periods.

REFERENCES

Ballukraya, P.N. (2001). Hydrogeophysical Investigations in Nammagiripettai Area, Namakal District, Tamil Nadu", Jour. Geol. Soc. India, V. 58, pp. 239-239.

B. Deepika, K. Avinash, K. S. Jayappa, (2013)Intregation of Hydrological Factors and Demarcation of Groundwater Prospects Zones: Insights from Remote Sensing and GIS Techniques, Environmental Earth Science, 70, 3, pp. 1319-1338.

Deepika, B., Avinash, K. and Jayappa, K.S.(2013) Intregation of Hydrological Factors and Demarcation of Groundwater Prospects Zones: Insights from Remote Sensing and GIS Techniques. Environ". Earth Sci., V.70, (3) pp. 1319-1338.

D. Nandi, J. Kant, C.K Sahu, (2015) Integrated Approach Using Remote Sensing and GIS for Hydrogeology of Moroda Block In Mayurbhanj District, Odisha, India, International Journal of Conservation Science, 6, Issue 3, pp. 383-390.

Jesiya, N.P. and Gopinath, G. (2015)"Delineation of Groundwater Potential Zones In Selected Urban and Peri Urban Clusters of Kozhikode District, Kerala, India". Int. Jour. Earth Sc.Engg. V.8, No.(2), pp. 391-396,.

Kumar, G. And Srinivasan, D. (2016) Evaluation of Groundwater Potential Index (GWPI) Using Geophysical Survey in Kollar Watershed, Tamil Nadu, India". Int. Jour. of Earth Sci. Engg, V.9 (5), pp. 1902-1906.

Magesh, N.S., Chandrasekar, N. and Soundranayagam, J. P., (2012). Delineation of Groundwater Otential Zones in Theni District, Tamilnadu, Using Remote Sensing, GIS and MIF", Geosciences Frontiers, V. 3(2), pp. 189-196.

Mahala, S. C., Naik, P.C., Samal, A.K. and Mohanty, S., (2013) Intregrated Geophysical Investigation for Selection of Bore Well Sites Near Rabanna Village, Jajpur District, Odisha, India". Int. Jour. Earth Sc. Engg., V.06, No. 5(1), pp. 1236-1242,

Muntari Mudi Yar Adua, Abbas Usman Kakale (2016) Sustainable Environment: Laterite As Sustainable Building Materials In Construction Industry. International Journal of Advances in Mechanical and Civil Engineering, ISSN: 2394-2827 Volume-3, Issue-2, pp. 70-73.

Nandi,D., Kant, J., Sahu, C.K.(2015). Integrated Approach Using Remote Sensing and GIS for Hydrogeology of Moroda Block in Mayurbhanj District, Odisha, India, International Journal of Conservation Science, 6(3), pp. 383-390.

Nandi.D, Mishra .S.R.,(2014). Groundwater Quality Mapping by Using Geographic Information System (GIS): A Case Study of Baripada City, Odisha, India, International Journal of Conservation Science, 5(1), pp. 79-84.

N. S. Magesh, N. Chandrasekar, J. P. Soundranayagam(2012), Delineation of Groundwater Potential Zones in Theni District, Tamilnadu, Using Remote Sensing, GIS and MIF, Geosciences Frontiers,3(2),pp. 189-196.

P.C. Sahu (2018) Geomorphological and Geoelectrical Studies for Targeting Groundwater in Hard Rock Terrain of Rairangpur Block, Odisha. International Journal for Science and Advance Research in Technology. ISSN [Online]: 2395-1052, pp-461-466.

P.C. Sahu (2019) Quantitative Assessment of Groundwater and Soil Fertility Management for Rural Development Using Remote Sensing and GIS Techniques. Journal of Emerging

Technologies and Innovative Research (JETIR), January 2019, Volume 6, Issue 1, pp. 261-275.

Reddy, P.R. (1999). Remote Sensing in Groundwater Studies; In Remote Sensing for Resources (Ed.D. P.Rao) Publ. of Asso. Expl. Geophysicists, Hyderabad, India (2nd Edn.) pp. 183-203.

Sahu, P.C. and Sahoo, H.K.,(2006). Targeting Ground Water in Tribal Dominated Bonai Area of Drought - Prone Sundargarh District, Orissa, India – A Combined Geophysical and Remote Sensing Approach. J. Hum. Ecol., 20(2): 109-115.

Sahu, P.C., (2017)"Groundwater Resource Conservation and Augmentation in Hard Rock Terrain: An Integrated Geological and Geo-Spatial Approach", International Journal of Conservation Science, V.8 (1), pp. 145-156

Sahu, P.C., (2017) Sustainable Groundwater Management in Drought Prone Bonai Sub-Division of Sundergarh District, Orissa, India" Water Resources: Mapping, Monitoring and Management, 1st Edn. Dis. Publ. House, New Delhi, pp. 10-29.

Sahu. P.C. (2016) Sustainable Development and Management of Groundwater Resources in Drought Prone Digapahandi block of Odisha, India. The Global Journal of Environmental Science and Research.Vol. 3, No. 1, PP. 105-114.

Selvarani, A.G., Maheswaran, G., Elangovan, K. and Sivakumar, C.,(2016) Evaluation of Groundwater Potential Zones using Electrical Resistivity and GIS in Noyyal River Basin, Tamil Nadu". Jour. Geol. Soc. India, V. 87 (5), pp. 573-582.

Sharma, A.K. and Ray, R.K.,(2015) A Remote Sensing and GIS based Approach to Evaluate the Groundwater Prospects of Baghain Watershed, Pann and Satna Districts of M. P., India; A Case Study", Journal of Geological Society of India, V. 86 (6) pp. 733-741,

V.M. Rokade, P. Kundal, andA.K Joshi,G (2007). Groundwater Potential Modeling through Remote Sensing and GIS : A Case Study from Rajula Taluka, Chandrapur District, Maharastra, Journal of Geological Society of India, 69, pp. 943-948.

Technologies for Water and Wastewater Management **Pages 63-90**
Edited by: Dr. Vijender Singh & Dr. Pawan Kumar 'Bharti'
ISBN: 978-93-88854-53-5
Edition: 2020
Published by: Discovery Publishing House Pvt. Ltd., New Delhi (India)

4

Water Scarcity in Agriculture
Watershed Development, Water Use Efficiency Challenges and Policy

Anitha G.[1] and Esakkimuthu M.[2]

Introduction

Water is one of the most important substances on earth. All plants and animals must have water to survive. If there was no water there would be no life on earth. Fresh water resources have faced a crisis worldwide for the last five decades. The crisis is growing rapidly. This is manifested in numerous challenges showing the various elements of the problem. These challenges include, increasing scarcity of fresh water, lack of accessibility to adequate clean drinking water and sanitation, deterioration of water quality, fragmentation of water management, nationally and globally, threat to world peace and security and a continuing lack of awareness of the magnitude of the problem by the decision makers and the public at large. The World Water Council was established as an international nongovernmental think tank to deal with these challenges. It has stated a target to define the vision for the world water, life and the environment for the next century. It is proposed that a number of key targets may include clean drinking water and sanitation for all inhabitants by 2015, adequate and secure food supplies to all by 2005, preservation of the environment and aquatic biodiversity by 2020, secured sustainable economic growth and promotion of world peace and security starting now.

Causes of Water Shortage - World and Indian Scenario

Today, one of the largest concerns around the world is the lack of freshwater for drinking and cooking. It is estimated that over one billion people, or about one-sixth of the world's population, does not have access to fresh water; of these one billion, the vast majority are living in developing nations.

[1] Assistant Professor (Soil Science and Agricultural Chemistry), Tamil Nadu Agricultural University, S. Thangapazham Agricultural College, Vasudevanallur, Tamil Nadu, India
[2] Assistant Professor (Agricultural Extension), Kerala Agricultural University, Regional Agricultural Research Station, Pilicode, Kerala, India

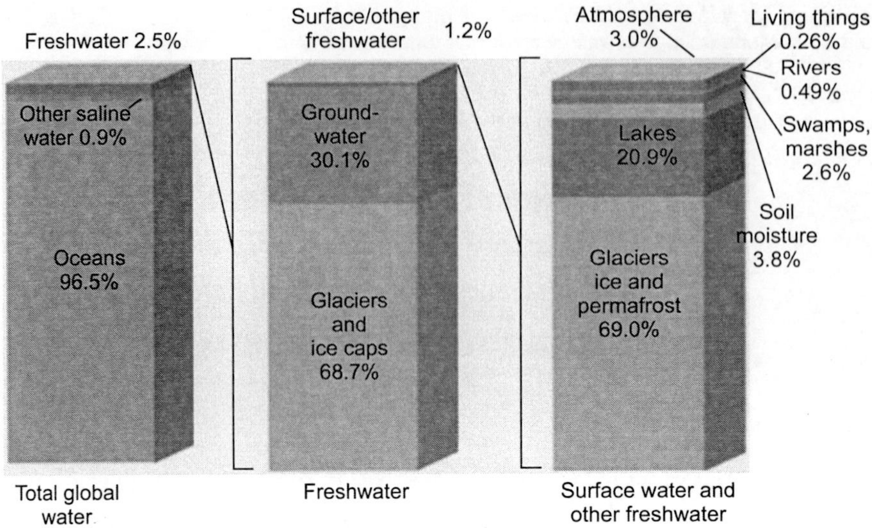

Fig. 4.1: Distribution of Earth's Water

Although water is one of the most common resources on the planet, only 2.5% of it can actually be consumed, and the rest is salt water. Of that only 2.5%, two-third is confined to glaciers and permanent snow cover. Only a fraction of world's water is liquid freshwater, and it is increasingly the subject of conflict and strife as it becomes less available.

Over Growth of Population

The world's population is growing at a rate of 80-81 million people each year. This means that each year we need to find a way to add about 64 million cubic meters of water the global water supply. The fast growing areas are Africa and Middle-east. The Sub-Saharan African population is growing at a rate of 2.2%. Africa is already one of the driest continents in the world, and with this constant changes its are facing water stress and water scarcity (***Hofwegenand Svendsen,* 2000**).

A country is said to experience water stress when annual water supplies drop below 1,700 cubic meters per person. At levels between 1,700 and 1,000 cubic meters per person, periodic or limited water shortages can be expected. When annual water supplies drop below 1,000 cubic meters per person, the country faces water scarcity.

As of 1999, 31 countries, with a total of 500 million people, faced either water stress or water scarcity than in past decades. Trying to farm in hot, arid countries is difficult, if not impossible at times. Agriculture uses 70% of the world's supply, with industry comes second with 22% of global use, and the only 8% used for domestic household purposes.

Agricultural users are getting better at limiting the amount of water they withdraw. New techniques such as drip irrigation, low pressure sprinklers, and even drip walls, can capture the water from rainfall before it drains away. In many parts of the world there is not enough rain for crops to be grown without farmers watering, or enough rain for crops to be grown without farmers watering, or irrigating them. If farmers start growing more crops they need a lot more water. It takes a least 2,000 litres of water to grow the food needed by one person for one day (***Seckler et.al*, 1998**).When areas get richer, with more developed economies, the way that people live often changes. They trend to use a lot more water in their homes for things like dishwashers and lawn sprinklers. In developed countries there are also more factories using water. This is not a bad thing in, but it can be a problem if there is not a big enough supply of water.

Exploiting Pollution

The world's population is increasing, towns and cities are growing quickly in places where there is not a lot of water. Pollution is becoming a huge and worsening factor in destroying the fresh water supply. Every day almost two million tons of wastes are dumped into lakes, rivers, and streams. At present there are about 12,000 square kilometers of polluted fresh water in the world, and if trends are not slowed are reversed, the total will reach 18,000 sq km by 2050, nearly nine times the total amount currently used for irrigation.

Some Alarming Facts

1. The 250 million U.S. residents living today have access to about the same amount of water as U.S. residents did 200 years ago, when the population was four million. (***National Drinking Water Alliance***)
2. If present consumption patterns continue, two out of every three persons on earth will live in water-stressed conditions by the year 2025 (***United Nations Environment Program***).
3. At least 1 billion people must walk 3 hours or more to obtain drinking water. Nearly 2% of U.S. homes have no running water. In Mexico, 15% of the population must haul or carry water (***National Geographic Society***).
4. In a one-hundred year period, an average water molecule spends 98 years in the ocean, 20 months as ice, only about 2 weeks in lakes and rivers, and less than a week in the atmosphere.
5. By 2050, per capita water supply is predicted to fall, leaving anywhere between 2 billion to 7 billion people with water scarcity (***CBC News***).
6. A billion people do not have enough clean water for drinking and cooking.

7. 2.4 billion People do not have proper sanitation, that means they don't have sinks and toilets that are the part of systems that remove waste safely.
8. Up to 2 million people die every year in the developing world from diseases that are to do with a proper water supply, poor sanitation or poor hygiene.
9. How many people have clean water piped into their homes?
   (a) Latin America and the Caribbean : 66%
   (b) Asia: 49%
   (c) Africa: 24%

Indian Facts

When humans use more water than we used to, it can cause problems. Below are the facts projected by National Training Project and Administration Institute.

1. In India about 303.6 million cubic of water is received by Asian rivers from Himalayan glaciers.
2. By the end of the year 2100 glaciers of Himalaya will dry up.
3. About 4.4 million of Indian Population is drinking polluted drinking water.
4. About 70% of water is obtained from ground water resources.
5. About 80% of water supply is done from ground water resources.
6. In Delhi the duration of water supply if for 4 hours daily while in Bombay it is for 5 hours.
7. In India there are about 1.90 million tube wells.
8. About 39% of families of India have developed their own drinking water resources in their own premises.
9. Drinking water is not available to about 2 lac students in schools.
10. **Not enough rain or drought:** For example if a river is dammed the areas below the dam might get a lot loss in water. If people living further up the river take a lot of water out, there is sometimes nothing left for people further down.
11. **Wells run dry:** In many parts of the world, humans rely on water from underground source. Underground reservoirs called aquifers, often take millions of years to fill up. If people remove the water faster than aquifer can refill, it can cause wells to run dry.
12. About 28.6% of families are procuring drinking water from a distance of more than 500 meters and only 22% families have tap-water facilities.

In 140 blocks of India the ground water level is dangerous zone. About 23297 villages are using ground water which has high level of fluoride (about recommended limit in Rajasthan).

Present Water Availability

1. India's population is 16% of the world population, whereas, water resources are only 4% that of the world.
2. Present water demand is 1122 billion m^3 (Surface water 690 billion m^3 and groundwater 432 billion m^3).
3. By 2010, groundwater demand would increase to 710 billion $m^{3.}$
4. By 2050, it would be 1180 billion m^3 i.e. less than availability.
5. In Rajasthan, total water availability is 10382 million m^3 at present, whereas the requirement is 12999 m^3.
6. Out of 236 blocks, 204 blocks are over-exploited due to above situation. The demand in 2025 would be doubled, we can imagine scenario of 2050.

When Plants Most Need Water?

Plants are in need of water when they being to wilt, but by the time wilting is visible, plant growth has already been reduced significantly wilt in is usually is due to insufficient soil moisture. Most plants have critical periods of growth during which lack of water is, most damaging. For plants producing, the period from flowering to seed set (fertilisation) is the most critical. If drought occurs during this period, grain or seed yield will be greatly reduced. In living tissues, water is the medium for many biochemical reaction extraction processes; inorganic nutrient, photosynthetic, bases and hormones are all transported in aqueous solution; evaporation of water can control the temperature of skin or leaf soil nutrients are available to plant roots only when dissolved in soil water in short, water is essential for life and plays and unique role in virtually or biological process.

World War for the Water?

Water scarcity in the world is not new. While some countries still do not feel their absence, other thousands of people die dehydrated. Many sources of fresh water disappeared, and a large percentage of which are contaminated. Since water is vital to the survival of human beings, their scarcity has serious consequences for the planet. If the international conflicts were aroused by the desire for more land or oil, the proximate cause of dispute is the fresh water.

In this decade, the media campaign on environmental issues has impacted the popular belief about a coming world war III. The foundation to affirm this belief is the impossibility of life without the vital element water, unlike oil, water is essential for any living being.

Therefore, the man will do anything to get that precious liquid. If its value, the oil was black gold, today gold water is transparent. But the exhaustion of this resource is not a phenomenon that is generated from the overnight.

Decades ago, human beings are engaged in activities that pollute, increasingly, their environment. The blame for the lack of water is pure and exclusively, human. The hyper land use, deforestation and overgrazing, are some of the causes that led to the reduction of potable water, and therefore distorted the water cycle. In addition, industries and lack of awareness in the daily habits of man, cause the pollution of many drinking water previously **(*Cooley*, 2008)**.

One could initiating a Third World war? Taking into account that only 3% is fresh water, and that 3% is mostly concentrated in the polar ice caps and glaciers, and at the same time, claiming that only a fifth of the world population has access to drinking water, leaving thousands of millions of people in unsanitary conditions.

The majority of the population without access to fresh water live in countries in process of development, that is to say, those who today are suffering the negative consequences of the lack of water resource and possibly suffer in the future, even coming to talk about regional and national wars.

Despite the above factors, it is perfectly conceivable in a war over water. It should be noted that current wars are already occurring at the regional level for this reason, such as the Jordan river in the Middle East; the case of Blue Nile river in Egypt and finally, in Latin American, exist the case of Guarani aquifer. These cases have been key players in the world of these domestic wars over water (access and distribution).

When man fell into the reality of the situation and the consequences of their reckless actions towards nature, he also realized that he must find a way to stop this process or, soon, the world would perish due to lack of water and of other natural resources.

Thus many scientists devoted themselves especially to the task of investigating possible ways to treat water. Thus, although not manage to generate new water sources, it could recycle those unused or contaminated by them. Through these studies, they found multiple ways to treat this water at the industrial level, but also to residential. Today, each family can purify your water if desired.

However, in the near future these methods will also become insufficient. While help the problem temporarily, they will not permanently. It is for this reason that many scientists are already looking for an effective and affordable way of treating salt water. If they move forward on the issue, could solve the shortage problem soon. What will happen when we get water from the sea? It is true that there is a hydrological cycle, but the number of individuals in need of this water resource will be extensive and not think it is the best solution to address this shortage (***Selby*, 2005**).

Although have described a serious of on-going conflicts in the conquest of water, do not forget that more countries are struggling to give states efficient and fair, through their governments and supranational bodies. Worthwhile for humanity help raise awareness about this global problem and that in the coming years the solution is not the terrible wars, but cooperation, solidarity and peace.

Bangladesh City: Decline of the Ground Water

Being one of the largest mega cities of the world Dhaka is facing continuing potable water-related problems over the last few decades. About 10 million people representing about 30% of the total urban population live in this capital city of the country. The population of the city rapidly increasing each day since this city is the center of all sorts of financial, business, medical, educational and political facilities and services.

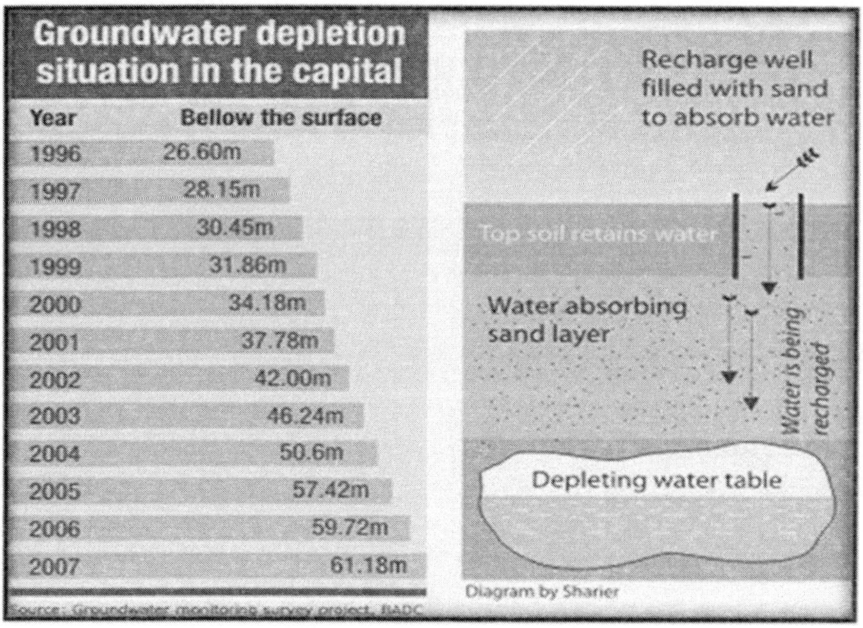

Fig. 4.2: Ground water depletion

According to the World Bank and World Health organization, 2 billion people lack access to clean water and 1 billion people do not have enough to even meet their daily needs.

Every day an increasing amount of pollution seeps into rivers and lakes making them toxic to humans and underground aquifers-our most significant sources of water- are being depleted **at an alarming rate.** By 2050 the number of people on the planet is projected to exceed 9 billion, and if current trends continue more and more usable water will be lost. Making an adequate supply of water available to everyone alive today is a monumental task, and ensuring that there is enough water for all future generations will require an **unprecedented level of international cooperation and compassion...**

Water Scarcity and Agriculture

Water Scarcity has a huge impact on food production. Without water people do not have a means of watering their crops and therefore, to provide food for the fast growing population. According to the international Water Management Institute, Agriculture which accounts for about 70% of global water withdrawals is constantly completing with domestic, industrial and environmental uses for a scarce water supply. In attempts to fix this ever growing problem, many have tried to form more effective methods of water management.

One such method is irrigation management. Irrigation is a method of transporting water to crops in order to maximize the amount of crops produced. Many of the irrigation systems in place do not use the water in the most efficient way. This causes more water thannecessary to be used or for there not to be enough water to ensure healthy crops. According to the World Bank, irrigation management works to upgrade and maintain irrigation systems, such as groundwater irrigation, that are already in place and expands the areas of irrigation to increase the amount of crops being produced.

Another method is water management for rainfed agriculture. Rainfed agriculture is the most common method of agriculture in developing nations. According to the book.

Rainfed Agriculture: Unlocking the potential, 80% of the land farmed around the world is rainfed and it "Contributes about 58% to the global food basket"

Some techniques in water management for rainfed agriculture include the use of supplemental irrigation and water harvesting techniques, such as rain catchment systems and weirs or sand dams. These techniques help provide much needed water to areas where rainfall is inconsistent. Harvesting this water helps to increase the number and quality of the crops grown. The water project works to combat this issue by helping to build water collection systems, such as weirs or sand dams. Water is collected and stored for drinking and the rest seeps into the ground and crates more fertile fields" (***The Water Project***).

Using these different methods of water management is essential for agriculture, as the increasing population calls for an increase in food production.

Water Resources are Becoming Scarce

Agricultural crisis

Although food security has been significantly increased in the past thirty years, water withdrawals for irrigation represent 66% of the total withdrawals and up to 90% in arid regions, the other 34% being used by domestic households (10%), industry (20%), or evaporated from reservoirs (4%). **(Source: *Shiklomanov*, 1998)**

As the per capita use increases due to changes in lifestyle and as population increases as well, the proportion of water for human use is increasing. This, coupled with spatial and temporal variations in water availability, means that the water to produce food for human consumption, industrial processes and all the other uses is becoming scarce.

Environmental crisis

It is all the more critical that increased water use by humans does not only reduce the amount of water available for industrial and agricultural development but has a profound effect on aquatic ecosystems and their dependent species. Environmental balances are disturbed and cannot play their regulating role anymore.

An increase in tensions

As the resource is becoming scarce, tensions among different users may intensify, both at the national and international level. Over 260 river basins are shared by two or more countries. In the absence of strong institutions and agreements, changes within a basin can lead to transboundary tensions. When major projects proceed without regional collaboration, they can become a point of conflicts, heightening regional instability. The Parana La Plata, the Aral Sea, the Jordan and the Danube may serve as examples. Due to the pressure on the Aral Sea, half of its superficy has disappeared, representing 2/3 of its volume. 36 000 km^2 of marine grounds are now recovered by salt.

Water stress results from an imbalance between water use and water resources. The water stress indicator in this map measures the proportion of water withdrawal with respect to total renewable resources. It is a criticality ratio, which implies that water stress depends on the variability of resources. Water stress causes deterioration of fresh water resources in terms of quantity (aquifer over-exploitation, dry rivers, etc.) and quality (eutrophication, organic matter pollution, saline intrusion, etc.) The value of this criticality ratio that indicates high water stress is based on expert judgment and experience. It ranges between 20% for basins with highly variable runoff and 60% for temperate zone basins **(*Alcamo et al*, 1999).** In this map, we take an overall value of 40% to indicate high water stress. We see that the situation is heterogeneous over the world.

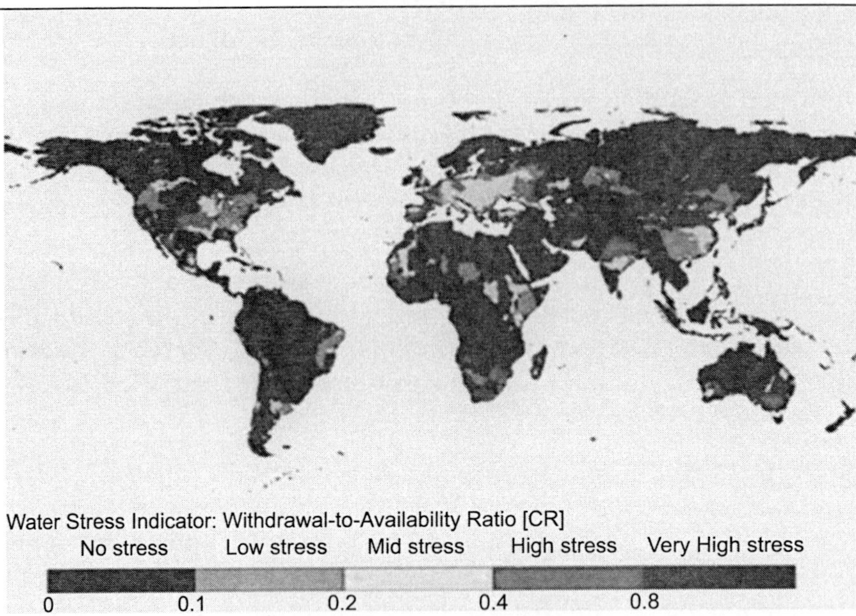

Fig. 4.3: Water Gap (1999)

Water Crisis

While the world's population tripled in the 20th century, the use of renewable water resources has grown six-fold. Within the next fifty years, the world population will increase by another 40 to 50%. This population growth coupled with industrialization and urbanization will result in an increasing demand for water and will have serious consequences on the environment.

Global Water Crisis

Water is life because plants and animals cannot live without water. Water is needed to ensure food security, feed livestock, maintain organic life, take up industrial production and to conserve the biodiversity and environment. Hence, there is no life without water. Earth is the only plant, so far known to have water and this makes it fit for human living. However, with reckless abuse and increasing demand, due to growing population and unsustainable lifestyle, many countries are facing severe water crisis. In the absence of suitable corrective measures, many developing countries including India will have to face crisis of food and water security in the near future.

Although, India is not a water poor country, due to growing human population, severe neglect and over-exploitation of this resource, water is becoming a scarce commodity. India is more vulnerable because of the growing population and in-disciplined lifestyle. This calls for immediate attention by the stakeholders to make sustainable use of the available water resources.

70% of the earth surface is covered with water, which amounts to 1400 million cubic kilometres (m km^3). However, 97.5% of this water being sea water, it is salty. Fresh water availability is only 35 m km^3 and only 40% of this can be used by human beings. Out of the total fresh water, 68.7% is frozen in ice caps, 30% is stored underground and only 0.3% water is available on the surface of the earth. Out of the surface water, 87% is stored in lakes, 11% in swamp and 2% in rivers **(*Camilleri*, 2003)**.

Long before, when the population was low and lifestyle was simple, water was available in plenty and was considered as a free resource. However, with growing demand for water and depletion of the available water, assured supply of good quality water is becoming a growing concern. As the water resources are not evenly distributed, across different continents, some countries have surplus water while many other countries are already facing scarcity of water. Skewed growth of population in different continents is further adding to this crisis.

Among various continents, Asia has 36% of the available fresh water reserves, with over 60% of the world population where water is a scarce commodity. Compared to Asia, Africa is in a better situation, where 13% of the population has access to 11% of the fresh water reserves. Australia and Oceana have plenty of water with 1% population owning 5% of the fresh water reserves, followed by North and Central America, with 8% population and 15% water reserves and South America with 6% global population and 26% fresh water reserves. Since generations, the pattern of water use in different countries is mostly dependent on their culture, lifestyle and industrial development, as availability of water was not a serious concern.

List of countries in Africa and Asia having Renewable Water Resources Below the Calculated Threshold of 1500 m^3/capita/year by the year 2030.

Afganistan	Egypt	Kenya	Niger	Tanzania
Algeria	Eritrea	Korea Republic	Nigeria	Togo
Bukina Faso	Ethiopia	Lebanon	Pakistan	Tunisia
Burundi	**India**	Libiya	Rwanda	Uganda
Cape Verde	Iran	Malawi	Saudi Arabia	Emirates
Comoros	Israel	Maldives	Somalia	Yemen
Cyprus	Jordan	Moroco	South Africa	Zimbabwe

Source: Yang et al. (2012) Environmental Science and Technology

Per Capita Water Use

The per capita water use in different continents. The data highlights a close correlation between economic prosperity and water use.

Continents	Per Capita Water Use (m^3/yr)
Africa	245
Asia	**519**
North and C. America	1861
South America	478
Europe	1280
USSR (Former)	713

Source: Yang et.al, (2012) Environmental Science and Technology

Major consumption of water is for agriculture, industrial production and domestic purposes, apart from being used for fishery, hydro-power generation, transportation and maintaining biodiversity and ecological balance. Developing countries are using comparatively less water for agriculture and more for industrial and domestic purposes, while the developing countries in Asia and Africa use 80-90% of the water for agriculture and only 5-12% of the water for industrial use. This is reflecting on inefficient use of water in agriculture and poor investments in industrial development. While the per capita water use in India will increase from the current level of 99 litres per day to 167 litres per day in 2050, the per capita consumption in USA will reduce from 587 litres to 484 litres per day in 2050. By then, India will be the highest water demanding country, needing 2413 litres/day, while China and USA would require 2192 billion litres and 1167 billion litres.

Current Water Usage

The proportion of water used for agriculture and industries varies from country to country depending on the lifestyle, extent of industrial development and water use efficiency;

Usage (%)	World	Europe	Africa	India
Agriculture	**69**	33	88	**83**
Industry	23	54	5	12
Domestic	8	13	7	5

Source: Wallace (2012) Agriculture, Ecosystems and Environment

Future Water Usage

With the urbanisation and industrial development, the usage of water is likely to increase in the coming years.

Year	Agriculture	Industry	Domestic	Total	Per Capita
India Billion Lit/Day Lit/Day					
2000	1658	115	93	1866	88.9
2050	1745	441	227	2413	167.0

China					
2000	1024	392	105	1521	82.7
2050	1151	822	219	2192	155.4
USA					
2000	542	605	166	1313	582.7
2050	315	665	187	1167	484.6

Source: Yang et.al, (2012) Environmental Science and Technology

Water Resources in India

India is blessed with good rainfall well distributed over 5-6 months in the year. The average annual rainfall in the country is 1170 mm with a wide range between 100 mm in desert areas of Rajasthan to 10000 mm in Cherapunji. The total available sweet water in the country is 4000 billion m^3 per annum. Out of this, over 1047 billion m^3 water is lost due to evaporation, transpiration and runoff, reducing the available water to 1953 billion m^3 and the usable water to 1123 billion m^3. It is disturbing to note that only 18% of the rainwater is used effectively while 48% enters the river and most of which reaches the ocean. Out of the total usable water, 728 billion m^3 is contributed from surface water and 395 billion m^3 is contributed by replenishable ground water. Against the above supply, the water consumed during the year 2006 in India was 829 billion m^3 which is likely to increase to 1093 billion m^3 in 2025 and 1047 billion m^3 in 2050, as estimated by the ***Government of India*(2009)**. As the potential for increasing the volume of utilisation of water is hardly 5-10%, India is bound to face severe scarcity of water in the near future.

While water for consumption is most crucial, it is equally important to provide water for irrigation to increase the food production and livestock husbandry, to ensure food security for the increasing population. Growing population, as everyone is aware, is a serious concern as it will create further burden on the per capita water availability in the future. As can be seen in Table 4.4, the per capita water availability in 1951 was 5177 m^3 per year when the total population was only 361 million. In 2001, as the population increased to 1027 million, the per capita water availability reduced drastically to 1820 m^3 per year. By 2025, the per capita water availability will further drop down to 1341 m^3 and to 1140 m^3 in 2050. Based on the average requirement of water for various purposes, the situation is considered as water stress condition when the per capita water availability ranges from 1000 to 1700 m^3 per year and it is considered water scarcity when the availability reduces to 1000 m^3 per year. As the water available within the country varies widely as a result of rainfall, ground water reserve and proximity to river basins, most of the Indian States will have reached the water stress condition by 2020 and water scarcity condition by 2025. This would further hamper the food security, as the scarcity of water will directly suppress agricultural production.

Per Capita Water Availability in India

Year	Population (Million)	Per capita water availability (m^3/year)
1951	361	5177
1955	395	4732
1991	846	2209
2001	**1027**	**1820**
2025	1394	1341
2050	**1640**	**1140**

Source: Government of India, 2009.

Presently, inspite of good rainfall distribution, the country is unable to make good use of rain water, because of lack of awareness and poor infrastructure to construct dams and reservoirs. As a result, only about 35-40% of the cropping area receives irrigation to take 1-2 crops in a year. Out of the total cultivable area of 182 m ha, only 140 m ha are under net cultivation and of this, 62 m ha are under irrigation. There is further potential to increase the area under irrigation to 140 m ha, 76 m ha through surface water and 64 m ha by using ground water. So far, the irrigation potentials have already been created to cover 107 m ha, although they are not utilised effectively. It is estimated that effective area under irrigation by 2025 will be 76 million ha, although the Government of India is estimating to cover 104 million ha. Ground water is the major source of irrigation and this trend will continue. By 2025, 60 million ha will be irrigated by using ground water and by 2050; the area underground water will increase to 70 million ha. In 2000, the area under canal irrigation was 17 million ha, which will increase to 27 million ha by 2050. There is further scope to increase the potential by 35 million ha, by inter-linking the rivers and harnessing 36 billion m^3 through artificial recharging of ground water (***Government of India***, **2009**).

River Pollution

Apart from irrigation, many rivers in India are also used for generating hydro power. Out of the estimated hydro power potential of 1, 50,000 mw, only 21% has been developed so far and additional 10% power generation projects are under implementation. Presently, the country is facing many difficulties in further tapping the potential, due to difficult sites, forest conservation concerns; inter State issues, poor implementation and lack of commitment. It is also possible to develop multipurpose projects for power generation and irrigation which can improve the project viability, while increasing water supply.

Pollution of water resources is another major concern which is affecting the water supply as well as human health conditions. Although, 5% of the total water is used for domestic use, 27% of the villages and 4 to 6% urban population in India do not have access to drinking water (***Keller et.al,* 1998**). Apart from inadequate supply of water, there is a serious concern about the quality of water, which is severely affecting the health. It is reported that over 70% of the water consumed by rural population in India does not meet the WHO standards. It has been reported that 80% of rural illnesses, 21% of transmissible diseases and 20% of deaths among children in the age group of 5 years, are directly linked to consumption of unsafe water.

Sewage and Industrial Pollution

The major causes of water pollution are discharge of untreated sewage and industrial effluent into rivers, excessive use of fertilisers in agriculture and contamination of ground water with salts and minerals present in the lower soil profiles. It is estimated that in New Delhi alone, 36 million tons of sewage is generated everyday of which only 50% is treated and the rest is let out into the Yamuna River directly. Same is the situation in other cities. Only 31% of the sewage water generated in 23 major cities is treated and the rest is polluting 18 major rivers in the country. Most of the rivers in the country are also contaminated by fluorides, nitrites and several toxic metals. Presently, over 66 million people are suffering from fluorosis after consuming water containing more than 1.5 ppm fluoride. Poor sanitation both in rural and urban areas is another reason for pollution of drinking water sources. Only 30% rural population has access to toilet facilities while 65% urban people use toilets. Nitrates and harmful germs from human excreta flow and percolate down to contaminate the water tanks and open wells.

Ground Water Pollution

There is no precise estimate available about the extent of ground water polluted by excessive application of chemical fertilisers and pesticides. The problem is not only that of application of higher doses of fertilisers but also excessive use of water for irrigation. As a result, most of the well water used for drinking in irrigated areas is polluted. Excessive irrigation has also been causing further damage to soil productivity, as the water reaching lower layers of soil and the salts present in this region are dissolved in water. Subsequently, these salts come to the top soil through capillary action. Such soils with high concentrations turn into sodic wastelands unfit for agricultural production. Presently, over 9 million ha fertile irrigated lands have turned into sodic wastelands and the water in these areas will have high salt concentration, unfit for human consumption as well as for agricultural production. As the people living in these villages are helplessly consuming such hard water, the incidences of illnesses are high.

Drivers of Water Usage

The demand for water in India is steeply increasing because of the following reasons (***Amarasinghe, et al. 2007***):

1. The primary reason is population as India's population which was 1.3 billion in 2005 is expected to rise to 1.66 billion in 2050.
2. There is also going to be a major impact on development in the form of urbanisation. In 2007, 28.2% of the Indian population was living in urban areas and the urban population is expected to increase to 55.2% by 2050.
3. The per capita income of Indians will increase from $468 in 2007 to $6735 in 2050.
4. Increased industrialisation will demand more water as its contribution to GDP will increase from 29.1% in 2000 to 40% by 2050. Thus, the demand for water will increase from 30 billion m^3 in 2000 to 161 billion m^3 in 2050.
5. The agriculture development will be more on water intensive cash crops and there will be 80% increase in the demand for water by 2050.

It is therefore necessary to address the bottlenecks affecting the water supply in India.

Challenges in Water Sector

The water supply in India is going to be a serious challenge due to various reasons. The most serious concern is the growing population which is likely to increase to 1.66 billion by 2050. With the increasing population, the annual food requirement in the country will exceed 250 million tons. The total demand for grains will increase to 375 million tons including grain for feeding livestock. With the growth in the National GDP, at 6.8% per annum, during the period from 2000 to 2025 and 6.0% per annum, during the years 2025 to 2050, the per capita income is bound to increase by 5.5% per annum. This will increase the demand for food. While the per capita consumption of cereals will decrease by 9%, 47% and 60%, with respect to rice, coarse cereals and maize, the per capita consumption of sugar, fruits and vegetables will increase by 32%, 65% and 78% respectively, during the period from 2000 to 2050. This will create an additional demand for water. The requirement of water for livestock will rise from 2.3 billion m^3 in 2000 to 2.8 billion m^3 in 2025 and 3.2 billion m^3 in 2050.

Over-exploitation of ground water is another concern. Presently, there are over 20 m wells pumping water with free power supply, provided by the Government. This has been depleting ground water, while encouraging wastage of water in many states. As a result, the water table in the country is dipping every year by 0.4 m. In many coastal areas, there has been heavy intrusion of sea water, making fertile agricultural lands unfit for cultivation. By and large, the infrastructure development in the water sector has been extremely slow and investment has not been optimum. Furthermore, the utilisation of created water facilities has been sub-optimal because of poor catchment area development resulting in heavy soil erosion and siltation and inefficient use of water because of distribution of water in open canals, flood irrigation and charging for water on the basis of area irrigated instead of quantity of water supplied. It has been estimated that over 70% of the irrigation water is wasted by depriving irrigation to other dry areas. Farmers in India have been traditionally practicing flow irrigation which is resulting in huge wastage of water, while causing severe soil erosion, leaching of fertilisers, increasing the infestation of pests, diseases and weeds and suppressing the crop yields. Nevertheless, farmers as well as policy makers are not serious about the discontinuation of this unscientific practice. Immediate attention is needed to shift from flood irrigation to micro irrigation and to increase the water use efficiency, which can ease the water scarcity to a great extent **(*Rosegrantet al.* 2002).**

With regard to the water use efficiency in agriculture, India is far below most of the developed countries. This is not only due to flood irrigation and over-watering, but also because of improper water conservation measures and crop varieties which demand more water. However, farmers are not motivated to conserve water as there is no incentive for them to do so. Global warming is posing further challenge, as the water requirement for crops will increase due to higher evapo-transpiration. The rivers emerging from the Himalayas are prone to heavy floods and subsequently face severe water shortage, thereby suppressing agricultural production.

Over 60-80 million ha of denuded forestlands and wastelands across the country are unable to retain rainwater which in turn would have ensured recharging of ground water and conservation of biodiversity. As a result, the rivers emerging from these mountains are unable to sustain the flow of water throughout the year. Heavy soil erosion has not only been causing floods but also forcing the rivers to change their courses. Such rivers will not be able to support agricultural production in the future.

Water Use Efficiency in Agriculture

Water Foot Print (Lit/kg)

Crops	India	World
Wheat	1654	1334
Rice	2850	2291
Sugarcane	1759	1735
Cotton	18694	8242

Source: Supriyakumar, Water footprint (2013)

It is therefore necessary to address these burning issues which are affecting the water availability, although India has adequate water resources to meet the growing needs.

The National Water Policy (NWP)

India had revised the NWP in 2002 with the following salient features (*Government of India*, 2009):

1. Establishment of National and State level data banks to monitor the demand and supply;
2. Facilitation for transformation of available water resources into utilisable water;
3. Non-conventional methods for efficient water use;
4. Supply of water from water surplus areas to water shortage areas;
5. Judicious allocation of water for different uses and pricing of water to ensure sustainable development;
6. Regulation on ground water exploitation and close monitoring of water table using modern scientific techniques;
7. Sustainability of existing water bodies, involving all the stakeholders and local communities;
8. PPP for water resource development and distribution;
9. Master plan for flood control, by linking different rivers and promoting soil conservation measures;
10. Development of drought prone areas through watershed development, afforestation and sustainable farming practices;
11. Interstate water sharing policy and timely addressing of disputes.

Over the last 10 years, the situation has changed drastically and the progress in the water sector has not been keeping up with the expected target. It was therefore felt necessary to bring further changes in the policy, particularly in the following areas:

Changes proposed in the National Water Policy

Agriculture Sector

1. Improvement in water usage efficiency.
2. Adoption of rainwater harvesting and watershed management techniques.
3. Reduction of subsidies on power supply particularly for pumping water.
4. Prevention of ground water exploitation by introducing differential pricing, rewards and punishments.
5. Implementation of National River Link project which aims to connect 30 rivers and canals to generates 175 trillion litres of water.

Industrial Sector

1. Encourage recycling and treatment of industrial wastewater through regulations and subsidies.
2. Encourage introduction of new technologies which consume less water.

Domestic Sector

1. Introduction of a policy for mandatory rainwater harvesting in cities;
2. Propagation of efficient water usage;
3. Creation of awareness about water conservation among common public.

Augmentation of Water Resources

While the consumption of water in India will increase by over 50%, the supply will increase only by 5-10% during the next 12-15 years. This will lead to water scarcity situation and most of the people, particularly those who are dependent on agriculture and living in poverty will suffer the most. Water scarcity will affect the food production, biodiversity and the environment. Environmental degradation will accelerate global warming, which in turn will accelerate water crisis (*Kijne et.al.*, 2003). This is a vicious cycle. The only solution is to tap all the possible water resources and make them available for sustainable use, while improving the water use efficiency. This can be done by addressing various concerns and initiating suitable actions for development of new water resources, augmentation of available resources, prevention of water pollution and improving the efficiency of water use in all the sectors. For creating additional water resources, the following activities should be initiated.

Increasing Water Storage Capacity

Activities such as farm ponds, percolation tanks, water reservoirs and construction of small and medium size dams and rivers can retain more surface water, while increasing the ground water recharge. Series of contour bounds particularly in undulating areas will facilitate percolation of water in the soil and improve the ground water table, while reducing soil erosion. Gully plugging, construction of series of small dams on rivulets will help in storing water in reservoirs.

In the absence of harnessing rainwater in the forests and denuded hilly terrains, inadequate soil and water conservation measures are leading to severe soil erosion, silting of rivers beds and reservoirs and frequent flooding across the country. Presently, over 40 million ha are prone to floods in the country. Invariably, 8-10 million ha are affected by floods over year. During the year 2007-08, floods in India have caused 3689 deaths, loss of 1.14 lakh livestock and damaged 3.5 million houses, causing huge losses to the people, society and the Government. One of the major reasons for soil erosion and silting of rivers is severe deforestation. As a result of soil erosion, many of the rivers have been changing their courses almost every year damaging fertile agricultural lands. Brahmaputra is a good example where the width of the river during summer is 3-4 km which increases to 10-12 km during the rainy season. This highlights the extent of flooding of the river and harassment to the people living along the river. Due to poor management of this river, only 22 billion m^3 of water is utilisable while over 607 billion m^3 water is wasted. Similar situation is prevailing with respect to other rivers such as Ganga, Godavari, Mahanadi, Narmada, etc.

Interlinking of rivers will help in preventing floods while improving water distribution in the country. Control of water flow and floods will prevent soil erosion. Presently, billions of tons of fertile soils along with precious nutrients are washed out of our fertile agricultural lands and forests. In fact, the amount of nutrients lost due to soil erosion is almost equivalent to the chemical fertilisers produced in the country. This highlights the impact of soil erosion control on the food production. Reforestation of degraded forests and development of wastelands through afforestation will help in soil and water conservation (*IDSA*, 2010).

Judicious distribution of water for different uses can help in preventing water scarcity. The water distribution for different purposes is influenced by powerful lobbies and vested interests. Many sectors receive more water than what is needed at the cost of others. Even within the same sector, like irrigation for agriculture, the locations for infrastructure development are often influenced by those who are politically powerful, with vested interests, while depriving others in needy regions. To overcome such inefficiency and wastage of resources, a suitable investment mechanism should be developed based on the needs and return on investments. A transparent programme implementation mechanism and regular monitoring for quality can improve the speed and quality of the projects.

Efficient Irrigation Practices

Efficiency in irrigation is most essential, if the country wants to face the challenge of water crisis. As most of the crops are watered through flood irrigation, over 70% of the water used for irrigation is wasted. Furthermore, as the water supplied is not measured, farmers have a tendency to flood the field with excessive water without any additional cost. Such a practice has been creating a negative impact by way of increased cost of leached nutrients, pollution of ground water, increase in soil salinity and increase of pests and diseases. It is high time that India compels the farmers to adopt micro-irrigation systems, which will not only reduce the water requirement but also bring down the cost of production, while increasing the area under irrigation. The Government of India should consider enforcing a ban on flood irrigation in the country. Simultaneously, metered supply of irrigation water, recovery of water cost, promotion of micro-irrigation systems and involvement of water users' group for water distribution would significantly help in improving the water use efficiency and reducing the cost of agricultural production.

Watershed Development

Development of watersheds is an important programme to make best use of the rainwater for agricultural production while improving soil conservation and biodiversity. Fortunately, the Government of India has given top priority for watershed development to provide assured water supply of agriculture in rain fed areas. Under the watershed development programme, the catchment area of a basin is considered as a unit and efforts are made to harness rainwater by treating the land from the ridge to the valley. It is estimated that over 63% of the cultivated lands in the rain fed areas need to be brought under watershed development to conserve soil and water, which in turn would improve the crop yields as well as ground water table. Watershed development programme introduced almost about three decades ago, had covered over 51 million ha by the end of the Tenth Five Year Plan. Additional 36 million ha were being developed under the watershed development programme during the Eleventh Five Year Plan. However, a large number of watersheds are still subjected to heavy soil erosion, due to poor quality soil conservation work undertaken in the past and lack of convergence with other agricultural development activities. Therefore, there is scope for developing over 125 m ha under the watershed. Out of these areas, 85 m ha are rain fed agricultural lands and 40 m ha are wastelands. The watershed development programme is presently focussing on contour bunding and gully plugging, as the budget provided by the Government of India is just adequate to carry out these activities. Additional funds are required to support the farmers to adopt improved agricultural practices.

Control of Water Pollution

Excessive use of water for agriculture, industries and domestic uses is leading to water pollution, because such excess water is transformed into saline water, sewage or effluent. Thus, rewards and punishments should be introduced for persuading people to make optimum use of the precious water. Discharge of sewage and affluent into water bodies and rivers must be banned and recycling of waste water must be pursued and enforced. This will help in keeping the water sources clean and reducing the future demand for water. Treated sewage and effluent can be used for agriculture and industrial production.

Desalination of Sea Water

Over 70% of the global water resources being saline, economic desalination of sea water is an excellent option to meet the future shortage of sweet water particularly to meet the human consumption. Presently, desalination of sea water is expensive and non-popular. However, with solar power, desalination can be a viable alternative to meet the water needs in coastal areas.

Research and Development

There is a need for investing in research related to ground water monitoring, weather forecasting, breeding water efficient and drought resistant crops and varieties which can cope up with the changing climatic conditions, arising due to global warming.

Priority Areas for Action

As the time is running out, it is necessary to act on priority in the following areas:

1. The irrigation projects should be well planned and different activities such as relief and rehabilitation of project affected population, micro level land use planning and capacity building of farmers, should be initiated simultaneously.
2. Afforestation on degraded forests, wastelands as well as river banks should be promoted on priority to facilitate soil conservation, recharging of ground water and preventing flooding of rivers and siltation of water reservoirs.
3. Increasing irrigation efficiency from the current level of 35% to 50% in surface irrigation systems and 65% to 75% in ground water irrigation systems, can be easily achieved if careful planning and distribution of water through water meters, judicious pricing of water to recover the investment and investment in micro irrigation facilities are carried out, while improving the capabilities of the farmers. Farmers should be enlightened about the importance of water conservation and judicious uses, which are needed for achieving sustainability.
4. Development of wastelands which are spread over 80 million ha and accelerating soil erosion and run off surface water, as improving the productivity of these barren lands, will help in conserving water while contributing to food production and biodiversity enrichment.
5. Development of local capabilities by grooming new generation water management technicians and managers to implement various innovative projects with greater efficiency. There is also a need for promoting multidisciplinary researchers to study various aspects of water resources, conservation, efficient storage, reduction of losses and sustainable utilisation.
6. Public Private Partnership, including civil society organisations and stakeholders in water resources development and conservation. So far, the State Governments were responsible for developing necessary infrastructure and managing water distribution, which lacked people's

cooperation. It is also necessary to organise small farms to enable them to get their due share of water, as the poor are excluded from most of the development projects due to their ignorance and inability to make necessary investments. Civil Society Organisations as well as Farmers' Organisations can help small farmers in adopting modern technologies and for establishing forward and backward linkage, required for increasing their income.

7. Convergence of various developmental programmes can help in increasing the outputs. There are many development programmes implemented by the Ministries of Water Resources Development, Agriculture and Rural Development, which are coordinated by a single agency at the grassroot level to ensure effective utilisation of the resources while creating better impact.
8. Review of the National Water Policy to enforce a ban on flood irrigation, discontinuation of free power supply to pump underground water and prevention of untreated sewage and effluent into rivers should be taken up immediately, as these practices do more harm than help the community. Realistic pricing of water based on the investment, followed by awareness and education for farmers, introducing reward and punishments for maintaining discipline in water management, would help in ensuring sustainable development.

Success Stories

Impact of Watershed Development

Several watershed development projects have demonstrated positive impacts such as enhanced soil productivity through soil and water conservation, increase in the ground water table, improvement in biodiversity and micro-climate and improved eco-system. Integration of watershed development with other related agriculture development activities such as efficient water use, organic farming and improved agriculture practices have enhanced agricultural production without depleting soil fertility and water resources. In several projects implemented by BAIF Development Research Foundation, farmers could increase their cropping intensity by 31-63% while enhancing the crop yields by 40-80%. As a result of soil conservation and percolation of rainwater, there has been a significant increase in the ground water table by 1.5 m to 4 m, within a short span of 2-3 years, which eased the problem of clean potable water supply for local villagers. Improvement in soil moisture facilitated vigorous growth of shrubs and grasses, which improved the green cover, while easing the fodder supply. With a well planned watershed development programme and required investment both by the development agencies and the farmers, it should be possible to bring all the wastelands and degraded lands under agricultural production and enhance the income by several folds within a period of 5-6 years.

Establishment of farm ponds of 8 × 8 m or 10 × 10 m size with 2-3 m depth is a unique concept for decentralised storage of surface runoff water. Farm ponds are very effective for reducing the soil erosion and recharging of ground water. In areas where the rainfall is over 750-800 mm per year, these farm ponds fill up and over flow at least 4-5 times during the rainy season and retain water for over 4-8 months, which can be used for cultivation of high value crops as well as establishing fruit orchards.

Networking of farm ponds, 1-2 ponds per ha, has been successful in increasing the water table, thereby reviving the dried bore wells in the programmes implemented by BAIF in Karnataka, Andhra Pradesh and Maharashtra. There are several locations where with efficient network of farm ponds, the rivulets which were retaining water for 4-5 months in the year are now able to retain water throughout the year. Introduction of efficient irrigation systems has significantly enhanced agricultural production. There are many micro irrigation techniques adopted by small farmers without even depending on the power supply. There are several success stories across the country where farmers and field practitioners have innovated different methods for efficient and low cost water harvesting. Such sustainable practices should be recognised and widely replicated across the country.

Tree-based Farming System

Tree-based farming has great promise in the areas covered under the watersheds as well as for developing denuded and wastelands. This is because trees demand less water and withstand water stress to a great extent. While taking up this programme, there are many options to select useful tree species particularly on private lands, based on the soil productivity, moisture availability and local needs. While shallow dry lands con be covered with shrubs and grasses, deep, fertile lands can be used for growing high value fruit crops. BAIF has demonstrated the feasibility of cultivating various dry land horticultural crops instead of timber and fuel wood species where farmers are able to generate income every year without destroying the trees. This programme of agri-horti-forestry has become very successful in rehabilitation of over two lakh tribal families across the country. Under the tree-based farming programme, the critical factor which needs to be considered is to provide livelihood to the participant families during the gestation period of 4-5 years, till the fruit trees start bearing. To address this concern, BAIF has promoted food crops in the inter space between fruit plants. Efficient use of available water resources and effective soil water conservation could enhance the crop yields, while ensuring food security. The orchard owners are able to come out of poverty, when the fruit trees start yielding. Trees in the field and farm bunds serve as wind breaks to reduce evaporation loss and to improve the soil fertility. Agro forestry is a viable option to mitigate global warming and to face the crisis of water scarcity.

Development of Wastelands

Reclamation of sodic lands is another important programme which needs to be pursued as over 9mha of good fertile lands are lying idle because of high salt content. Efficient reclamation of these lands and recognition of the water use will bring this area under multiple cropping while making surplus water available to bring additional 8-10 ha under irrigation. Reclamation of sodic lands for agriculture can enhance food production by 50 million tons per year.

India also has 2 million ha of ravine lands particularly in the states of Uttar Pradesh, Madhya Pradesh and Rajasthan, where excessive soil erosion is damaging good agricultural lands, while flooding the rivers. Public Private Partnership for development of ravine lands owned by the farmers and community can prevent soil erosion and formation of ravine lands, while helping the farmers to grow 1-2 crops every year. BAIF has demonstrated the process of soil and water conservation, resulting in increased ground water table, which could enable small farmers to drill tube wells at cost and water sharing basis to grow multiple crops.

Livestock Development

Animal Husbandry is another important sector requiring water for feeding 500 million heads of livestock and to produce fodder for them. However, as over 75% of these animals are of inferior quality, farmers let them loose in the field for free grazing. This has been causing denudation of vegetation and heavy soil erosion. BAIF has demonstrated a new approach of improving the productivity of these animals which will motivate the farmers to take up stall feeding for reducing the herd size. Such a practice will reduce the pressure on natural resources, particularly water stress, while enhancing their income. Dairy husbandry is one of the most reliable sources of livelihood for small farmers, as the families maintaining 2-3 good quality cows or buffaloes are able to come out of poverty.

There are many voluntary organisations as well as National and International research and development organisations, who have implemented several successful projects with active participation of farmers. These success stories need to be widely publicised and replicated across the country with the financial support from the on-going Government schemes. Showcasing of successful holistic water-resource management projects can motivate the water users, particularly the farmers to adopt new practices and change their lifestyle to make efficient use of precious water.

Conclusion

The world faces an unprecedented crisis in water resources management, with profound implications for global food security, protection of human health, and maintenance of all ecosystems on Earth. Therefore increased efforts will be needed to plan and manage water supplies in future, through increased monitoring and understanding of the interrelationships between population size, climate change and water availability I order to bring about water security. Without water security, social, economic and national stability are imperiled.

Individuals need to realise that the choices that they make, the lifestyles that they live, the food that they eat and nearly every other component of their lives has a direct affect on the environment. We need to accept that as a species are living our lives based on a on a linear system in a planet that only has access to finite resources. It is therefore so important that we cannot continue pumping water from the ground without thought to how it may be restored in years to come. The human race faces a challenge that could see the end of life on Earth. We need to adopt the approach of environmental justice discourse by prioitising the rights of nature as being of equal importance to human rights.

Fortunately, the human race has a reputation for having the irrepressible ability to adapt in times of great adversity by rising to meet great challenges. We need to realise that it is not too late to make the necessary changes and that even in our own personal capacity, we have the ability to change the world.

REFERENCES

Aaron, T. and Wolf, A. K. (2006). Water Can Be a Pathway to Peace, Not War, *Environmental Change and Security program*, 1-6.

Amarasinghe, U. A., Shah, T., Turral, H. and Anand, B.K. (2007). India's Water Future to 2025-2050: Business as Usual Scenario and Deviations. Research Report 123, IWMI.

Camilleri, F. (2003). The World's Water Crisis: Present Developments and Future Conditions. *Division for Industry, Research, Energy, Environment and STOA* , 1-39.

Christopher, M. (2013). Water Wars: The Brahmaputra River and Sino-Indian Relations. *Center on Irregular Warfare & Armed Groups*, 1-39.

Cooley, J. K. (2008). World War for Water. *Foreign Policy*. **54**, 3-26.

George williamsherk, P.W. (2012). Water Wars in the Near Future? Reconciling Competing Claims for the Worlds Diminishing Fresh Water Resources- The Challenge of the Next Millennium. *The Centre for Energy, Petroleum and Mineral Law and Policy*, 1-8.

Govt. of India. 2009. Background Note for Consultation Meeting with Policy Makers on Review of National Water Policy. Ministry of Water Resources. 50.

Hofwegen, P.V and Svendsen, M.(2000). A Vision for Water for Food and Rural Development. The 2nd World Water Forum, 1-73.

HRH Rijsberman, F.R. (2000). Summary Report of the 2nd World Water Forum: Water Policy 2(2000):387-395.

Hull, J. W. (2000). The War Over Water. *Regional Resource of Strategic Management* , 1-12.

IUCN (2000). Vision for Water and Nature: A World Strategy for Conservation and Sustainable Management of Water Resources in the 21st Century, 1-34.

IWMI (2000). World Water Supply and Demand in 2025. World Water Scenario Analyses.

Kijne J.W., Barker, R. and Molden, D.J. (2003). Water Productivity in Agriculture: Limits and Opportunities for Improvement, 1-31.

Keller,J., Keller,A. and Davids,G.(1998). River Basin Development Phases and Implications of Closure. *Journal of Applied Irrigation Science*. 33(2):145-164.

Kumar, S. (2013). The Looming Threat of Water Scarcity. *World Watch Institute* , 1-7.

Lemly, A.D., Kingsford, R.T. and Thompson, J.R. (2000). Irrigated Agriculture and Wildlife Conservation: Conflict on a Global Scale. *Environmental Management* 25(5): 485-512.

Meigh, J.R., McKenzie, A., Austin, B.N., Bradford, R.B., and Reynard,N.S. (1998).

Assessment of Global water Resources – phase II. Estimates of Present and Future Water Availability in Eastern and Southern Africa, 1-17.

Mehta, P. (2012). Impending Water Crisis in India and Comparing Clean Water. *Archives of Applied Science Research*, 4 (1):497-507.

Narayanamoorthy, A. (2004). Drip Irrigation in India: Can it Solve the Water Crisis? Water Policy 6(2):117-130.

Postel, S. (1998). Water for Food Production: Will there be Enough in 2025. *Bio Science* 48(8): 629-637.

Postel, S. (2001). Safeguarding Our Water - Growing More Food with Less Water. *Scientific American Journal*, 40-45.

Pruss, A, Day K, Fewtrell, L and Bartram, J. (2002). Estimating the Global Burden of Disease from Water, Sanitation and Hygiene at a Global Level. *Environmental Health Perspectives*, 110, 537-542.

Raskin, P., Gleick, P., Kirshen, P., Pontius, G. and Strzepek K. (1997) Water Futures: Assessment of Long Range Patterns and Prospects, 1-19.

Renault, D. and Wallender, W.W. (2000) Nutritional Water Productivity and Diets. *Agricultural Water Management* 45, 275-296.

Richard,A., Lane, M. L. (2010) The Water Crisis in Third World Countries. *Monterey Starkey*, 1-30.

Rijsberman, F.R. and Molden D.J. (2001) Balancing Water Uses: Water for Food and Water for Nature. *International Conference on Freshwater*, 43-56.

Rijsberman, F. R. (2004). Water Scarcity: Fact or Fiction? *International Water Management Institute*, 1-14.

Rijsberman, F.R. (2004). The Water Challenge. *Global Crises, Global Solutions*, 1-15

Rijsberman, F.R. (2002). Troubled Waters, Water Troubles: Overcoming an Important Constraint to Food Security. Sustainable Food Security for all by 2020: *Proceedings of an International Conference*, 141-144.

Rijsberman, F.R and Mohamed, A. (2003). Water, Food and Environment: Conflict or Dialogue? *Water Science and Technology* 47, 53-62.

Robb, J. (2012). World War III: War for Water? *The Omega Letter Christian Intelligence* 1-3.

Rosegrant, M.W., Cai, X. and Clire, S.A. 2002. Global water outlook to 2025: Averting an Impending Crisis. *Food Policy Report, IWMI*. 36.

ShamaPerveen, R. S. (2012). India's Deepening Water Crisis. *Water Risks for Indian Industries* , 1-19.

Seckler, D., Molden, D.J. and Sakhtivadivel, R. (2003). The Concept of Efficiency in Water Resources Management and Policy, 1-9.

Seckler, D., Amarasinghe,Molden, U D.J,de Silva, R., Barker,R. (1998). World Water Demand and Supply, 1990 to 2025: *Scenarios and Issues*. IWMI Research Report 19.

Selby, J. (2005). The Geopolitics of Water in the middle east: fantasies and realities. *Third World Quarterly* , 1-21.

Shiklomanov, I.A. (1998). World Water Resources: An Appraisal for the 21st Century. IHP Report, 1-23.

Smakthin, V., Revenga, C.and Doll, P. (2004). Environmental Water Requirements in Global-scale Water Resources Assessments. Comprehensive Assessment of Water Management in Agriculture Research Report, 445-471.

UNWWDR (United Nations World Water Development Report) (2003). Water for People, Water for Life, 1-25.

Wallace, J.S. and Gregory, P.J (2002). Water Resources and their Use in Food Production. *Aquatic Sciences* 64, 363-375.

Wallace, J.S. (2000). Increasing Agricultural Water Efficiency to Meet Future Food Production. *Agriculture, Ecosystems and Environment* 82, 105-119.

Wathab, A. (2009). Water and War. *ICRC Response, Ecosystem and Environment,* 1-24.

Yang, H, P., Reichert, K., Abbaspour and Zehnder, A.J.B. (2012) A Water Resources

Threshold and its Implications for Food Security. *Environmental Science and Technology* **37**, 3048-3054

Technologies for Water and Wastewater Management **Pages 91-96**
Edited by: **Dr. Vijender Singh & Dr. Pawan Kumar 'Bharti'**
ISBN: 978-93-88854-53-5
Edition: **2020**
Published by: **Discovery Publishing House Pvt. Ltd., New Delhi (India)**

5 Basic Concept of Ground Water Movement, Monitoring and Modeling

Pawan Kumar 'Bharti'

ABSTRACT

In water cycle, rainfall is the main source that provides water for all living organisms in different ecosystems. Water from rain, enters in to soil and then flow vertically and down slope through the soil profile. Water flow may vary at place to place according to the physical conditions of soil of a particular area. Water movement beneath the earth may be measured with the help of Darcy's law by using various form of formula according to the physio-geography and soil profile of the area.

Key words: *Darcy's law, ground water movement, water flow, ground water modeling*

Introduction

In the last three decades, the rapid growth of industrialization and urbanization has created negative impacts on the environment. Due to industrial, municipal and agricultural wastes containing pesticides, insecticides, fertilizers residues and heavy metals with water; ground water has been polluted (Sastry *et al.* 1999). Ground water is used for domestic supply, industries, and agriculture in most part of the world as it is a replenishable resource and has inherent advantage over surface water. There has been a tremendous increase in the demand of fresh water due to growth in population, advanced agriculture practices and industrial usages (Bachmat, 1994). Industries are discharging their metal & hazardous substances containing effluents in to fresh water with out any adequate treatment (Canter, 1987). The seepage of effluents posed serious threat to the ground water resources (Groff, 1993).

Movement of Ground Water

Contamination of ground water is more complex than surface water pollution mainly because of difficulty in its timely detection and slow movement, which requires special expertise to predict the path and rate of ground water movement (Malik and Bharti, 2010).

Generally, it is believed that movement of ground water flows according to ground elevation or the general topography of the area. Ground water in its natural state is invariably moving and this movement is governed by established hydraulic principle and can be expressed by Darcy's Law. According to Darcy's Law "flow rate through porous media is proportional to the head loss and inversely proportional to the length of the flow path".

$$Q = \frac{K(h_1 - h_2)}{L}$$

Where,

Q – Specific discharge,

K – Hydraulic conductivity,

h_1-h_2 – Head loss, and

L – Distance of travel by ground water.

In addition the complex geo-chemical reactions taking place in the subsurface between myriad contaminants and earth materials are not always well-understood. Ideally speaking contamination should be prevented from occurring. After several contaminants are found in ground water, a decision must be made on whether to rehabilitate the aquifer or find alternative ground water resources. So, ground water must be managed and protected carefully for the most beneficial use in the future.

Ground water movement is basically depends upon the altitude, water table, soil characteristics and also soil profile. However, some basic equations and formulas may be applied for the measurement of ground water flow and also the movement of pollutants migrated in the ground water regime of a particular area.

Groundwater Flow Pattern

Geology offers control on the rate of ground water movement. The size of the pores and their relative connectivity (permeability) determine the rate at which water moves in to, though and out of aquifer (Bharti, 2007).

The flow of ground water in saturated soil is described well by Darcy's law, which, for steady flow in one dimension (linear), may be given by (Wainwright and Mulligan, 2004)-

$$q = -K\frac{dH}{dx}$$

Where, q is the discharge per unit area, K is the hydraulic conductivity; H is the hydraulic head and x is the distance in the direction of flow.

To make q positive, a minus sign appears before K. this correction is necessary because water flows down the hydraulic gradient, i.e. it flows along a negative gradient from areas of higher H to areas of lower H (Fetter, 1994).

Richards Equation

The water flow through unsaturated soil also be described by modified Darcy's law, where K is assumed to be a function of water content (θ), i.e.-

$$q = -K(\theta)\frac{dH}{dx}$$

L.A. Richards was the first person to realize that the Darcy's law could be applied to unsaturated flow, so the equation may be called as Richards equation.

Where flow is unsteady such as in natural conditions, water content will change and so will K. Thus, in unsaturated flow, unlike saturated one, K is time-variant, except for some very simple cases.

The simplest of this class of model ignore or greatly simplify flow in the unsaturated zone and assume that flow in the soil is parallel with the soil surface, and that the hydraulic gradient at any point with in the saturated zone is equal to the slope (Beven, 2000). Thus, the Darcy's law becomes-

$$Q = Kh \sin \beta$$

Where, Q is the discharge per unit width of hill slope in the down slope direction, h is the depth below the water table measured orthogonally to the impermeable plane at the base of the soil and β is the slope of the plane and soil surface (Masters, 1998).

Ground water moves more quickly in coarse sand sometimes as much as several meters per day while in case of clay which are generally impermeable the movement may seldom move not more than an inch per year (CPCB, 2003).

The general direction of ground water flow can be established on the basis of the local topography using topographical maps or aerial photos and the presence of stream or river which act as ground water discharge boundaries. The near surface ground water flow generally follow surface drainage pattern. If the flow direction can not be established, three small diameter wells are temporarily installed in the aquifer (CPCB, 2003). Relative water level in these wells reveals the direction of flow. Other methods of delineating ground water flow pattern include electromagnetic induction, earth resistivity survey, radioactivity and temperature logging (Bharti, 2007).

Darcy and Linear Velocity/Flow Velocity

If we combine the usual relationship between flow rate, velocity and cross section area, than-

$$Q \quad A$$

With Darcy's law we can calculate velocity,

$$\upsilon = \frac{Q}{A} = \frac{KA(dH/dL)}{A} = K\frac{dH}{dL}$$

Where, υ is known as the Darcy velocity, not a real velocity because much of the cross section area is made up of solids, the actual area through which all of the flow takes place is much smaller, so the real groundwater velocity is considerably faster than the Darcy velocity (Masters, 1998). A represent the cross section area, and A′ being the area of voids filled with water, than υ' be the actual average linear velocity, as

$$Q = A\upsilon = Av'$$

$$\upsilon' = \frac{Q}{A'} = \frac{AL\upsilon}{A'L} = \frac{\text{Total volume} \times \upsilon}{\text{Void volume}}$$

The actual average linear velocity through the aquifer is the Darcy velocity divided by porosity, so-

$$\upsilon' = \frac{\text{Darcy velocity}}{\text{Porosity}} = \frac{\upsilon}{\eta}$$

$$\upsilon' = \frac{K(dH / dL)}{\eta}$$

Where, υ' is the average linear velocity of groundwater, υ is Darcy velocity and η is the porosity of soil medium, which is the important physical factor may influence the ground water movement.

Retardation Factor

If a contamination moves at the same speed as the groundwater, some contaminants are absorbed on the soil particles, which reduce the overall solute flow rate relative to that of the ground water itself (Masters, 1998). This reduction in speed is called the retardation factor,

Where, υ' is the average linear velocity of groundwater, υ_s is the average linear velocity of retarded constituent.

$$\text{Retardation factor} = R = \frac{\upsilon'}{\upsilon} \geq 1$$

Ground water monitoring involves various investigations prior to the actual assessment of groundwater quality. The topography, geology, soil profile, aquifer characteristics, source of pollution, land-use pattern and above all the extent of ground water development are some of the important pre-requisites to decide the scheme of ground water monitoring. For representative information on ground water quality the first information to look for is the movement of ground water. From the above conditions of the ground water and related factors along with there equation, it is cleared that the ground water movement may be measured easily by applying some basic techniques.

Groundwater Monitoring Techniques

Monitoring of ground water quality involves collection of representative sample and simultaneous collection of hydro-geological information or data about the location of sampling station. The sampling and hence the ground water quality data may adversely affect if one or more of the following factors are not appropriately looked into (CPCB, 2003).

1. Samples are not taken at appropriate time intervals, seasonally and at improper locations.
2. Sample was taken from stagnant water in the open dug well or suddenly in case of bore well without removing the casing storage effect. The error can be largely overcome if three to ten well bore volumes are removed, and in case of hand pumps sufficient water is pumped out before taking the sample.
3. Contamination due to entrained sediment.
4. Hydraulic characteristics of the soil formation near the screen, resulting in possible dilution of the contaminant.
5. Release of carbon dioxide during pumping and hence increase in pH which may cause many metallic ions to come out of solution.
6. The sample preservation is not properly done and analyzed without considering the parameter- specific prescribed period of retention time.

Concept of Ground Water Modeling

According to many instances of ground water monitoring, the ability to predict how the contaminant plume will behave in future can be done by using the mathematical modeling techniques to estimate the spread of a contaminant and its strength at any point in the plume. A model is a device that represents an approximation of a field situation and provides a frame work for synthesizing field information and for testing of ideas about how the system works.

The concept of groundwater modeling is chiefly based on following factors:

1. Advection of the constituent with the water flowing through the aquifer.
2. Dispersion of the constituents.
3. Characteristics of recipient medium.
4. Sources of pollution.

Water chemistry data also provided a more reliable spatial measure of hyporhiec/ground water interface seasonal fluctuation (Fraser & Williams, 1998)

The steps to build the model are shown in the structure given below:

Factors > Processes > Model > Prediction > Assessments

Table 5.1: The Basic Step of Ground Water Monitoring and Modeling

Step 1.	Step 2.	Step 3.	Step 4.	Step 5.
Factors	**Processes**	**Model**	**Prediction**	**Assessments**
Hydrology / Hydraulics. Physical & chemical soil characteristics. Waste leachate properties.	Dispersion / Dilution. Precipitation. Adsorption. Biological activity. Etc.	Attenuation and Convection.	Contaminant concentrations in space and time.	Comparison of model results with field data.

REFERENCES

Bachmat, Y. (1994). Ground Water as Part of the Water System. In: Ground Water Contamination and Control, Ed. V. Zoller. *Marcel Dekker, Inc.* New York, pp. 560.

Beven, K. (2000). On the Future of Distributed Modeling in Hydrology, *Hydrological Processes*, 14: 3183-3184.

Bharti, P.K. (2007): Effect of Textile Industrial Effluents on Ground Water and Soil Quality in Panipat Region (Haryana), *Ph.D. Thesis*, Submitted to Gurukula Kangri University, Hardwar, pp. 191.

Canter, L.W. (1987). Ground Water Quality Protection, *Lewis Publications. Inc.*, Chelsea, Ml, pp. 650.

CPCB (2003). Ground Water: Parivesh, *Central Pollution Control Board*, Delhi-32, July, pp. 40.

Fraser, B.G. and Williams, D.D. (1998). Seasonal Boundary Dynamics of a Ground Water/ Surface-water Ecotone, *Ecology*, 79(6): 2019-2031.

Fetter, C.W. (1994). Applied Hydrology, 3rd edition, Macmillan, New York.

Groff, K.A. (1993). Textile Waste, *Environmental Research*. 65: 421.

Malik, D.S. and Bharti, P.K. (2010). Textile Pollution, Daya Publishing House, Delhi, pp. 383.

Masters, G.M. (1998). Introduction to Environmental Engineering and Science, *Prentice-Hall India*, pp. 460.

Sastry, K.V. and Pratima Rathee (1999). Ground Water Quality in Three Villages of Rohtak District. *J. Natcon*, 11(2): 175-182.

Wainwright, John and Mulligan, Mark (2004). Environmental Modeling, *John Wiley & Sons Ltd.* pp. 408.

large quantity of soluble organic matter and plant nutrients. It does not contain any toxic elements, but the only problem is with its very high BOD, COD, electrical conductivity and colour. The direct application of spent wash to the soil would return the nutrients to the soil yet continuous application to the soil may be harmful. However, the TDE is also widely used in agriculture as a nutrient source and organic manure for maintaining soil fertility.

Characteristics of Raw Spent Wash

The distillery spent wash is concentrated with soluble forms of organic matter and highly acidic in nature with pH ranging from 3.8 to 4.2 with considerable quantities of Ca and Mg, which could be well utilized as an amendment for reclamation of alkali soils as reported by Jayachandran *et al.* (1999), Soundararajan (2003) and Saliha (2005).

The Raw spent wash is a dark brown coloured liquid with unpleasant odour of burnt sugar. It is acidic (pH 3.8 to 4.2) and has all the ingredients found in the molasses except fermentable sugar. The dark brown colour of spent wash is due to the presence of melanoidin of cane molasses with high similarity to synthetic melanoidin and humic acid (Samuel Raj and Ramasamy, 1997; Soundararajan, 2003), which are not decomposed effectively by yeast and methane bacteria in activated sludge process.

Bustamante *et al.* (2005) characterized the vinasse (effluent discharged after the production of alcohol in the winery industries) and it showed an acidic pH, a high organic load and notable polyphenol content (318 mg L^{-1}). Rajukkannu and Manickam (1996) and Thiyagarajan (2001) reported that the unpleasant bad and abnoxious odour of the spent wash is due to the presence of skotole, indole and other sulphur compounds. The spent wash contains about 90 - 93 per cent water and 7 - 10 per cent solids, of which 2 - 20 per cent is sugar and 10 - 11 per cent is protein in dry spent wash as observed by Rajannan *et al.* (1998) and Joshi (2001). They also found that organic compounds extracted from spent wash using alkaline reagents are humic in nature.

Murugaragavan (2002) enumerated the population of different groups of micro organisms in the distillery raw spent wash. He reported that the population of bacteria, fungi and yeast in raw spent wash were higher ranging from 16 to 33.5 × 10^6 CFU ml^{-1}, 4.33 to 12.5 × 10^3 CFU ml^{-1} and 3 to 4 × 10^4 CFU ml^{-1} of spent wash, respectively. Veeresh *et al.* (2007) characterized the raw spent wash and found that the pH of the raw spent wash was acidic (3.03-5.40) with high EC (4.93 to 23.70 dSm^{-1}), BOD (31,400 to 48,079 mg L^{-1}) and COD (2276-12496 mg L^{-1}). The high BOD, COD and other organic compounds like phenols, lignin and oil and greases in spent wash are likely to deteriorate soil and environmental health. The unpleasant odour due to the presence of skatole, indole and other sulphur compounds which are not effectively decomposed by yeast or methanogenic bacteria during distillation and biomethanation is also an issue of public concern.

General Characteristics and Composition of TDE

The primary treated spent wash otherwise known as biomethanated spent wash (or) TDE is near neutral (pH of 7.2) in reactions (Rajukkannu *et al.*, 1996), Sridharan (2007) and Janaki (2008). The treated distillery spent wash had the temperature of 22-36°C, dissolved oxygen of 0.5 to 1.0 ppm, pH of 3.8-5.0, BOD of 12,000-19,000 ppm and COD of 17,300-25,000 ppm as reported by Vasisht and Kapoor (1981). Bories *et al.* (1998) observed that treated distillery wastewater had high BOD of 21.3 g L^{-1}, COD of 57.66 g L^{-1} and total suspended matter of 2.15 g L^{-1}, and the contents of N, K, Ca, Mg, Na, Zn, Fe, Cu and Mn were 616, 3900, 1460, 870, 150, 8.50, 87.47, 4.95 and 4.47 mg L^{-1} respectively.

According to Kulkarni *et al.* (1987) reported that nitrogen is mostly present in colloidal form and behaves as a slow release fertilizer better than most of the inorganic nitrogen sources. Two-third of phosphorous is also in organic form, the metabolic activity of which is more than that of inorganic sources. The TDE also contains large amount of important secondary nutrients like Ca, S and Mg and trace elements of Cu, Mn and Zn.

Rajaram and Janardhana (1988) observed that processed effluent is rich in organic constituents like ammoniacal nitrogen (18 mg L^{-1}), chloride (1,270 mg L^{-1}), sulphide (26 mg L^{-1}), sulphate (1000 mg L^{-1}), fluoride (0.63 mg L^{-1}), sodium (5 mg L^{-1}), suspended solids (12,600 mg L^{-1}), dissolved solids (2,11,180 mg L^{-1}), volatile solids (78,865 mg L^{-1}) and traces of heavy metals. The post methanation distillery effluent is characterized by dark coffee colour, purifying odour and highly biodegradable in nature (Pathak *et al.*, 1998). Most of the distilleries have installed biomethanation digester which reduces the biological oxygen demand (BOD) by 90 per cent. The post methanation effluent has EC of 8.5 dSm^{-1} and pH of 7.5. In India annually 40 × 10^8 litre of effluent is produced by methanation process and this will supply 13,000, 800 and 2, 40,000 t of N, P and K, respectively (Chhonkar *et al.*, 2000)

Spent wash is of purely plant origin and contains large quantities of soluble organic matter and plant nutrients that the sugarcane plant has adsorbed from soil. The spent wash when subjected to bio-methanation process looses up to 85 per cent of BOD and becomes distillery effluent. Different terminologies viz., stillage, vinasse, slop and still residue etc are used for this type of effluent in different countries (Baskar *et al.*, 2003). Sukanya and Meli (2004) reported the characteristics and composition of distillery effluent. It possessed dark reddish brown colour with unpleasant odour and a pH of 7.8. In addition to this, distillery effluent possesses high salt content (EC 20.8 dSm^{-1}), total dissolved solids (14634 mg L^{-1}), organic carbon (8%) and total suspended solids (3800 mg L^{-1}). It also has very high BOD (4620 mg L^{-1}) and COD (26000 mg L^{-1}) along with

N (0.19%), P (6 ppm), Ca (100 moles L^{-1}) and Mg (200 moles L^{-1}). It contained a good amount of potassium (5356 ppm), iron (38 ppm), sulphate sulfur (4.2 mmoles L^{-1}) and chlorides (14.40 mmoles L^{-1}). Maheswari (2011) reported that the effluent contains all plant nutrients in the order of K>S>Ca>Mg>N>P (macronutrients) and Fe>Zn>Mn>Cu (micronutrients).

Methods of Application

The treated distillery effluent could not be directly applied to the growing crops because of their excessive BOD, COD and EC. Therefore it should be applied to the field well before the planting of crop to give sufficient time for the natural oxidation of organic materials or diluted with normal water to bring down the excessive BOD, COD and EC and then applied to the growing crops. Application of TDE will be used as a nutrient source for many crops in different types of soil. So care should be taken to safeguard the soil and plant growth method of application play a vital role in sustaining the crop productivity.

1. Application of TDE through fertigation

The study result conceived by Devarajan *et al.* (1993) and Rajannan *et al.* (1996) have concluded that distillery effluent at 40 to 50 times dilutions increased the yield of sugarcane, banana, gingelly and rice. Devarajan *et al.* (1996) stated that the significant increase in the organic carbon content of the soils, with effluent irrigation, could be attributed to the high organic load of the effluent. Kayalvizhi (2000) found that the cane yield was higher at 1:10 dilution of distillery effluent in sugarcane. Chandraju *et al.* (2010) reported that dilution of 1:3 distillery spent wash shows more uptakes of nutrients when compared to 1:2 spent wash. This could be due to the maximum absorption of nutrients by plants at more diluted effluent. The results of the post harvest soil samples showed that was no adverse effect on characteristics. Hence the distillery spent wash can be conveniently used for irrigation purpose with required dilution without affecting environment and soil.

2. Pre-plant application of treated distillery effluent

Research work carried out in South American countries revealed that sugarcane yield could be increased from 3 to 35 per cent when vinasse was applied as pre-sown one time application at the rate of 150-600 m^3 ha^{-1} (Scandaliaris *et al.*, 1987) and there was no adverse effect on sprouting of cane (Perez-Zamore *et al.*, 1990). A field experiment was conducted by Devarajan *et al.* (1994) to study the effect of one time application of TDE @ 25, 50, 125, 250 and 500 t ha^{-1} before planting. The results revealed that all the levels of effluent application recorded significantly higher yield than control. Devarajan and Oblisami (1995) reported that pre-plant application of distillery effluent @ 125 t ha^{-1}

registered the highest cane yield. Pre-plant application of distillery effluent at 150 and 300 t ha^{-1} increased the sugarcane yield by 53.8 and 44.0 % respectively when compared with untreated control. The distillery effluent when applied in fallow lands during summer facilitates oxidation of organic matter and reduction of BOD levels. It could take care of the soil fertility problems and increase the crop yield (Rajukkannu *et al.*, 1996). Baskar *et al.* (2001) reported that application of pre-treated distillery effluent at graded doses (0, 1.25, 2.5, 3.75, 5.0 and 6.25 lakh litres per acre) progressively increased the cane yield of sugarcane when it was applied well before (40 days) planting in sandy soil.

Mohammed Haroon and Subash Chandra Bose (2004) reviewed the use of untreated distillery spent wash for reclamation of sodic soil. According to them, distillery spent wash application is recommended in summer when the ground water table is low. The distillery spent wash alone or in combination with gypsum is effective in spot reclamation of alkali soils particularly for agro forestry system under rainfed conditions. The primary treated distillery effluent (PTDE) can be used as source of fertigation either as onetime pre-plant application or frequent application of diluted (1:20 or 1:30) effluent. Suganya and Rajannan (2009) revealed that the application of distillery spent wash @ 100 KL ha^{-1} + RD-NP and distillery spent wash @ 100 KL ha^{-1} + 75% of RD-NP recorded the highest grain yield of maize. The method of application of distillery spent wash viz., pre-sown and post sown did not show much differences in the grain yield, growth attributes and yield attributes of maize crop. Hence any of these two methods could be adopted for the utilization of distillery spent wash for cultivation of crops.

Chidunkumar et al. (2009) noticed that the yields of all vegetables were high in the case of 33% and moderate in 50% spent wash and low in raw water irrigation. In 33% spent wash irrigation, the plants are able to absorb maximum amounts of nutrients both from the soil and the distillery spent wash resulting good yields. Previna (2012) revealed that application of TDE @ 3.75 lakh litres ha^{-1} either as pre-plant application or with irrigation water at 1:20 dilution (4 times) along with 75 per cent N and P fertilizer significantly enhanced the cane yield in medium textured soil viz., sandy loam soil. Long term application of TDE at above doses significantly improved the soil fertility without any deleterious effect. Previna (2012) observed the increased sugarcane yield was recorded to the tune of 15 per cent for foliar spray treatment with TDE and micronutrients. Similarly, the yield increase was 3 per cent for TDE combination with micronutrient over micronutrient spray alone.

Effect of TDE on Soil Properties

The effect of TDE on soil physical properties, physico-chemical properties, nutrient availability and rice growth are reviewed as follows.

1. Physical Properties of Soil

The distillery effluent contains appreciable amount of organic matter and hence, its application significantly improves the physical properties of soil. Escober (1966) had earlier observed that an increase in hydraulic conductivity and infiltration rate and improvement in aggregate stability following addition of distillery slops and molasses to the column of saline sodic soils. Increase in saturated hydraulic conductivity was attributed to increased porosity (Weil and Kroontje, 1979; Khaleel *et al.*, 1981), better aggregation and lower bulk density of the soil with effluent addition. Heavy dose of organic carbon compounds added through distillery effluent may cause high oxygen demand for microbial activities under anaerobic conditions, which will in turn cause a decrease in infiltration rate and hydraulic conductivity due to accumulation of solids. The effluent irrigation forms a hard crust on the surface due to sugar compounds and consequently blocks the pores which in turn may reduce the infiltration rate (Epstein *et al.*, 1976). Scandaliaris *et al.* (1987) reported a decrease in hydraulic conductivity at high rate of effluent application.

Tisdall and Oades (1982) reported that stimulation of higher microbial activity and secretion of microbial polysaccharides due to high carbon load causing stabilization of soil aggregates. Haynes and Naidu (1998) and Celik *et al.* (2004) also reported a reduction in bulk density with addition of organic matter. Soil permeability and porosity are the important parameters to be considered while planning for liquid waste disposal to agricultural land (Sweeney and Graetz, 1991). Higher concentration of treated distillery effluent solutions maintained permeability of soil by reducing dispersion of clay particles and breaking of soil aggregates. Joshi and Kalra (1995) observed that distillery effluent when applied makes the top surface hard, thereby reduces the water infiltration rate of the soil and also restrict the moisture losses due to evaporation. They also noted that the effluent application increases the per cent of micro pores that enhances the moisture retention and storage capacity of soil. Devarajan *et al.* (1996) also reported that the infiltration rate of the soils was significantly reduced with effluent irrigations and the reduction was marginal at 50 times dilution (5.2%) and appreciable at 10 times dilution (54.5%).

According to Pathak *et al.* (1998) observed that the saturated hydraulic conductivity of the soil was improved due to application of effluent after wheat harvest. The reduction in Na content in soil with TDE applications was also observed to be dependent on soil texture. Singh and Raj Bahadur (1998) reported a significant increase in infiltration rate of an Inceptisol with application of spent wash. Zalawadia and Raman (1994) found that application of Post methanation spent wash (PMSW) improved the water retention characteristics of the soil. Similar result was reported by Tripathi *et al.* (1988). Valliappan (1998) also observed that the saturated hydraulic conductivity and pore space in raw spent wash treated leached sodic soils were increased considerably from 0.44 to 2.57 × 10^{-6} m s^{-1} and 44.7 to 47.7 per cent respectively, with simultaneous reduction in the bulk density and water dispersible clay from 1.62 to 1.36 Mg m^{-3} and 7.29 to 2.26 per cent respectively., indicating the unique feature of distillery spent wash on the reclamation of sodic soils.

Increase in total and micro porosity of the soil in effluent treatments was attributed to higher organic matter content, better aggregation and changing distribution of pore sizes of the soil (Aggelides and Londra, 2000). Subash Chandra Bose *et al.* (2002a) observed that application of graded dose of primary treated distillery effluent from 1.25 to 6.25 lakhs litre ha^{-1} in sandy soil progressively reduced the bulk density from 1.51 to 1.46 Mg m^3 and increased the water holding capacity from 32.12 to 35.2 per cent which might be due to increased soil organic matter content added through distillery effluent. Soundararajan (2003) revealed that bulk density of the soil was decreased and the particle density remained unchanged in the spent wash applied soils. Celik *et al.* (2004) also found that total porosity of soil increases with organic fertilizers and compost application depending on the amount of materials added. Experiments conducted by Chandra *et al.* (2005) revealed that application of distillery effluent increases the hydraulic conductivity of the soil. Increasing dose of effluent significantly reduced the bulk density of the surface soil due to the high organic matter content and better aggregation in the treated distillery effluent applied soil (Hati *et al.*, 2007).

2. Effect on Physico-chemical Properties

The major physico-chemical properties considered are pH, EC and organic carbon of soil. The distillery effluent contains appreciable amount of basic cations, organic matter and higher salt load, its application to soil may affect the physico-chemical properties of soil.

(*i*) Soil pH: Subba (1972) recorded an increase in soil pH from 7.5 to 8 by the application of distillery effluent. The soil pH increased slowly due to periodical addition of spent wash to a non-calcareous medium black soil (Jadhav and Savant, 1975). Mattiazo and Ada Gloria (1985) found that the organic matter oxidation brought out by microbial activity was responsible for increased pH of the soil treated with distillery effluent. Sweeny and Graetz (1991) reported that addition of distillery effluent regardless of rate raised the soil pH, owing to increase in soil K, Ca, Mg and Na levels. Jhosi *et al.* (1996) reported that the soil pH registered no significant change with effluent amendment in wheat crop. Devarajan and Oblisami (1995) found a significant increase in soil pH in effluent irrigated rice field from 7.15 to 7.95, while Joshi *et al.* (1996) and Pathak *et al.* (1998) observed no significant change in the soil pH for the effluent irrigated wheat crop.

According to Selvalakshmi *et al.* (2001) also indicated a reduction in soil pH due to application of effluent with significant increase in organic carbon, EC, CEC and available N, P, K and micronutrients (Fe, Zn, Cu and Mn) contents in the soil. Subash Chandra Bose *et al.* (2002a) observed a significant increase in the pH of the post harvest soil due to the application of graded doses of primary treated distillery effluent. However the increase was only by 0.2 units which fall within neutral reactions even at higher dose of distillery effluent (6.25 lakhs litre ha^{-1}). Dinesh (2011) and Leninraja (2012) observed a significant decrease in the pH of the post harvest soil due to the application of graded doses of treated distillery effluent.

***(ii)* Electrical conductivity:** According to Jadhav and Savant (1975), Ajmal and Khan (1988) and Pathak *et al.* (1999) reported that the highest soil EC of 0.79 dSm^{-1} was recorded in treatment that received effluent water having BOD of 2000 mg L^{-1} followed by 0.64 dSm^{-1} in treatment that received effluent water having BOD of 1500 mg L^{-1} which might be due to the higher EC of the effluent (8.5 dSm^{-1}).The study results revealed by Singh and Raj Bahadur (1998) reported that the EC of the soil slightly increased with increase in number of pre-sowing distillery effluent irrigations. EC of the soil increased significantly when treated with effluent, which can be due to the presence of soluble salts in the effluent (Rajukkannu *et al.*, 1996). Baskar *et al.* (2001), Balasubramaniam *et al.* (2007) and Previna (2012) reported that the application of graded dose of distillery effluent significantly increased the EC of the soil and it was well within the safe limit. According to Raverkar *et al.* (2000) soil EC increased linearly with increase in the concentration of post methanated spent wash application. Subash Chandra Bose *et al.* (2002a) indicated that one time application of treated undiluted distillery effluent before planting of the crop did not raise EC of the soil beyond 0.25 dSm^{-1} even at 6.25 lakh litres ha^{-1} of treated effluent application.

***(iii)* Effect on soil fertility:** According to Mena *et al.* (1986) also reported that the vinasse (distillery effluent) application to soil increased the total N, C and organic matter contents and modified the C: N ratio. Cruz *et al.* (1991) found that the organic material added with the vinasse mineralized rapidly releasing nutrients, maintaining soil fertility and increasing Ca, S, N and P contents of the soil. Sweeny and Graetz (1991) also reported that the digested distillery effluent application increased the soil concentration of most elements particularly K. Application of vinasse @ 80 m^3 ha^{-1} increased the soil N, Ca, Mg, K and P content (Taluk and Medeiros, 1989) and soil humic acid (Palma *et al.*, 1989). Singh and Raj Bahadur, (1997) reported buildup in soil fertility status with effluent irrigation particularly in organic carbon and potassium status. Thiyagarajan and Mahimairaja (2002) reported that spent wash being originated from plant source, contained almost all plant nutrients besides high level of organic carbon and small amount of micronutrients. Mineralization of organic material as well as the nutrients present in the distillery effluent is responsible for increasing the availability of plant nutrients in soil (Somashekar *et al.*, 1984; Rajukkannu *et al.*, 1996 and Baskar *et al.*, 2004).

Selvakumar (2006) reported that the nutrient status of the soil was tremendously improved by the addition of 84 m^3 ha^{-1} of post methanated distillery spent wash with many fold increase in organic carbon content and the availability of N, P, K, and Fe, Zn, Cu, and Mn and also maintained higher availability of these nutrients even after the harvest of sweet sorghum crop. Biswas *et al.* (2009) studies clearly showed that optimum level of spent wash or post methanated effluent application could substitute chemical fertilizer and manure without sacrificing the yield of the crops in vertisol. The soil treated with spent wash contained more macro and micro aggregate associated carbon and soil organic carbon. The organic carbon content of effluent treated soils varied from 0.70 to 1.08 per cent. Addition of organic matter through the effluent could be the reason for this improvement in organic carbon content (Pathak *et al.*, 1998). Similar results were also reported by Ajmal and Khan (1988). Previna (2012) revealed that application of TDE @ 3.75 lakh litres ha^{-1} either as pre-plant application or with irrigation water at 1:20 dilution (4 times) along with 75 per cent N and P fertilizer significantly enhanced the cane yield in medium textured soil viz., sandy loam soil. Long term application of TDE at above doses significantly improved the soil fertility without any deleterious effect.

***(iv)* Organic carbon:** The effluent addition in soil significantly increased the organic carbon content in the soil and it is due to higher organic carbon of the effluent (Jadhav and Savant, 1975; Ajmal and Khan, 1988; Pathak *et al.*, 1998 and Maheswari, 2011). Recault (1990) reported that the distillery effluent was concentrated with soluble forms of organic matter. Zalawadia and Raman (1994) reported that the organic carbon content was significantly more in the distillery effluent irrigated soils. Devarajan *et al.* (1996) stated that the significant increase in the organic carbon content of the soil with effluent irrigation could be attributed to high organic content of the effluent. Singh and Bahadur (1997) and Balasubramaniam *et al.* (2007) reported that soil organic carbon increased significantly with increase in number of pre-sowing distillery effluent irrigation. Rajendra Gupta and Khan (2009) reported that addition of distillery effluent increased organic carbon content in all three textures (sandy loam, silty loam, clay loam). Increase in soil organic carbon was more in the soils which were treated with TDE applications of higher concentrations.

***(v)* Available Nitrogen:** According to Sengik and Kiel (1995) observed low volatilization loss of NH_3 in the vinasse applied soil when compared to cattle manure, refuse compost and peat. Devarajan *et al.* (1996) observed a significant increase in available N (from 276 to 412 kg ha^{-1}), when irrigated with 10 times diluted distillery effluent. Increase in the N availability in soil due to effluent application was reported by Devarajan and Oblisami (1995); Baskar *et al.* (2001) and Subash Chandra Bose *et al.* (2002b). Sukanya and Meli (2004) conducted studies in wheat to substitute distillery effluent as nitrogen source. The highest yield of 53.14 q ha^{-1} was obtained at nitrogen substitution through 50 per cent solid effluent and 50 per cent through inorganic source. It also supplies other nutrients in addition to nitrogen when applied as a source of nitrogen. Similar results were reported by Zalawadia and Raman (1994) in onion. Kalaiselvi and Mahimairaja (2010) observed that transformation and plant availability of N in soil was greatly influenced by the effluent application. Both the methods of effluent application (one time and continuous) differed significantly in affecting the N dynamics. Maheswari (2011) stated that the application of TDE increases the nitrogen availability in soil.

(*vi*) Available Phosphorus: The distillery effluent irrigation helps in buildup of soil fertility by increasing available soil phosphorous status (Singh and Bahadur, 1997; Zalawadia *et al.*, 1997; Pathak *et al.*, 1999). Application of distillery effluent had solubilised the native insoluble P and thus helped to increase the available P (Rajukkannu *et al.*, 1996). The application of TDE increased the available P status of the soil to the tune of two to three times from the initial soil test value in spite of the crop removal which might be due to the higher P content of the effluent (Devarajan *et al.*, 1996; Baskar *et al.*, 2001 and Kayalvizhi *et al.*, 2001). Vantour *et al.* (1987) observed that effluent increased the P fractions in saline soils especially calcium phosphate. Further, the proportion of organic P was also increased with spent wash application due to the associated rise in organic charge. The phosphorus as well as the HCO_3 content of distillery effluent and the organic acids produced during the decomposition of distillery effluent would have helped to solubilize the native soil P (Baskar *et al.*, 2001). Leninraja (2012) reported that the application of TDE @ 1.5 lakh litres ha^{-1} results in high available P in soil.

(*vii*) Available Potassium: According to Someshekar *et al.* (1984) opined that the mineralization of organic material as well as the nutrients present in the effluent is responsible for the increase in the availability of plant nutrients. Chang and Li (1988) found that the application of vinasse to the main crop of sugarcane increased the available K content of the surface soil and remained high even after the harvest of the first ratoon. Thus the effluent had not only supplied the nutrients to the existing crop but also maintained and improved the soil fertility for the next crop. Bertranou *et al.* (1989) reported that the available K was increased by 4 to 5 times due to effluent irrigations which might be due to the fact that K is supplied in large quantities. Zalawadia *et al.* (1994) stated that the available K content is increased to the tune of 1139 mg kg^{-1} of soil by the application of distillery effluent. The experiment conducted by Joshi *et al.* (1996) revealed that at surface layer the available K content of the post harvest soil (after wheat crop) has substantially increased from 87 ppm (control) to 1075 ppm due to onetime application of distillery effluent @ 240 m^3 ha^{-1}. The distillery effluent irrigation increases the available K content of post harvest soil (Singh and Bahadur, 1997 and Pathak *et al.*, 1999). Application of TDE @ 1.5 lakh litres ha^{-1} results in highest available K (Maheswari (2011) and Previna (2012)).

Secondary Nutrients

According to Devarajan *et al.* (1996) observed an increase of Ca and Mg from 1400 ppm to 2200 ppm and 126 ppm to 470 ppm, respectively due to the application of 10 times diluted distillery effluent. The distillery effluent contains appreciable amount of Calcium, magnesium and potassium and hence its application significantly increase the exchangeable cations in the soil (Baskar *et al.*, 2001). The exchangeable Ca, Mg and Na contents of the post harvest soil were significantly increased due to the application of graded doses of distillery effluent. This might be due to Ca, Mg, Na contents of the effluent (Devarajan *et al.*, 1996; Kayalvizhi *et al.*, 2001). Thitakamol and Kaewpinthong (2004) reported that application of increasing doses of distillery slop increased the exchangeable magnesium. Dinesh (2011) and Leninraja (2012) reported that the concentration of Ca, Mg were significantly higher due to application of TDE, whereas Na concentration in soil was decreased resulting in low exchangeable sodium percentage.

Available Micronutrients

According to Devarajan *et al.* (1996) reported that the available micro nutrients viz., Fe, Zn, Cu and Mn of the post harvest soil increased from 2.2 to 3.9 ppm, 22.9 to 31.6 ppm, 4.1 to 7.3 ppm and 15.5 to 25.8 ppm, respectively due to fertigation with 10 times diluted distillery effluent. Similar increases in the availability of micro nutrients were observed by Kayalvizhi *et al.* (2001). Baskar *et al.* (2001) reported that the available micro nutrients viz. Fe, Zn, Cu and Mn, were progressively increased by the graded levels of distillery effluent and the availability being maximum with the application of distillery effluent @ 2.5 lakh litres ac^{-1}. They also stated that the increased availability might be due to direct contribution from the effluent as well as solubilization and chelation effect of organic matter supplied by the effluent. The available micro nutrients were significantly increased due to application of TDE. The highest DTPA-Fe, Zn, Cu and Mn were recorded in the higher dose of 1.5 lakh litres ha^{-1} (Maheswari, 2011 and Leninraja, 2012)

Effect on Biological Properties of Soil

As this distillery effluent contains highly bio-degradable organic matter with high content of dissolved salts of essential plant nutrients, it is expected to alter soil biological health as well as enzyme activity. Soil enzyme activity is considered as a tool for microbial activity in soil. Therefore any management practices that influence the microbial population of the soil would be expected to produce changes in the soil enzyme activity and the levels of enzyme activity can be used as an indicator of soil fertility (Burns, 1982). Perucci (1990) observed that soil phosphatase activity was stimulated by the addition of compost. The biological N fixation was considered to be higher in the post methanated distillery effluent treatment as organics amendment known to stimulate N_2 fixation (Roper and Ladha, 1995). Tauk *et al.* (1990) also lend support for the increased number of fungi, bacteria and actinomycetes owing to the addition of biomethanated distillery spent wash.

According to Devarajan *et al.* (1993) reported that the population dynamics of bacteria, actinomycetes, fungi, *Azospirillum* and *Azotobacter* were enhanced or maintained in the field soils of turmeric, paddy, sesame, cotton, banana and groundnut when the crops were irrigated with 50 times diluted treated distillery effluent. Batch *et al.* (1993) observed that the vinasse sugar factory effluent (1:5) at 250 m^3 ha^{-1} rate stimulated the soil microorganism and increased the dehydrogenase activity in soil. Goyal *et al.* (1995) have also reported higher dehydrogenase activity in soil due to distillery effluent application. Lakshmanan and Gopal (1996) also found that the population of bacteria, fungi, actinomycetes and azetobactor in the soils irrigated with 50 times diluted effluent was higher than the soils irrigated with other dilutions viz., 40, 30, 20 and 10 times dilutions and they reported that the population varied with period under effluent irrigation and the peak was recorded in the fifth month. Goyal *et al.* (1995) have also reported higher dehydrogenase activity in soil due to distillery effluent application. Garcia *et al.* (1997) have suggested that dehydrogenase activity can be taken as an index of overall microbial activity of degraded soils. Kaushik *et al.* (2005) reported that soil invertase activity (IA) also increased in effluent irrigated soil from 180 to 528 μg glucose g^{-1} d^{-1}. According to Omar *et al.* (2002) the concentrated vinasse as a soil conditioner under two levels of nitrogen fertilizers (50 and 100 %) did not reduce the faba bean rhizospheric bacterial counts.

According to Murugaragavan (2002) reported that the addition of raw spent wash at 125 m^3 ha^{-1} in dry land soils increased the activity of soil enzymes, phosphatase, dehydrogenase and urease. Selvakumar (2006) reported that though there was an initial set back in the fungi and actinomycetes population due to the application of post-methanated distillery effluent @ 84 m^3 ha^{-1}, the population of bacteria, fungi and actinomycetes and the activities of phosphatase, dehydrogenase and urease enzymes were substantially increased on 25th day of its application. Nagaraju *et al.* (2009) reported that discharge of effluents from distillery industry has enhanced the soil protease activity but it declined with the time. Potassium which is present in abundance in the PME has also been reported to enhance microbial activity (Chandra *et al.*, 2002). By increasing the effluent concentration, the enzyme activity was improved up to 100 per cent. Maheswari (2011) and Dinesh (2011) reported that application of treated distillery effluent increased the population of bacteria, fungi and actinomycetes as well increased the enzyme activities of the soil.

Effect of Treated Distillery Effluent on Growth of Rice and Other Crop

A research study conducted by Forester (1976) reported an increase in total chlorophyll content in rice at lower concentration of treated distillery effluent. This might be due to the fact that potassium had the beneficial effect on increasing leaf chlorophyll. Sahai *et al.* (1983) observed that the growth of rice seedlings were better in five per cent effluent dilution than control. Besides chlorophyll 'a' and 'b' the carotenoids content recorded was higher at five per cent effluent concentration. Rajaram and Janardhana (1988) conducted germination studies and early seedling growth of rice and found that lower concentration of effluent did not affect the germination. The root and shoot length were maximum at 2.5 per cent distillery effluent concentration. Arora *et al.* (1992) stated that the spent wash treated rice plant showed better growth and development as compared to control plants grown in full nutrient solution. Behra and Mishra (1982) reported an increase in total chlorophyll content in paddy at lower concentration of distillery effluent. Tripathi *et al.* (1988) stated that pre-sown application of diluted distillery effluent @ 20 m^3 ha^{-1} was optimum for building up soil fertility and increasing the yield of rice in sandy loam soil. Application of spent wash with 50 times dilution in rice (CO 43) resulted in normal yield. The maximum grain yield was recorded in rice variety ADT 42 due to 75 times diluted distillery effluent treatments which was on par with 100 times diluted spent wash application. The primary treated spent wash is rich in potassium, sulphur, nitrogen, phosphorous and its application to soil has been reported to increase rice yield (Devarajan and Oblisami, 1995). Pathak *et al.* (1998) reported that soil amended with diluted post methanated distillery effluent increased the yield of wheat and rice grown in sequence. This might be due to the fact that potassium had the beneficial effect on increasing leaf area, chlorophyll content and succulence of flag leaf in crop (Forster, 1976).

According to Rajannan *et al.* (1998) reported that fertigation of distillery effluent at 40 to 50 times dilution increased the yield of rice, maize, sugarcane, banana and gingelly. Rajukkannu and Shanmugam (1998) observed that the spent wash when diluted suitably (1:10 to 1:50) there was reduction in its BOD and EC, hence it can be made amenable for irrigation to rice crop. They also visualized an increase in nutrient content of soils and the yield of rice crop without any adverse effect on soil physical, chemical and biological properties. The field experiment conducted by Valliappan (1998) showed that application of spent wash (150 ml kg^{-1} soil) without NPK fertilization to sodic soil had recorded the rice grain and straw yields of 5,720 kg ha^{-1} and 10,480 kg ha^{-1}, respectively which accounted an additional grain yield of 2755 kg ha^{-1} (93 per cent) and straw yield of 6305 kg ha^{-1} (151 per cent) over the absolute control. Chinnusamy *et al.* (2001) studied the effect of treated distillery effluent on two cultivars of *Oryza sativa* L. Cv. Saka 4 and Pusa 44 after diluted with tap water at 100, 50 and 25 per cent in petri plates. The root length, shoot length, fresh weight of shoot and root, dry weight of shoot and root, germination relative index, vigour index, emergence index and chlorophyll content were higher in 25 per cent over control. Jintaridth *et al.* (2002) reported that application of effluent @187.5 m^3 ha^{-1} gave the highest response of rice yield (3,533 kg ha^{-1}) followed by the application of effluent @ 125 m^3 ha^{-1} (3248 kg ha^{-1}). The lower dilution level of 1:5 increased the uptake of nitrogen (195.45 kg ha^{-1}) and found better in terms of productivity and quality (Sukanya and Meli, 2004). Saliha (2005) reported that grain and straw yield of rice crop (CO 43) was 7,125 kg ha^{-1} and 11,025 kg ha^{-1}, respectively with one time application of spent wash @ 75 to 150 m^3 ha^{-1} to the air dried non- saline sodic soil. Sharma *et al.* (2008) reported the maximum dry matter yield was obtained for both grain and straw with the application of post methanated spent wash (PMSW) equivalent to one pre sowing irrigation (PSI) along with 100 per cent of recommended fertilizers. In comparison to the control, pre sowing irrigation with spent wash at 125 m^3 ha^{-1} (62.5 ml kg^{-1} soil) increased the grain yield of rice by 1.7 times under field conditions (Mahimairaja and Bolan, 2004).

According to Madhumita Das *et al.* (2010) reported that the application of highly saline (EC 20.7 dSm^{-1}), near neutral, cane molasses based treated TDE was found beneficial by correcting soil constraints and improving yield at 25 kg grain m^{-3} along with nutrients uptake in paddy. Application of TDE at the rate of 120 m^3 ha^{-1} was found to be the most favourable concentration for growing paddy crop in red and laterite soil type (pH < 7.0). Maheswari (2011) stated that the application of graded dose of TDE could be effectively used up to 1 lakh 1itres ha^{-1} for rice grown in sandy clay loam soil. Leninraja (2012) reported that the application of TDE @ 1.0 lakh litres ha^{-1} or TDE @ 1.5 lakh litres ha^{-1} along with 37.5% N as urea + 37.5% N as biocompost recorded the highest yield and uptake of nutrients by paddy.

Other Crops Farming

1. Sugarcane

According to Janaki (2008) reported that the yield attributes like cane length, cane girth, number of millable canes and number of internodes per cane and yield in sugarcane were enhanced with the application of TDE @1.0 lakh litres ha^{-1} along with NPK or NP alone with an yield increase to the tune of 46.5 and 42.5 t ha^{-1}, respectively over the control. Previna (2012) revealed that the application of graded doses of TDE significantly increased the yield of sugarcane, but failed to modify the juice quality. The graded doses of TDE along with NPK significantly increased the soil available nutrients, organic carbon content and also favoured the microbial population and promoted the enzyme activities in soil besides improving soil physical properties.

2. Sweet sorghum

The highest yield of grain (2.96 t ha^{-1}), cane juice (16.62 t ha^{-1}) and ethanol (2184 litres ha^{-1}) in sweet sorghum were observed for one time land application of post methanated distillery effluent @ 84 m^3 ha^{-1} when compared to 100 per cent recommended fertilizer - NPK and control (Selvakumar, 2006).

3. Millets

Kaushik *et al.* (2005) reported that application distillery effluent with 1:50 dilution favoured successful germination and improved seedling growth of pearl millet. Dinesh (2011) reported that the application of TDE and organic manures favoured an increase in the grain and stover yield; growth and yield attributes and nutrient uptake by maize crop and the magnitude of increase was markedly higher with the application of TDE @ 1.0 lakh litres ha^{-1} than other treatments.

4. Pulses

Results from the pot experiment demonstrated that spent wash > 50 m^3 ha^1 was found detrimental for germination and establishment of green gram in Vertisol, whereas in Alfisol even @ 25 m^3 ha^1, the spent wash was found to inhibit the germination and growth of green gram. However, in Vertisol the germination, growth, nutrient contents and yield of green gram were significantly improved with spent wash application @ 25 m^3 ha^1 (Murugaragavan, 2002). Hati *et al.* (2007) recorded increased electrical conductivity (EC) and organic carbon content surface soil (0-10 cm) in increased levels of effluent from 1.25 to 5 cm compared to the treatments with control (no fertilizer or manure or effluent) and 100 per cent NPK + FYM at 4 mg per ha to soybean (T2) in soybean – wheat sequence cropping system.

5. Vegetable crops

Sharma (2001) reported that vinasse (2.5 – 3.5 t ha^{-1}) increased the yield of sugar beet, potatoes and other vegetables and due care should be taken before using the distillery effluent for pre-sowing irrigation purposes in vegetable crops. The results showed that 5 per cent concentration of distillery effluent was critical for seed germination in tomato and bitter gourd, and 25 per cent in case of chilli, cucumber and onion. Soundarrajan and James Pitchai (2007) reported that 50 times dilution of TDE increased the crop quality and yield in bhendi crop.

Rice Growth with Graded Doses of NPK Application

According to Anandakrishnan *et al.* (2007) reported in a study with application of post methanated effluent @ 1.5, 2, 2.5 lakh 1itres ha^{-1} and a control with no

PME and the sub plot treatment at 50% N + 100% P, 100% N +75% P and a control with no fertilizer. The results of the study indicated that the application of distillery effluent @ 1.5 lakh 1itres ha^{-1} along with 50 % N and 100 % P found to be the best for getting higher grain and straw yield of rice (white ponni) was also observed up to 2 lakh 1itres ha^{-1}.

On farm trial was carried out to optimize the fertilizer N, P and K requirement of rice for a yield target of 6 t ha^{-1} using site specific nutrient management (SSNM) approach. The mean N requirement for a yield target of 6 t ha^{-1} was 152, 112 and 30 kg N ha $^{-1}$ during first trial and 138, 219 and 134 kg ha^{-1} with no amendment, gypsum and distillery spent wash reclamation respectively in second trial. In both the trials, mean P requirement varied between 25 to 30 kg P_2O_5 ha^{-1} irrespective of amendment used. The fertilizer K requirement varied between 66 to 75 kg K_2O ha^{-1} under no amendment and gypsum in both the trials (Ravichandran *et al.*, 2007). Anandakrishnan *et al.* (2007) reported that an experiment was carried out with the application of post bio-methanated distillery effluent as one-time pre-plant application for rice in clay loam soil texture along with graded levels of N, P and K fertilizer. The results of the field experiment showed the application of increasing doses of PME significantly increased the grain and straw yield of rice. An increased grain yield of 26.8 per cent was recorded due to the application of PME @ 1.5 lakh 1itres ha^{-1} over control. The grain yield increased to the tune of 455,667, 573 and 778 kg ha^{-1} due to application of N, NP, NK and NPK fertilizers, respectively over control (without NPK).

According to Sharma *et al.* (2008) reported that one-time pre sowing irrigation with post methanation distillery effluent along with inorganic fertilizer proved most effective in increasing the grain and straw yield of rice. Rodrigo *et al.* (2008) reported that the average grain yield of 5.52 t ha^{-1} with straw weight of 6.27 t ha^{-1} was obtained with distillery slop treatment in rice under field condition. Maheswari (2011) stated that the nitrogen availability in soil is greatly influenced by different levels of TDE, N fertilizer treatment and their interaction. At all stages of rice growth, the available N in the soil were greater in soil that received 1.5 lakh 1itres h^{-1} of TDE with 100 % recommended dose of nitrogen (RDN) treatments. At all stages the amount of NH_4-N and NO_3- N was greater in soil that received 1.5 lakh 1itres ha^{-1} of TDE with 100 % RDN treatment and apart from that the K fertilizer could be skipped from the fertilizer schedule. Angelin Silviya (2012) reported the highest rice yield was recorded by the application of TDE @ 40,000 L ha^{-1} with 100 per cent NPK addition which was being comparable with TDE @ 40,000 L ha^{-1} with 75 per cent NPK.

Conclusion

The large number of experiments it has been found that the TDE is very useful in increasing the yield of several crops and improving physical properties like bulk density, hydraulic conductivity and infiltration rate also improves the soil fertility in terms of organic carbon and all the available nutrients. Application of TDE increases the microbial biomass and their by it enhances the dehydrogenase, phosphatase and urease activity. The TDE could be advantageously used as a source of plant nutrients to supplement the nutrient requirement in some of the field crops. Though the beneficial effects of TDE as a source of nutrient on crop production are well documented, the information is scares on long term application of TDE at different time intervals along with inorganic fertilizers. Therefore, the present study was undertaken to assess the suitability of TDE for substitution exclusion of N and K fertilizer for improving the rice production.

REFERENCES

Aggelides, S.M. and P.A. Londra. (2000): Effect of Compost Produced from Town Wastes and Sewage Sludge on the Physical Properties. Bioresour. Technol., 71: 253–259.

Ajmal, M. and A.U. Khan. (1988): Effect of Sugar Factory Effluent on Soil and Crop Plants. Environ. Pollut., 30: 135.

Anandakrishnan, B., M. Soundarrajan, M.S. Dawood, S. Jebaraj and R. Pushpavalli. (2007): Studies on the Long Term Effect of Distillery Effluent on Sugarcane Yield and Soil Properties. In: Abstracts of National Conference on "Ecofriendly Utilization of Recyclable Organic Resources from the Sugar and Distillery Industries for Sustainable Agriculture" held at Anbil Dharmalingam Agricultural College and Research Institute, Tiruchirappalli-9, Tamil Nadu Agricultural University, Tamil Nadu, during 6 to 7th March, p. 42.

Aneja, K. R. (2005): Experiments in Microbiology, Plant Pathology and Biotechnology. New Age Publishers, p 69.

Angelin Silviya. (2012): Study on the Impact of Treated Distillery Effluent on Yield of Rice and Quality of Soil and Water. M.Sc., Thesis, Tamil Nadu Agricultural University, Coimbatore.

Anonymous. (2010): Area, Production and Productivity of Principal Crops. Department of Economics and Statistics, Chennai.

APHA. (1989): Standard Methods for the Examination of Water and Waste Water ,16th ed. American Public Health Association, Washington, DC, pp. 83.

Aruna, L., G. Selvakumari and R. Mohan. (1999): Nitrogen Release Pattern of Green Manures in Sodic Soil. Madras Agric. J., 86: 356-359.

Arora, M., D. K. Sharma and B. K. Behera. (1992): Upgrading of Distillery Effluent by *Nitrosococcus oceanus* of Its Use as a Low Cost Fertilizer. Res. Cons. and Recycling, 64: 347-353.

Balasubramaniam, P., S.Santhanabosu and K.Selvakumar. (2007): Effect of Graded Levels of Distillery Effluent on Quality of Leachate and Soil Properties in Column Experiment. In : Abstracts of National Conference on Ecofrieldly Utilization of Recyclable Organic Resources from Sugar and Distillery Industries for Sustainable Agriculture, Held at ADAC & RI, TNAU, Tiruchirapalli, Mar. 6-7, pp: 62.

Balasubramanium, P., R.Angelin silviya, R.Nagarajan and A.Tajuddin. (2013): Effect of Graded Levels of Treated Sugarcane Distillery Effluent with Soil Test Based NPK on Yield and

Nutrient Uptake of Rice (*Oryza sativa* L.) in Sandy Clay Loam Soil. Intl. J. Chem, Envt and Biological Sci., 2(1).

Baskar, M., H. Gopal, C. Kayalvizhi, M. Sheik Dawood, M. Subash Chandra Bose and K. Rajukkannu. (2001): Influence of Pre-plant Application of Distillery Effluent and Fertilizers on Soil Properties and Yield of Sugarcane. In: National Seminar on Use of Poor Quality Water and Sugar Industrial Effluents in Agriculture, ADAC & RI, Tiruchirappalli, Tamil Nadu Agricultural University, Feb. 5, pp. 76-82.

Baskar. M., M. S. Dawood, V. Balamurugan, S. A. Raj, K. G. Kunduswamy and K. Ravindran. (2004): Potential Use of Molasses and Distillery Industry Waste Water in Agriculture Through Environmentally Safe Technologies. Sustainable Sugarcane and Sugar production Technology. In: *Proceedings of Intern. Symp.* Nanning, Guangxi, China on Nov. 29th, pp. 718-724.

Baskar, M., C. Kayalvizhi and M. Subash Chandra Bose. (2003): Ecofriendly Utilization of Distillery Effluent in Agriculture—A Review. Agric. Rev., 24: 16-30.

Batch, T., A. Martinez, A. Mustelier-L-del, D. R. Villegas and D. Ponce-de- Leon. (1993): Agricultural Use of Vinasse Mixed with Effluent from Brown Sugar Production. Quimica Fiscay Biologia de Suelos, 1: 229-232.

Becker, M., J. K. Ladha and J.C.G. Ottow. (1994): Nitrogen Losses and Low Land Rice Yield as Affected by Residue N release. Soil Sci. Soc. Am. J., 58: 1660-1665.

Behera, B.K. and B.M. Misra. (1982): Analysis of the Effect of Industrial Effluent on Growth and Development of Rice Seedlings. Environ. Res., 28: 10-20.

Bertranou, A.V., C. Fasciola, C. Gomez, M. Javregui and O. Valez. (1989): Land Treatment of Winery Wastewaters : A Case Study of Irrigated Arid Zones. Wat. Sci. Tech., 19: 1243-1246.

Bhaskar, S., D.P. Dhanaraj, H Kavitha, C.A. Srinivasamurthy, H.M.A. Rehman, B. Lingaiah and N. Vijayakrishna. (2007): Effect of Distillery Effluent as Ferti-irrigation on Soil Properties of Alfisols of Karnataka. In: Abstracts of National Conference on " Ecofriendly Utilization of Recyclable Organic Resources from the Sugar and Distillery Industries for Sustainable Agriculture" Held at Anbil Dharmalingam Agricultural College and Research Institute, Tiruchirappalli-9, Tamil Nadu Agricultural University, Tamil Nadu, on March 6-7th , p.59.

Biswas, A.K., M. Mohanty, K.M. Hati, A.K. Misra. (2009): Distillery Effluents on Soil Organic Carbon and Aggregate Stability of a Vertisol in India. Soil Tillage Res., 104: pp. 241-246.

Bories, A., J. Raynal and F. Bazile. (1998): Anaerobic Digestion of High Strength Distillery Wastewater (cane Molasses Sillage) in a Fixed Film Reactor. Biol. Wastes, 23: 251 - 267.

Bose, S.C.M., M. Baskar, C. Kayalvizhi, H. Gopal and M. Sivanandham. (2002): Utilization of Distillery Effluent in Coastal Sandy Soil to Improve the Soil Fertility and Yield of Sugarcane. In: Proceedings of 17th World Congress of Soil Science Held in Thailand, pp. 1980-1 to 8.

Bremner, J. M and R. L. Mulvany. (1978): Urease Activity in Soils. In: Soil Enzymes. (Ed.) R.G. Burns, Acadamic Press, New York, USA, p. 149-196.

Burns, R. G. (1982): Enzyme Activity in Soil Location and Possible Role in Microbial Ecology. Soil Biol. Biochem., 14:423-427

Bustamante. M. A., C. Paredes, R. Moral, J. Moreno-Caselles, A. Perez-Espinosa and M. D. Perez-Murcia. (2005): User of Winery and Distillery Effluents in Agriculture. Wat. Sci. Tech., 51: 145 – 151.

Celik, I., I.Ortas and S. Kilic. (2004): Effects of Compost, Mycorrhiza, Manure and Fertilizer on Some Physical Properties of a Chromoxerert Soil. Soil Tillage Res., 78: 59–67.

Chandra, S., Joshi, H.C. Pathak, H. Jain and M.C. Kalra. (2002): Effect of Potassium Salts and Distillery Effluent on Carbon Mineralization in Soil. Bioresour. Tech., 83 (3): 255-257.

Chandra, S., H. C. Joshi and H. Pathak. (2005): Impact of Distillery Effluent and Salts on Hydraulic Conductivity of a Sandy Loam Soil. Caspian J. Env. Sci., 3(1): 9-14.

Chandraju, S. C.S. Chidankumar and R.V. Chalapathy. 2010. Irrigational Impact of Distillery Spentwash on the Growth, Yield and Nutrients of Leafy Vegetables. Res. J. Agric. Sci., 2: 255-257.

Chang, S.J. and S.W.Li. (1988): Effect of Spentwash Application on Yield and K availability in Sugarcane. Annual Report of Taiwan Sugar Research Institute, pp. 11-12

Chendrayan, K., T. K. Adhya and N. Sethunathan. (1980): Assay of Dehydrogenase Activity in Soils. Soil Biol. Biochem., 12: 271-273.

Cepro, G.S. and A.J. Machado. (1987): Centro Agric. 14(4): 76-80.

Chhonkar, P.K., S.P.Datta, H.C. Joshi and H. Pathak. (2000): Impact of Industrial Effluents on Soil Health and Agriculture – Indian Experience. Part I – Distillery and Paper Mill Effluents. J. Scientific Ind. Res., 59: 350-361.

Chidankumar, C.S. and S. Chandraju and R.Nagendraswamy. (2009): Impact of Distillery Spentwash Irrigation on the Yield of Top Vegetables (Creepers). World Applied Sciences Journal. 6(9): 1270-1273.

Chinnusamy, C., K. Annadurai, C. Jayanthi, R. Veerapathiran and S. Karunanithi. (2001): Organic Amendments and Distillery Effluent on Soil Fertility and Productivity of Rice. In: National Seminar on Use of Poor Quality Water and Sugar Industrial Effluents in Agriculture ADAC & RI, Tiruchirappalli, Tamil Nadu Agricultural University, Feb 5, p. 84.

Cruz, R. L., A. M. Righetto and M. O. Nogueira. (1991): Experimental Investigation of Soil and Ground Water Impacts Caused by Vinasse Disposal. Water Sci. Tech., 24: 77 - 85.

Devarajan, L.,G.Rajannan, G. Ramanathan and G. Oblisami. (1993): Sugarcane Cultivation with Distillery Effluent. SSISTA Sugar J., 20: 23-25

Devarajan, L., G. Rajannan, G. Ramanathan and G. Oblisami. (1994): Performance of Field Crops Under Distillery Effluent Irrigation. Kisan World, 17: 48-49.

Devarajan, L and G. Oblisami. (1995): Effect of Distillery Effluent on Soil Properties, Yield and Quality of Sugarcane. Madras Agric. J., 82: 397-399.

Devarajan, L., G. Rajannan and G. Oblisami. (1996): Effect of Distillery Effluent with Fertilizer Levels on Soil Fertility Status, Yield and Quality of Sugarcane. In: Proceedings of National Seminar on Use of Distillery Waste on Agriculture Held at ADAC & RI, Tiruchirappalli, Tamil Nadu Agricultural University, 28 and 29th Oct 1996. pp. 80 – 88.

Devarajan, L., G. Rajannan and G. Oblisami. (1998): Effect of Distillery Industry Effluent Irrigation on Soil Properties, Yield and Quality of Oilseed Crops. In: Proceedings of National Seminar on Application of Treated Effluent for Irrigation, Held at REC, Tiruchirappalli, Mar. 23, pp. 19-23.

Dinesh, D. (2011): Utilization of Distillery Industrial Wastes as Sources of Nutrients for Maize (*Zea mays* L.). Ph.D. Thesis, Tamil Nadu Agricultural University, Coimbatore.

Escober, R.P. (1966): Stability of Aggregates Treated with Distillery Slop or Black Strap Molasses. J. Agric. Univ. Puerto Rico., 50:174–185.

Epstein, E., I.M. Taylor and R.L. Chaney. (1976): Effect of Sewage Sludge Ans Sludge Compost Applied to Soil on Some Soil Physical and Chemical Properties. J. Environ. Qual, 5: 422 426.

Forster, E.H. (1976): The Role of Potassium in Crop Production. In: Proc. 11th congr. Int. Potash. Inst. Berne (Switzerland), pp. 111-112.

Garcia, C., Hernandez and T.Costa. (1997): Potential Use of Dehydrogenase Activity as an Index for Microbial Activity in Degraded Soils. Commun. Soil Sci. Plant Ann., 28: 123-134.

Ghosh, A.K., Pankaj Kumar and N. P. Ray. (1999): Physico-chemical Analysis of Distillery Effluent and their Effect on Germination of Some Legumes. Neo Botanica., 7(1): 27-32.

Gomez, K.A. and A.A. Gomez. (1984): Statistical Procedures for Agric. Res., John Wiley and Sons, New Delhi, p. 680.

Goyal, S., K. Chander and K.K. Kapoor. (1995): Effect of Distillery Wastewater Application on Soil Microbial Properties and Plant Growth. Environ. Eco., 13 (1): 89-93.

Gupta, A.P., R.S.Antil and V.K.Gupta. (1986): Effect of Pressmud and Zinc on the Yield and Uptake of Zinc and Nitrogen by corn. J. Indian Soc. Soil Sci., 34: 810-814.

Hati, K. M., A. K. Biswas, K. K. Bandyopadhyay and A. K. Misra. (2007): Soil Properties and Crop Yields on a Vertisol in India with Application of Distillery Effluent. Soil Tillage Res., 92:60-68.

Hayase, F., Kim, S.M., Kato, H. (1984): Decolorization and Degradation Products of the Melanoidin by Hydrogen Peroxide. Agric. Biol. Chem. 48 (11), 2711–2717.

Haynes, R.J., R. Naidu. (1998): Influence of Lime, Fertilizer and Manure Applications on Soil Organic Matter Content and Soil Physical Conditions: A Review. Nutr. Cycl. Agroecosyst., 51:123–137.

Jackson, M. L. (1973): Soil Chemical Analysis. Pub: Prentice Hall of India. Pvt. Ltd., New Delhi.

Janaki.D. (2008): Utilization of Distillery Spentwash as Manure to Crops and Its Impact on Soil, Crop and Ground Water Quality. Ph.D. Thesis, Tamil Nadu Agricultural University, Coimbatore.

Jadhav, H.D. and N.K.Savant. (1975): Influence of Added Spent Wash on Chemical and Physical Properties of Soil. Indian J. Agric. Chem., 8: 73–84.

Jayachandran, J., T. S. Manickam, G. Rajasekaran, M. Mathivanan and S. Balu. (1999): Bioremediation of Sodic Soil (Alkali Soil) with Distillery Spentwash in Manikandam Block - A Case Study. In: Proceedings of National Seminar on Bioremediation of Polluted Habitat, Mar. 22 - 23, pp. 18-19.

Jintaridth Bunjirtluk, Kanjanathanset Khamchai, Inthasothi Tippawan, Leaungvutuviroj Chaveevan and Charoenchamratcheep Charoen. (2002): Utilization of Spent Wash Liquor for Rice Production in Acid Sulphate Soils. In: Symposium No.63, 17th WCSS, 14-21 Aug, Thailand, pp. 2282-2295.

Joshi, H.C and N. Kalra. (1995): Distillery Waste Utilization in Agriculture. Yojana, 39(8): 10-38

Joshi, H. C., H. Pathak, A. Choudhary and N. Kalra. (1996): Distillery Effluent as a Source of Plant Nutrients. Fert. News, 41: 41 – 47

Joshi, H. C., H. Pathak, A. Chaudhary, T. P. Joshi, V. K. Phogat, and N. Kalra. (2000): Changes in Soil Properties with Distillery Effluent Irrigation. J. Environ. Res., 6 (4): 153 - 162.

Joshi, H. C. and G. Singh. (2010): Use of Distillery Effluent in Agriculture. J. Socio. Environ. Res. Org., pp. 20-23.

Joshi, H. C. (2001): Bio-energy Potential of Distillery Effluents. URL: http://www.undp.org.in/ Programme/ GEF/ june/ page 10 - 15. html.

Kalaiselvi, P and S. Mahimairaja. (2010): Effect of Spent Wash Application on Nitrogen Dynamics in Soil. International J. of Environ. Sci. Development, 2: 16-28.

Kamalakumari, K and P. Singaram. (1995): Relationship Among Soil Chemical, Biochemical Properties and Enzyme Activities. Madras Agric. J., 82: 69-70.

Kaushik, A., R. Nisha, K. Jagjeeta and C.P. Kaushik. (2005): Impact of Long and Short Term Irrigation of a Sodic Soil with Distillery Effluent in Combination with Bioamendments. Bioresource Technol., 96: 1860-1866.

Kayalvizhi, C., H. Gopal, M. Baskar, M. Sheik Dawood, M. Subash Chandra Bose and K. Rajukkannu. (2001): Effect of Fertigation with Distillery Effluent on Soil Properties and Yield of Sugarcane. In: Proceedings of National Seminar on "Use of Poor Quality Water and Sugar Industrial Effluents in Agriculture", held at ADAC & RI, Tiruchirappalli, Tamil Nadu Agricultural University, Feb. 5th, pp. 75.

Khaleel, R., Reddy and K.R. Overcash. (1981): Changes in Soil Physical Properties Due to Organic Waste Application: A Review. J. Environ. Qual. 10: 133–141.

Kulkarni, A.D., H.M. Modak and S.J. Jadhav. (1987): Fertilizer from Spentwash-A Review, Bhartiya Sugar., 12(9): 1-17.

Lakshmanan, A and N. O. Gopal. (1996): Effect of Distillery Effluent Irrigation on the Microbial Population of the Soil. In: Proceedings of National Symposium on Use of distillery and Sugar Industry Wastes in Agriculture, ADAC & RI, Tiruchirappalli, Tamil Nadu Agricultural University, p. 5.

Leninraja. D. (2012): Ecofriendly Utilization of Distillery Wastes for Sustaining Soil Health and Crop Production. Ph. D. Thesis, Tamil Nadu Agricultural University, Coimbatore.

Lindsay, W. L and W. A. Norvell. (1978): Development of DTPA Soil Test for Zinc, Iron, Manganese and Copper. Soil Sci. Soc. Am. J., 42: 421 - 428.

Madhumita D., H. Chakraborthy, R.B. Singandhupe, S.D. Muduli and A. Kumar. (2010): Utilization of Distillery Wastewater For Improving Production in Unproductive Paddy Grown Area in India. J. Sci. Ind. Res., 69: 560-563.

Maheswari, K. (2011): Eco-friendly and Effective Nitrogen Management with Treated Distillery Effluent and Its Impact on Rice Yield and Soil Properties. M. Sc., Thesis, Tamil Nadu Agricultural University, Coimbatore.

Mahimairaja, S., N.S. Bolan, M.J. Hedley and A.N. Macgregor. (1995): Dissolution of Phosphate Rock During the Composting of Poultry Manure. An Incubation Expriment. Fertilizer Research, 40: 93-104.

Mahimairaja, S and N.S. Bolan. (2004): Problems and Prospects of Agricultural Use of Distillery Spentwash in India. In: Proceedings of Supersoil 2004: 3rd Australian New Zealand Soils Conference, Dec.5-9, University of Sydney, Australia., pp. 1-6.

Mallika, S. (2001): Ecofriendly Utilization of Distillery Spentwash for Enhancing Soil Fertility and Crop Productivity. M.Sc Thesis., Tamil Nadu Agricultural University, Coimbatore, India.

Mattiazo, M.E and N. Ada Gloria. (1985): Effect of Vinasse on Soil Activity. STAB (Portuguese), 4(2): 38- 40.

Mena, M.A. et al. (1986): Cien. Agric., 29: 122-127.

Mohamed Haroon, A. and M. Subash Chandra Bose. (2004): Use of Distillery Spentwash for Alkali Soil Reclamation, Treated Distillery Effluent for Fertigation of Crops. Indian farm., 53(11): 48 - 51.

Moore, W. A., R. C. Kronel and C. C. Ruchhoff. (1949): Dichromate Reflux Method for Determination of Oxygen Consumed. Anal. Chem., 21: 953.

Murugaragavan, R. (2002): Distillery Spent Wash on Crop Production in Dryland Soils. M.Sc., Thesis, Tamil Nadu Agricultural University, Coimbatore.

Nagappan, M., K. Jothinathan and S. Sivakumar. (1996): Effect of Secondary Treated Distillery Effluent Irrigation on Soil Properties and Yield of Crops. In: Proceedings of National Symposium on Use of Distillery and Sugar Industry Wastes in Agriculture, ADAC & RI, Tiruchirappalli, Tamil Nadu Agricultural University, pp. 62-65.

Nagaraju, M., G. Narasimha and V. Rangaswamy. (2009): Influence of Sugar Industry Effluents on Soil Protease Activity. Ecol. Environ. Conserv., 15: 2.

Ojha, N.J and M.C. Talukdar. (2000): Yield and Yield Attributes of Direct Seeded Rainfed Summer Rice (*Oryza sativa* L.) as Influenced by Levels of Potassium and Sources of Organic Matter. Indian J. agric. Sci., 70 (11): 774-776.

Olsen, S. R., C. V. Cole, F. S. Watanabe and A. L. Dean. (1954): Estimation of Available Phosphorous in Soils by Extraction with Sodium Bicarbonate. (USDA) Circular No. 939.

Omar, M. N. A., A. T. Mostafa and A. S. Ahmed. (2002): Concentrated Vinasse as a Novel Diazotrophs Growth Medium (biovinasse inoculant) and Soil Conditioner to Improve Faba Bean Yield Under Dripping Irrigation System. In: Symposium No.03, 17th WCSS, 14-21 Aug, Thailand, pp. 137-144.

Palma, M. S., S. M. Tauk and O. Raymundo (1989): Aspects of Humification in Reddish-yellow Latosol of Medium Texture Treated with Vinasse, Under Maize Culture. Ciencia e Culture Sao Paulo, 4: 1125-1128.

Pathak, H., H. C. Joshi, A. Chaudhary, R. Chaudhary, N. Kalra and M. K. Dwivedi. (1999): Soil Amendment with Distillery Effluent for Wheat and Rice Cultivation. Water, Air Soil Pollut., 113: 133-140.

Pathak, H., H.C. Joshi, A.Chaudhary, R.Chaudhary, N.Kalra and M.K. Dwivedi. (1998): Distillery Effluent as Soil Amendment for Wheat and Rice. J. Indian Soc. Soil Sci., 46(1):155-157.

Patil, G. D., Pingat, S. M. and Yelwande. (2000): Effect Spentwash Levels on Soil Fertility, Uptake, Quality and Yield of Fodder Maize. J. Maharashtra Agri. Univ., 25 : 168-170

Perez-Zamora,F. (1990): Revista Industrialy Agricola de Tucuman., 67: 79-89

Perucci, P. (1990): Effect of the Addition of Municipal Solid Waste Compost on Microbial Biomass and Enzyme Activities in Soil. Biol. Fertil. Soils, 10: 221 - 226.

Piper, C.S. (1966): Soil and Plant Analysis. Inter Science Publication Inc., New York., pp. 368.

Prabu, P.C. (2003): Bioremediation of Paper Mill Effluent Polluted Habitat. Ph.D. Thesis, Tamil Nadu Agricultural University, Coimbatore.

Previna, S. (2012): Ecofriendly Utilization of Treated Distillery Effluent in Sugarcane (Saccharum officinarum L.). Ph. D., Thesis., Tamil Nadu Agricultural University, Coimbatore.

Rajannan, G., J. Helkiah, K.S. Parwin Banu and P.P. Ramasami. (1996): Preparation of Quality Compost from Pressmud and Distillery Effluent. In: Proceedings of National Seminar on Use of Distillery and Sugar Industry Wastes in Agriculture, Held at ADAC & RI, TNAU, Triuchirapalli, Oct. 28-29, pp. 149-151.

Rajannan, G., L. Devarajan and G. Oblisami. (1998): Impact of Distillery Effluent Irrigation on Growth of Banana Crop. In: Proceedings of National Seminar on Application of Treated Effluents for Irrigation, Held at REC, Triuchirapalli, Mar. 23., pp. 56.

Rajaram, N. and K Janardhana. (1988): Effect of Distillery Effluent on Seed Germination and Early Seedling Growth of Soybean, Cowpea, Rice and Sorghum. Seed Research, 16 (2) : 173-177.

Rajendra Gupta and Khan. (2009): Evaluation of Distillery Effluent Application Effect on Physic-chemical Properties and Exchangeable Sodium Content of Sodic Soils. Sugar Tech., 11(4): 330-337.

Rajukkannu, K., T. S. Manickam, K. Shanmugam, A. Chandrasekaran and R. Gladis. (1996): Distillery Spent Wash Development of Technology for Using it as an Amendment for Reclamation of Sodic Soils. In: Proceedings of National Symposium on "Use of distillery and Sugar Industry Wastes in Agriculture", held at ADAC & RI, Tiruchirappalli, Tamil Nadu Agricultural University on 28 & 29 October, 1996, pp. 30-39.

Rajukkannu, K and T. S. Manickam. (1996): Use of Distillery Effluent and Sugar Industry Wastes in Agriculture- Problems and Prospects. In: Proceedings of National Symposium on "Use of Distillery and Sugar Wastes in Agriculture" Held at ADAC & RI, Tiruchirappalli, Tamil Nadu Agricultural University, Feb 5th, pp. 22-25.

Rajukkannu, K and T.S. Manickam. (1997): Use of Distillery and Sugar Industry Waste in Agriculture. In: Proceedings of the 6th National Symposium on Environmental Issues Related to Agriculture, Textile and Leather, Tamil Nadu Agricultural University, Coimbatore, Tamil Nadu, India, pp. 286-290.

Rajukkannu, K and K. Shanmugam. (1998): Recycling of Distillery Wastes in Agriculture. In: Proceedings of National Seminar on Applications of Treated Effluent for Irrigation, Held at REC, Tiruchirapalli, Mar. 23, pp. 19.

Ramana, S., A. K. Biswas, S. Kundu, J. K. Sana and R. B. R. Yadava. (2002): Effect of Distillery Effluent on Seed Germination in Some Vegetable Crops. Bioresource Technol., 82: 273-275.

Ramaswami, P.P. (1999): Recycling of Agricultural and Agro Industrial Wastes for Sustainable Agriculture Production. J. Indian Soc. Soil Sci., 47: 661-665.

*Ramteke, D. S and C. A. Moghe. (1988): A Course Manual on Water and Waste Water Analysis. National Environmental Engineering Research Institute, Nagpur.

Raverkar, K. P., S. Ramana, A. B. Singh, A. K. Biswas and S. Kundu. (2000): Impact of Post Methanation Spentwash (PMS) application on the Nursery Raising and Bio-chemical Parameters of Glyricidia Sepium and Biological Activity of soil. Ann. Plant Soil Res., 2: 161-168.

Ravichandran, N.S., A.R. Mohamed Haroon, A. Bhaskaran, K.Vidya, S.P. Ramanathan and S. Jebaraj. (2007): Site Specific Nutrient Management for Rice in Distillery Spentwash Reclaimed Alkali Soils. In: Abstracts of National Conference on Ecofrieldly Utilization of Recyclable Organic Resources from Sugar and Distillery Industries for Sustainable Agriculture, Held at ADAC & RI, TNAU, Tiruchirapalli, Mar.6-7, pp. 32

Recault, Y. (1990): Treatment Distillery Waste Water Using an Anaerobic Downflow Stationary Fixed Film Reactor. Performance of a Large Plant in Operation for Four Years. Wat. Sci. Techn., 22 (1/2): 361-372.

Roper, M. M. and J. K. Ladha. (1995): Biological N_2 Fixation By Heterotrophic and Phototrophic Bacteria in Association with Straw. Plant Soil, 174: 211-224.

Rodrigo B. Badayos, Nertila M. Manalili and Prof. Moises A. (2008): Dorado SEAMEO Regional Center for Graduate Study and Research in Agriculture. In: Results and Findings on the Use of Treated Distillery Wastes as Inputs for Agricultural Production – A Waste Management Approach to Cleaner Productions. pp. 16.

Sahai, R., S. Jabeen and P.K. Saxena. (1983): Effect of Distillery Waste on Seed Germination, Seedling Growth and Pigment Content of Rice. Indian J. Ecol., 10: 7-10

Saliha, B. (2005): Distillery Spentwash for Sustainable Soil Health. Kissan World, 32: 50-51

Samuel Raj, H and K. Ramasamy. (1997): Characterization of Colouring Principle in the Distillery Effluent. In: Proceedings of National Symposium on Environment Held at Tamil Nadu Agricultural University, Coimbatore, Jan. 7-9, pp. 108-113.

Scandaliaris, T., C. N. Datur and M.Rancedo. (1987): Influence of Vinasse on Sugarcane Production and Soil Properties. Review of Indian Agroforestry, Tucuman., 64: 41-44.

Selvakumar, K. (2006): Impact of Post-methanated Distillery Spentwash on the Yield and Quality of Sweet Sorghum and on Soil Health. M.Sc., Thesis, Tamil Nadu Agricultural. University, Coimbatore.

Selvalakshmi, M., J. Balamururgan, K. Rajukkannu, S. Pazhanivelan and M. Subash Chandra Bose. (2001): Fertigation of Rice with Primary Treated Distillery effluent. In: Proceedings of National Seminar on Use of Poor Quality Water and Sugar Industrial Effluents in Agriculture, Held at ADAC & RI, TNAU, Tiruchirappalli., Feb. 5, pp. 82.

Sengik, E and J.C. Kiel. (1995): Effect of Organic Residues and Monocalcium Phosphates on Ammonium Volatilization in Soils Treated with Urea. Revista Brasileira de Ciencia do solo, 19: 321-326.

Sharma, D.R. (2001): Response of Rice and Wheat to Sodic Soil Water Irrigation and Gypsum Application. J. Indian Soc.Soil Sci., 49(2): 324-327.

Sharma, P., K.S. Dhillon and S.K. Dhillon. (2008): Impact of Distillery Effluent Application along with Inorganic Fertilizers on Dry Matter Yield and Mineral Composition of Rice. Acta Agronomica Hangarica, 56: 2

Singh, Y. and Raj Bahadur.(1997): Effect of Distillery Effluent Irrigation on Maize Grain Crop and Soil Fertility. Indian J. Eco., 24: 563-59.

Singh, Y. and Raj Bahadur. (1998): Effect of Application of Distillery-effluent on Maize (*Zea mays* L) Crop and Soil Properties. Indian. J. Agric. Sci. 68: 70-74.

Sivasamy, N. (2004): Phytoremediation Potential of Fodder Crops in Paper Mill Effluent Polluted Soil Habitat. M.Sc., Thesis, Tamil Nadu Agricultural University, Coimbatore.

Somashekhar, P., K.Gowda, L. N. Shattigar and K. P.Shrinath (1984): Effect of Industrial Effluents on Crop Plants. Indian J. Environ. Health, 26(2): 36-46.

Soundararajan, M. (2003): Studies on Impact of Distillery Effluent (spentwash) with Amendment on Soil Physico- chemical Properties, Yield and Quality of Bhendi (*Abelmoschus esculentus* (L.) Moench) M.Sc., Thesis, Tamil Nadu Agricultural University, Madurai.

Soundarrajan, M and G. James Pitchai. (2007): Impact of Distillery Spentwash on Seed Germination, Seedling Growth and Yield of Bhendi (*Abelmoschus esculentus*). J. Ecobiol., 20 (4): 385-389.

Sridharan. B. (2007): Recycling of Post Methanated Distillery Spentwash in the Soils of Vasudevanallur for Maize Crop. M.Sc., Thesis, Tamil Nadu Agricultural University, Coimbatore.

Subash Chandra Bose, M., M. Baskar, C. Kayalvizhi, H. Gopal and M. Sivanandham. (2002a): Utilization of Distillery Effluent in Coastal Sandy Soil to Improve the Soil Fertility and Yield of Sugarcane. In: Proceedings of 17th World Congress of Soil Science Held in Thailand, pp. 1-8

Subash Chandra Bose, M., M. Baskar, C. Kayalvizhi, H. Gopal and M. Sivanandham. (2002b): Utilization of Distillery Industrial Wastewater as a Source of Plant Nutrients for Rice Production in the East Coast of Tamil Nadu. In: Extended Summaries- NCCAR., pp. 91-92.

Subba, R . (1972): Utilization of Anaerobically Treated Spentwash for Sugarcane Crop. D.S.T.A. (India) Annual Convention. pp. 29-32.

Subbiah, B. V and C. L. Asija. (1956): A Rapid Procedure for Estimation of Available Nitrogen in Soils. Curr. Sci., 25: 259-260.

Suganya, K. and G. Rajannan. (2009): Effect of One Time Post-sown and Pre-sown Application of Distillery Spentwash on the Growth and Yield of Maize Crop. Botany Res. International, 2: 288-294.

Sukanya, T.S and S.S. Melli. (2004): Effect of Distillery Effluent Irrigation on Growth, Yield and Quality of Maize Grown on Sandyloam in Northern Transitional Zone of Karnataka. Karnataka J. Agric. sci., 17 (3): 405-409

Sundaramoorthy, K., T. M. Thiyagarajan, K. Valliappan and P. Singaram. (2005): Utilization of Distillery Spentwash in agriculture. In: Proc. of an International Symposium on Transitions in Agriculture for Enhancing Water Productivity Held at AC & RI, Killikulam, Vallanadu, Tamil Nadu, India, Sept. 23 - 25. pp. 205-222.

Sweeney, D. W and D. A. Graetz. (1991): Application of Distillery Waste Anaerobic Digester Effluent to St. Augustine Grass Agriculture, Ecosystems and Environment, 33: 341 - 351.

Tabatabai, M. A and M. J. Bremner. (1969): Use of *p*-nitrophenol Phosphate for Assay of Soil Phosphatase Activity. Soil Biol. Biochem., 1: 301-307.

Tauk, S. M., I. H. Schoenlein Crusius and A. Petenate. (1990): Ecological Model of Nutrients, Microorganisms and Enzymatic Activity of Soil in a Cerrado Area Treated with Vinasse, Corumbati. Reviste de Microbiologia., 1: 99-108.

Taluk, S. M. and A. M.Medeiros. (1989): Nutrient and Enzymatic Activity in Red Yellow Medium Textured Latosol Treated with Vinasse Under Maize Crop. Ecletica Quaimica., 14: 83-93.

Thitakamol, T. and S. Kaewpinthong. (2004): Utilization of Distillery Slop for the Rice Production in Khonkaen Province. In: Research Report Submitted to National Research Council of Thailand. Bangkok, Thailand. pp. 23-56.

Thiyagarajan, T.M. (2001): Use of Distilley Effluents in Agriculture: Problems and Perspectives. In: Proc. Nat. Sem. On Use of Poor Quality Water and Sugar Industrial Effluents in Agriculture. ADAC & RI, Tiruchirapalli, Feb. 5., pp. 1-15.

Thiyagarajan, T.M and S. Mahimairaja. (2002): Use of Distillery Spent Wash in Agriculture Present Research Results and Future Priorities. In: Conference on "Towards sustainable Distillery Spentwash Management with Recycle-reuse-reduce Concepts". The South Indian Sugar Mills Association, Bannari Amman Sugars Limited, Sathyamangalam, Tamil Nadu, pp. 12-25.

Thiyagarajan, T. M., H. Hengsdijk and P. S. Bindraban. (2005): Utilizing Distillery Spentwash in Agriculture. In: Proceedings of an International Symposium held in AC & RI, Killikulam, Tamil Nadu Agricultural University, Sep. 23-25, pp. 205-222.

Tisdall, J.M. and J.M. Oades. (1982): Organic Matter and Water-stable Aggregates in Soil. J. Soil Sci., 33:141-163.

Tripathi, B.D., D. Kumari and R.K. Diwedi. (1988): Utilization of Distillery Effluent in Coastal Sandy Soil to Improve Soil Fertility. Geo. Eco. Trop., 12: 133.

USEPA. (1979): Method 218.1, Atomic Absorption Direct Aspiration. In: Methods for Chemical Analysis of Water and Wastes. Environmental Monitoring and Support Laboratory, Cincinnati.

Valliappan, K. (1998): Recycling of Distillery Spent Wash—An Eco-friendly Effective Reclamation Technology for Sodic Soils. Ph.D. Thesis., Tamil Nadu Agricultural University. Coimbatore, India.

Vantour, A., M. Mena, A. Martinez-Cruz and V. Martinez.(1987): Organic Residues from Cane Sugar and Alcohol Factories as Amendments for Saline Soils. III. Effects on the Forms and Content of Phosphorus. Ciencias de la Agricultura, 30: 92-101.

Vasisht , H. S and N. K. Kapoor. (1981): The Ecology of Polluted Waters of Yamuna River (Haryana). Indian J Ecol., 8: 134-135.

Veeresh, H., R. Muthuraja, A. H. M. Rehman, T. Jayanthi, S. Bhaskar and C. A. Srinivasamurthy. (2007): Characterization of Distillery Spentwash from Karnataka. In: The abstracts of National Conference on "Ecofriendly Utilization of Recyclable Organic Resources from the Sugar and Distillery Industries for Sustainable Agriculture" held at ADAC & RI, Tiruchirappalli, Tamil Nadu Agricultural University, March 6-7, pp. 3.

Venkatakrishnan, D and M. Ravichandran. (2007): Effect of Integrated Nutrient Management on Growth and Yield of Sugarcane. Int. J. Trop. Agr., 25: 163-168.

Verma, T. S., V. K. Suri and J. Paul. (2002): Prescription-based Fertilizer Recommendations for Rice, Maize and Wheat in Different Agro-climatic Zones of Himachal Pradesh. J. Indian. Soc. Soil Sci., 50: 272-277.

Waksman, S.A and E.B. Fred. (1922): A Tentative Outline of the Plate Method for Determining the Number of Microorganisms in Soil. Soil Sci., 14: 27-28.

Walkley, A and C.A. Black. (1934): An Estimation of Methods for Determining Organic Carbon and Nitrogen in the Soils. J. Agric. Sci., 25: 598-609.

Weil, R.R. and W.Kroontje, (1979): Physical Condition of a Davidson Clay Loam After Five Years of Heavy Poultry Manure Applications. J. Environ. Qual., 8: 387–392.

Yadvinder Singh, Bijay-Singh, J. K. Ladha, J. S. Bains, R.K. Gupta, Jagmohan Singh and V. Balasubramanian. (2007): On-farm Evaluation of Leaf Color Chart for Need-based Nitrogen Management in Irrigated Transplanted Rice in Northwestern India. Nutrient Cycling Agroecosyst., 24: 25-46.

Yaduvanshi, N. P. S. (2001): Effect of Five Years of Rice-wheat Cropping an NPK Fertilizer Use with and Without Organic and Green Manures on Soil Properties and Crop Yields in a Reclaimed Sodic Soil. J. Indian Soc. Soil Sci., 49: 714-719.

Young, J. C., G. N. McDermott and D. Jenkins. (1981): Alteration in the BOD Procedure for the 15th Edition of Standard Method for the Examination of Water and Waste Water. J. Water Pollut. Control Federation, 53: 1253.

Zalawadia, N. M and S. Raman. (1994): Effect of Distillery Waste Water with Graded Fertilizer Levels on Sorghum Yield and Soil Properties. J. Indian Soc. Soil Sci., 42: 575-579.

Zalawadia, N. M., S. Raman and R. G. Patel. (1997): Influence of Diluted Spentwash of Sugar Industries Application on Yield and Nutrient Uptake by Sugarcane and Changes in Soil Properties. J. Indian Soc. Soil Sci., 45: 767-769.

Technologies for Water and Wastewater Management Pages 123-144
Edited by: Dr. Vijender Singh & Dr. Pawan Kumar 'Bharti'
ISBN: 978-93-88854-53-5
Edition: 2020
Published by: Discovery Publishing House Pvt. Ltd., New Delhi (India)

7 Thermodynamics, Kinetics Study and Statistical Approach of Arsenic Removal in Waste Water Utilizing Activated Carbon from Saw Dust in Different Impregnation Ratio

Swapnila Roy[1*], Ashok Kumar Shaw[2]

ABSTRACT

The present study is highlighted on arsenic removal efficiency in synthetic water utilizing low-cost starting material converted to activated carbon (AC), activated by magnesium chloride ($MgCl_2$) in different impregnation ratio (IR) (0.25, 0.5, 1.0) upon thermal treatment. Comparative batch studies were conducted in different experimental conditions to investigate the influence of different process parameters on arsenic removal. The phenomenon of arsenic ion uptake was realized by Langmuir and Freundlich adsorption model. Langmuir isotherm showed satisfactory fit to the experimental data. The rate of adsorption implied that the pseudo-second-order rate well fitted the adsorption kinetics better than the pseudo-first-order rate equation. Significant process parameters including adsorbent dosage, pH and contact time were optimized using Response surface methodology (RSM). Results of RSM analysis indicated good correlation between experimentally recorded and theoretically predicted % arsenic removals. The mechanism of adsorption process was illustrated by calculating Gibbs free energy, enthalpy and entropy from thermodynamic studies. In this present investigation, it was represented that regeneration % of activated carbon (IR:1.0) prepared from saw dust in 5 adsorption-desorption cycles are 90.92%, 86.46%, 80.13%, 71.01%, and 62.53% respectively. The optimum contact time, dosage of adsorbent and pH for activated carbon with I.R. (1.0) were found to be 70 min, 1.5 g L^{-1} and pH 2.00 respectively. In that condition, it was performing high level of arsenic removal efficiency (92.4%). So it may be concluded that as saw dust is easily available material, so chemically synthesized activated carbon can be used for arsenic removal in waste water.

***Keywords**: Arsenic removal, Activated Carbon, Isotherm model, Kinetics, Thermo-dynamics, Process Optimisation, Response surface methodology.*

1 Regent Institute of Science and Technology, Kolkata, India
2 Regent Education and Research Foundation, Kolkata, India

Introduction

For many years, groundwater is assumed to be as the most safe for drinking without any treatment[1]. But now it is considered to be polluted as because of presence of arsenic ion. Dissolution of minerals depends on the water composition and the time of contact between the source minerals and the water. Fish, shellfish, meat, poultry, dairy products and cereals can also be dietary sources of arsenic, although exposure from these foods is generally much lower compared to exposure through contaminated groundwater. In seafood, arsenic is mainly found in its less toxic organic form.The maximum limit of arsenic in drinking water is 0.01 mg/L according to the guidelines of water quality.The greatest threat to public health from arsenic originates from contaminated groundwater[2,3]. Inorganic arsenic is naturally present at high levels in the groundwater of a number of countries, including Argentina, Bangladesh, Chile, China, India, Mexico, and the United States of America. Drinking-water, crops irrigated with contaminated water[4] and food prepared with contaminated water are the sources of exposure. Due to natural effects,the arsenic dispersed into the nearest water courses or agricultural fields in the forms of arsenate ion [As (V)] and arsenite ion [As (III)], leading to a high arsenic concentration in thewater courses around the mines. Arsenic exists in the −3, 0, +3 and +5 oxidation states. Environmental forms include arsenious acids, arsenic acids, arsenites, arsenates, methyl arsenic acid, dimethyl arsinic acid, arsine, etc. Arsenic(III) is a hard acid and preferentially complexes with oxides and nitrogen.

Arsenic is used industrially as an alloying agent, as well as in the processing of glass, pigments, textiles, paper, metal adhesives, wood preservatives and ammunition. Arsenic is also used in the hide tanning process and, to a limited extent, in pesticides, feed additives and pharmaceuticals. The first symptoms of long-term exposure[5,6] to high levels of inorganic arsenic (for example, through drinking-water and food) are usually observed in the skin, and include pigmentation changes, skin lesions and hard patches on the palms and soles of the feet (hyperkeratosis). These occur after a minimum exposure of approximately five years and may be a precursor to skin cancer. In addition to skin cancer, long-term exposure to arsenic may also cause cancers of the bladder and lungs. The International Agency for Research on Cancer (IARC) has classified arsenic and arsenic compounds as carcinogenic to humans, and has also stated that arsenic in drinking-water is carcinogenic to humans.A great deal of research over recent decades has been done to lower the concentration of arsenic in drinking water and still there is a need to develop low cost viable techniques[7] Existing major arsenic removal[8,9,10] technologies include oxidation, adsorption, precipitation, coagulation and membrane separation[11,12].

The present study focused on arsenic uptake[13,14]where activated carbon was used, prepared from saw dust which was impregnated by magnesium chloride in different ratio and synthesized chemically.

Objective of the Study

The present study on arsenic removal was investigated with the objective to prepare chemically activated carbon from saw dust[15]using magnesium chloride as an activating agent. The physical and chemical properties of the prepared activated carbon were determined and estimation of arsenic removal efficiency using different experimental procedure by adsorption as a function of contact time, adsorbent dose and pH.

Materials and Methods

Materials

Magnesium chloride($MgCl_2.6H_2O$)[Merck, Germany],Saw dust(available in local market) were collected for preparation of activated carbon. All chemicals of reagent grade and ultrapure distilled water were used in all the preparations.

Preparation of Adsorbents

In this present study activated carbon was prepared from saw dust using magnesium chloride($MgCl_2$) as an activating agent. The particular quantity of washed and dried saw dust was mixed with required amount of activating agent ($MgCl_2$), according to different impregnation ratio (I.R. = 0,25,0.50,1.0).

$$\text{Impregnation ratio (I.R)} = \frac{\text{Weight of active agent added}}{\text{Weight of carbonising material added}} \quad ...(1)$$

The required quantity of distilled water was added and boiled until slurry like mixture was obtained. Then the mixture was dried in a container for one day at 105 ± 5°C. Then these three containers were placed in Muffle furnace at 800°C for 4 hours. After that when these containers were attained steady state temperature, these were kept in cool environment for about 10 hours. Finally these were taken out. The prepared activated carbon was washed by dilute HCl to remove excess HCl present in the activated carbon. Then these three activated carbon were oven dried and kept in desiccators for further experiment.

Physicochemical Properties of Adsorbents

The different physiochemical properties[16,17] (oil yield, bulk density, porosity, moisture content, ash content and pH)of the prepared activated carbons were estimated using standard procedures. All the experiments were performed thrice and results are given in Table 7.1.

Table 7.1: Physicochemical Analysis

Sl. No.	Characteristics	Chemically Activated ($MgCl_2$)		
		0.25	0.5	1.0
1.	Moisture content (%)	6.21	5.32	3.87
2.	Ash content (%)	16.24	15.06	13.07
3.	Decolorizing power, (mg/g)	30.87	35.83	43.64
4.	pH	7.8	7.6	7.2
5.	Yield of carbon (%)	61	72	86
6.	Bulk Density	0.67	0.73	0.78
7.	Porosity	0.63	0.69	0.75

Yield of Carbon

After carbonization followed by cooling, the activated carbonwas weighed. Then the percentage yield of carbonizing was achieved by applying this formula

$$\%\text{ yield of carbon} = \frac{\text{Weight of char}}{\text{Weight of raw material}} \quad ...(2)$$

Determination of Bulk Density

The dry empty 10 mL centrifuge tube was cleaned and weighed (*W*1) and then the centrifuge tube was filled with the prepared activated carbon powder and then weighed (*W*2). The difference in the weights denotes the weight of the activated carbon powder in tube. The bulk density was estimated using the following equation:

$$\text{Bulk Density} = \frac{W_2 - W_1}{\text{volume of centrifuge tube}} \quad ...(3)$$

Porosity Determination

The porosity of the activated carbon was estimated using the formula:

$$\text{Porosity} = \frac{\text{pore volume}}{\text{total volume}}$$

The pore volume of prepared activated carbon was achieved using the formula:

$$\text{Pore volume} = \frac{\text{Bulk density of activated carbon}}{\text{density of water}}$$

$$\text{Hence, porosity} = \frac{\text{Bulk density of activated carbon}}{\text{density of water} \times \text{total volume}} \quad ...(4)$$

Determination of Moisture Content

The empty crucible was dried at 110°C and then cooled in a desiccatorand weighed (W_1). Then the prepared known weight of activated carbon powder with crucible were weighed (W_2) and dried in an oven at 110°C. This weight was taken constantly at 30 minutes interval until the weight became constant. Then activated carbon with crucible was cooled in a desiccator and reweighed (W_3). The weight difference of the activated carbon was used to measure the moisture content (X_o) of the activated carbon from saw dust.

$$X_o = \frac{W2 - W3}{W2 - W1} \times 100 \qquad ...(5)$$

Determination of Ash Content

The empty crucible was oven dried at 110°C and cooled in a desiccator and weighed (*W1*). The known weight of prepared dried activated carbon powder was put in the crucible and weighed (*W2*) and then kept in the muffle furnace at 800°C for 1 hour and then allowed to cool .Finally the crucible was reweighed (*W3*). The percentage ash content of activated carbon sample was obtained from the following equation:

$$\text{Ash\%} = \frac{W_{ash}}{W_0} \times 100 = \frac{W3 = W1}{W2 - W1} \times 100 \qquad ...(6)$$

Where W_{ash} = weight of ash (g)

Determination of pH

1 g activated carbon from saw dust was weighed. Then it was dissolved in 3 ml distilled water. The mixture was heated and stirred for few minutes. Then it was filtered and pH was determined using a digital pH meter.

Preparation of Synthetic Arsenic Solution

Stock arsenic ion solution(1000 mg L^{-1}) was prepared by dissolving accurately weighed quantity in double-distilled water. Experimental arsenic solution of different concentrations were prepared by diluting the stock solution with suitable volume of distilled-water.

Experimental

Experimental set up

Experiments were conducted in temperature controlled incubator shaker (INNOVA 4430, New Brunswick Scientific, Canada). Temperature fluctuations in the reactor were negligible .The samples were collected for stirring for particular time interval. The dissolved arsenic in each conical flask was estimated by using ion AAS[18](Perkin Elmer).

Percentage of arsenic removal efficiency was calculated with a standard RSM design (CCD) and20 experiments were carried out. The percent removal (%) of arsenic is determined by using the following equation:

$$R(\%) = \frac{C_i - C_0}{C_i} \times 100 \qquad ...(7)$$

Where C_i is the initial fluoride concentration (mg L^{-1}) and C_0 is the final fluoride concentration in solution (mg L^{-1}).

Batch Experiment

In this present batch study, the required quantity of activated carbon was added to the arsenic solution, then it was stirred for different contact time with different dosage of adsorbent in different pH of solution. This powder like activated carbon is very suitable for arsenic removal in water.

Thermodynamic and Kinetics Studies

Adsorption Isotherm

The Langmuir and Freundlich isotherms study were carried out by using AC (different IR ratio)for arsenic removal in water. The interaction between arsenic ions and adsorbents can be better explained by these isotherm models.

Langmuir Isotherm

The linear form of Langmuir model is given by the following equation:

$$\frac{C_e}{Q_e} = \frac{1}{Q_0 b} + \frac{C_e}{Q_0} \quad ...(8)$$

Where C_e is the residual fluoride concentration at equilibrium, Q_e is the fluoride concentration adsorbed on the sorbent at equilibrium, Q_o denotes maximum fluoride concentration and b is the Langmuir constant.

Freundlich Isotherm

From the following equation Freundlich constants were calculated as follows or batch sorption studies.

$$\text{Ln } Q_e = \ln K_F + \left(\frac{1}{n}\right) \ln C_e \quad ...(9)$$

Where Q_e is the amount of arsenic adsorbed at equilibrium, and K_F and n are Freundlich constants indicates adsorption capacity and adsorption intensity respectively.

Adsorption Kinetics

The adsorption process was carried out at various temperatures to determine the optimum temperature for maximum adsorption efficiency and for obtaining the reaction rate constant activation energy. 100 mL of arsenic solution of concentration 50 mg L^{-1} was taken in 250 mL conical flask and 1.5 g adsorbent was added to it. Then this mixture was agitated at 150 rpm for 1 hour.From this experiment kinetic rate constantat different temperatures were estimated.

Pseudo First Order Kinetics

The rate constant was estimated using the following equation:

$$\frac{dq_t}{dt} = k_1(q_e - q_t) \qquad ...(10)$$

where, q_e= arsenic adsorbed at equilibrium/unitweight of adsorbent (mg/g), q_t is the amount of arsenic adsorbedat any instant (mg/g) and k_1 is the rate constant (min^{-1}).

Integrating at these conditions as $t = 0$ and $q_t = 0$ to $t = t$ and $q_t = q_t$, the final equation is written as given below:

$$\text{Log}(q_e - q_t) = \log q_e - \frac{k_1 t}{2.303} \qquad ...(11)$$

Pseudo Second Order Kinetics

The model equation is described as follows :

$$\frac{1}{q_t} = \frac{1}{k_2 qe2} + 1/q_e(t) \qquad ...(12)$$

Where k_2 denotes the pseudo-second-order rate constant of adsorption (g mg^{-1} min^{-1}) and q_e and q_t are the amount of arsenic adsorbed (mg/g) at equilibrium and at time t respectively.

Activation Energy

From the obtained the rate constant, activation energy of the adsorption of arsenic was calculated using Arrhenius Eq (6) given as follows:

$$\text{Ln}k_2 = \ln A_0 - \frac{E_a}{RT} \qquad ...(13)$$

Where E_a= activation energy ($kJmol^{-1}$); R = gas constant (8.314 J mol^{-1} K^{-1}); and A_0= Arrhenius constant.

Adsorption thermodynamics

The adsorption thermodynamic parameters of arsenic were estimated using the following formulas:

$$K_c = \frac{C_a}{C_e} \qquad ...(14)$$

Where, K_c = coefficient of distribution for the adsorption; C_a = arsenic adsorbed per unit mass of the adsorbent (mg L^{-1}); C_e = equilibrium concentration of adsorbate in aqueous phase (mg L^{-1}).

$$\Delta G_0 = -RT\ln K_c \qquad ...(15)$$

Where, G_0 (kJ mol^{-1}) = change of Gibb's free energy; R = universal gas constant; and T = absolute temperature (K); and

$$1nK_c = \frac{\Delta S_0}{R} - \frac{\Delta H_0}{RT} \qquad ...(16)$$

Where ΔH_0 (kJ mol^{-1}) = change of enthalpy; ΔS_0(J mol^{-1} K^{-1}) = change of entropy.

Technologies for Water and Wastewater Management **Pages 97-122**
Edited by: **Dr. Vijender Singh & Dr. Pawan Kumar 'Bharti'**
ISBN: 978-93-88854-53-5
Edition: **2020**
Published by: **Discovery Publishing House Pvt. Ltd., New Delhi (India)**

6 Utilization of Treated Water Effluent for Crop Farming

Anitha G.[1] and Esakkimuthu M.[2]

Introduction

In a developing country like India, distilleries have become a major source of pollution as 88% of its raw materials are converted into waste and discharged into water bodies, causing water pollution. There are about 600 sugar mills in India, which release about 7.5 million tonnes of molasses as by product (Ramaswami, 1999). Nearly 90 per cent of molasses goes to produce industrial and potable alcohol and about 7-8 per cent is utilized for animal feed. Alcohol (ethanol) is produced mainly by the fermentation of diluted sugarcane molasses. In the distillery, for every litre of alcohol produced, about 15 litres of spent wash is released as wastewater. After fermentation, the alcohol is separated by distillation and the residual liquid (1:10 ratio of alcohol and residual liquid) is discharged in large volume as wastewater, which is generally known as spent wash. Different terminologies viz., stillage, vinasse, slop, bottom slop, still residue are used for this type of effluent in different countries, 'stillage' and/ or 'vinasse' is the most common term used in most of the European and South American countries. The term 'dunder' is used in Australia, while the term distillery effluent or wastewater is used in other countries (Valliappan, 1998).

Distillery spent wash, after the recovery of biogas is known as biomethanated distillery spent wash (BDS) or post methanated distillery effluent or primary treated effluent. However, biological oxygen demand (BOD) of this primary treated effluent still remains quite high necessitating further treatment, which would be difficult as all easily degradable organics are already consumed (Joshi *et al.*, 1996). Moreover, it contains considerable amount of N and P, rich in K, Ca, Mg, S and trace amount of Fe, Zn, Cu and Mn (Devarajan *et al.*, 1993; Valliappan, 1998; Mohammed Haroon and Subash Chandra Bose, 2004). The distillery effluent is waste water which is purely of plant origin containing a

[1] Assistant Professor (Soil Science and Agricultural Chemistry), Tamil Nadu Agricultural University, S. Thangapazham Agricultural College, Vasudevanallur, Tamil Nadu, India

[2] Assistant Professor (Agricultural Extension), Kerala Agricultural University, Regional Agricultural Research Station, Pilicode, Kerala, India

Results and Discussion

Characterisationof Activated Carbon (saw dust)

XRD(X-ray Diffraction) analysis

X-ray diffraction analysis of activated carbon was conducted using X-ray diffractometer equipment (Bruker,D8 Advance)with a Cu Kα radiation. The diffraction patternof activated carbon from saw dust (IR:1.0)as prepared,was represented in **Figure 7.1.**

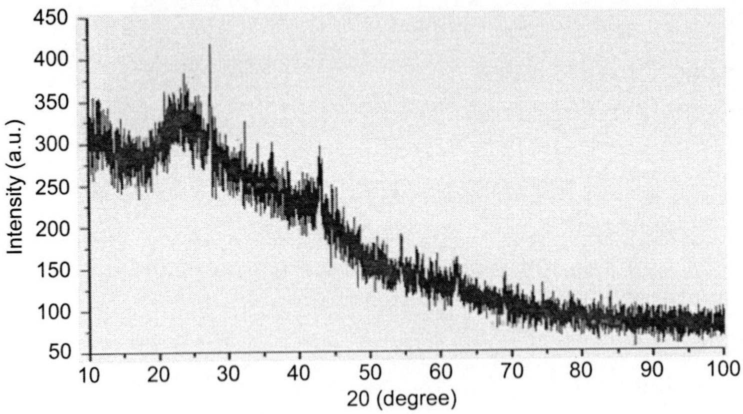

Fig. 7.1: XRD of activated carbon from saw dust

Boehm Titration

The acidic and basic properties of surface of the samples were estimated by the Boehm Titration method. In this method, 0.2 g AC (different impregnation ratio) sample was added to 25 ml of 0.1 M $NaHCO_3$ and similarly to 25 ml of 0.1 M Na_2CO_3. The mixtures were stirred for 24 hours and then it was filtered. After removal of carbon, the excess of base and acid was titrated with 0.1 M HCl solution and 0.1 M NaOH solution, respectively. Chemically number of acidic sites were estimated by chemical neutralization of carboxyl, phenolic and lactonic groups by NaOH; carboxyl and lactonic groups by Na_2CO_3; and carboxyl groups by $NaHCO_3$. Similarly, the number of basic sites was estimated from the amount of consumed hydrochloric acid by AC (Table 7.2).

Table 7.2: Acidic and Basic Surface Characteristics of the Activated Carbons

Sample: (AC from saw dust)	Groups			Total acidity (meq g^{-1})	Total basicity (meq g^{-1})
	Carboxylic (meq g^{-1})	Phenolic (meq g^{-1})	Lactonic (meq g^{-1})		
IR:0.25	0.16	0.2	0.24	0.86	0.98
IR:0.5	0.17	0.23	0.22	0.87	0.99
IR:1.0	0.18	0.27	0.23	0.85	1.01

Determination of Optimum Contact Time

Contact time play a significant role in adsorption study. To study the effect of contact time, 100 mL of arsenic solution of 100 mg $L^{-1}$and pH 2.0±0.02, was mixed with 1.5 gL^{-1} activated carbon, stirred at different contact times (10-100 min) and then filtered. These filtrates were analyzed for residual arsenic concentration using AAS.

Determination of Optimum Dosage of Adsorbent

Theoptimum dosage of activated carbon was added to the conical flask in different dosage varying from (200-1500 mg) which contains 100 mL of 50 mg L^{-1} arsenic solution and pH was maintained as 2.0 ± 0.02. The solution in the conical flask was subjected to stirring for optimum contact time and then filtered, and finally analyzed. The dosage which gives maximum arsenic removal efficiency was selected as optimum dosage of adsorbent.

Determination of Optimum pH

The effect of pH on arsenic adsorption was experimented by performing equilibrium adsorption at different pH (2.00, 4.00, 6.00, 8.00, 10.00) values. The pH at which maximum arsenic removal happened that was optimum pH.

Interaction Effect

Effect of Adsorbent dose

Within the experimental range of adsorbent dose in between 0.2 g-1.5 gL^{-1}, percent removal of arsenic firstly increased (upto1.0 gL^{-1}), then decreased slowly. The adsorbent dose in the range of 0.2-1.0 gL^{-1}, arsenic removal efficiency increased due to the number of ions increases on the adsorbent surface as the attraction force between adsorbate ions and adsorbent. While increasing dosage of adsorbent higher than 1.5 gL^{-1}, number of arsenic ions

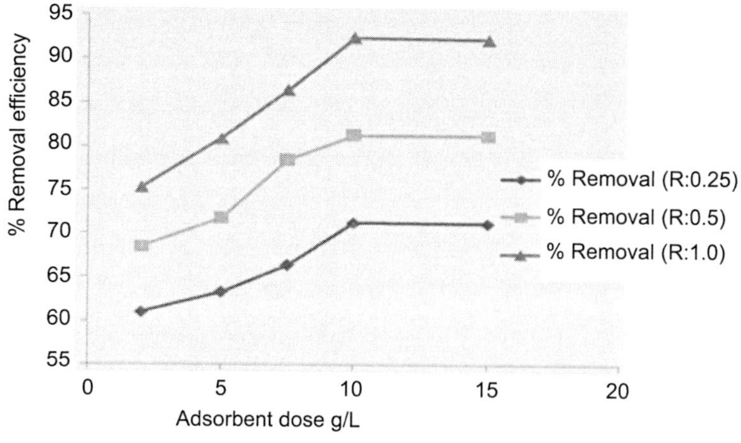

Fig. 7.2: Effect of adsorbent dose on arsenic removal by AC-Saw Dust (IR:0.25,0.5,1.0)

decreased gradually on the adsorbent surface because surface of adsorbent was saturated by adsorbate ions, and in that case the repulsive force occurred between arsenic ions and adsorbent surface. Comparing three adsorbents (different IR ratio), weight of active agents were increasing according to the increased ratio. So the adsorption capacity of adsorbate was higher, with increasing ratio. From Figure 7.2, it was observed that the removal efficiency of arsenic increased with increasing IR, so it can be inferred that activated carbon (IR = 1.0)was the best adsorbent for arsenic removal among three adsorbents.

Effect of Contact Time

It was observed from Figure 7.3 the experimental results that on increasing the contact time at pH 2 and optimum dosage of adsorbent, arsenic removal efficiency increased. As the contact time increased, higher the number of arsenic ions attached on the adsorbent surface. Chemically the accumulation of arsenic ions on adsorbent surface increased due to attractive force which resulted in increasing the arsenic removal in solution. But after certain point (70 min), removal efficiency decreased. The reason behind this phenomena was that maximum number of the arsenic ions attached on adsorbent surface when reaction time was 70 minutes. Comparing three adsorbents (IR:0.25,0.5,1.0), the number of pores were higher (IR:1.0) than two other adsorbents due to presence of more activating agents for preparation of carbon, consequently the adsorption capacity was the highest for that activated carbon (IR:1.0). As a result in particular contact time, adsorption capacity was highest shown by AC(IR:1.0) than other two adsorbents. From Figure 7.3, it was observed that the removal efficiency of arsenic increased in case of AC (IR:1) which was reflected in the plot.

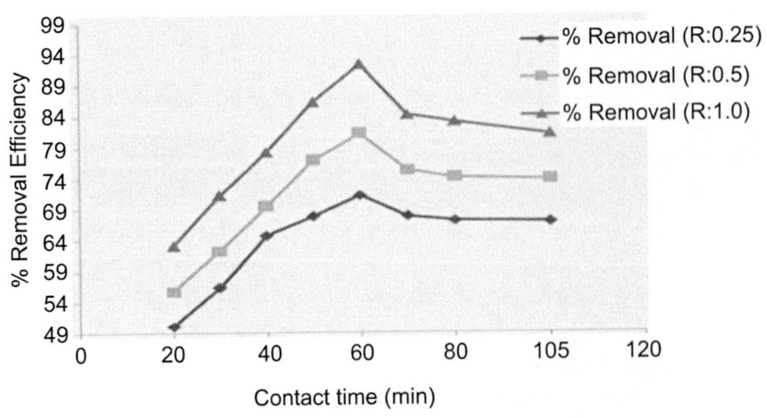

Fig. 7.3: Effect of contact time on arsenic removal by AC-Saw Dust(IR:0.25,0.5,1.0)

Effect of pH

In the above experiment, it was showed that with increasing pH, the percent removal of arsenic decreased sharply for three adsorbents. Following the adsorption process, increasing the pH the acidity of the medium increases, which is the feasible condition for removal of arsenic (Figure 7.4).Consequently, the removal efficiency decreased. As the adsorption capacity of activated carbon (IR:1) was the highest than other two adsorbents(explained before),so at particular pH (optimum dosage of adsorbent and optimum contact time) the number of adsorbate ions increased on AC(IR:1) than AC(IR:0.25) and (IR:0.5). Overall, AC(IR:1) was the best adsorbent among three for further experiment.

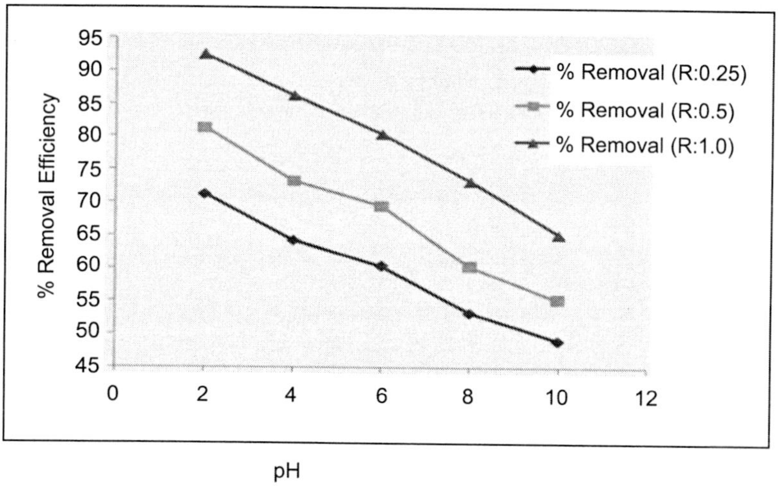

Fig. 7.4: Effect of pH on arsenic removal by AC-Saw Dust(IR:0.25,0.5,1.0)

Thermodynamics and Kinetics study

Estimation of thermodynamic parameters of three activated carbon for arsenic removal

From the experimental study following equation (8-10) it was depicted that the negative value of ΔG^0 increased with increasing in the temperature (up to 333 K). It implied that the adsorption was thermodynamically feasible in nature and the positive values of ΔH^0 indicated endothermic nature of the reaction due to consuming energy from the reaction system. The values of ΔH^0 and, ΔS^0 were estimated from the slopes and intercept of the plot ln K_c vs. (1/T) (Fig. not given) and the values were listed in Table 7.3. It was observed that the negative value of ΔG^0 at all temperatures represented that the arsenic removal reaction was spontaneous in nature. In this case ΔG^0 decreased up to 333K and after that it increased which denoted that the adsorption reaction was feasible up to 333K. As a result the randomness in between arsenic ion and activated carbon surface was increased. Due to endothermic reaction, it was expected that the adsorption capacity of arsenic ions by activated carbon was increasing with temperature. But after 333K,the reverse reaction occurred. Mathematically entropy of the reaction was estimated from the experimentally obtained data that was positive for these adsorbents. So it can be inferred that as temperature was increased above 333K, the desorption took place on the adsorbent surface, consequently the concentration of arsenic in solution was increased in small amount in solution.

Table 7.3: Thermodynamic Parameters for the Adsorption of Arsenic onto AC-Saw dust (IR:0.25,0.5,1.0)

Sl. No.	T, K	ΔG, kJ/mol			ΔH, kJ/mol			ΔS,J mol^{-1} K^{-1}		
		IR:0.25	IR:0.5	IR:1.0	IR:0.25	IR:0.5	IR:1.0	IR:0.25	IR:0.5	IR:1.0
1	293	-8.93	-9.13	-9.83	62.33	72.19	79.43	252.11	257.13	267.39
2	313	-10.23	-10.86	-11.93						
3	333	-12.45	-12.97	-13.54						
4	343	-13.32	-13.86	-14.29						
5	353	-11.45	-11.74	-12.56						

Batch adsorption isotherm

The estimated adsorption equilibrium data for AC (IR:0.25,0.5,1.0) was modeled applying Langmuir and Freundlich isotherms model (Figure 7.5 & 7.6). Using these two models the probable mechanism of interaction between arsenic ions and prepared adsorbents were well explained . The isotherm parameters were shown in Table 7.4. From that Table 7.4 it implied that Langmuir model showed good agreement with three adsorbents than Freundlich model in present study of arsenic sorption. According to the Langmuir model, the monolayer arsenic adsorption occurred in these three adsorbents which depends on the nature of surface.

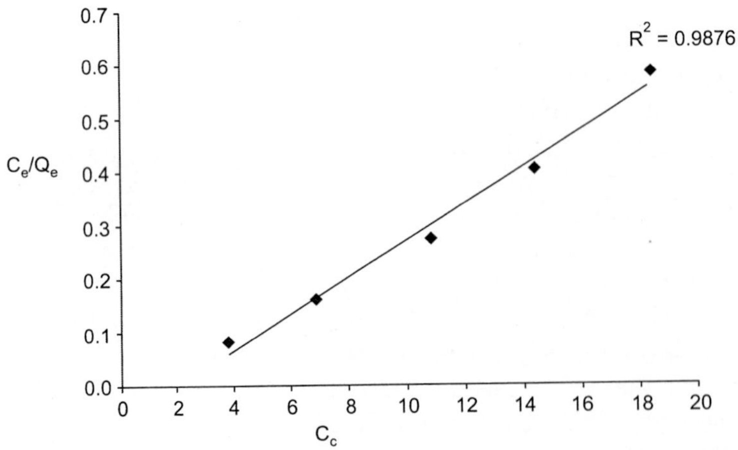

Fig. 7.5: Langmuir Isotherm plots of arsenic removal onto AC-Saw dust (IR:1.0)

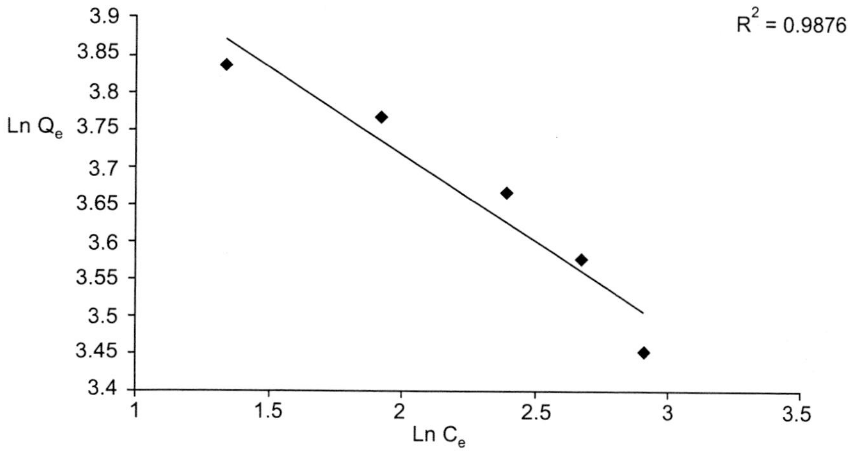

Fig. 7.6: Freundlich Adsorption Isotherm plots of arsenic removal onto AC-Saw dust (IR:1.0)

Table 7.4: Langmuir and Freundlich Isotherm Model Constants and Correlation Coefficients for Arsenic Adsorption onto AC-Saw Dust (IR: 0.25, 0.5, 1.00) at Optimized Conditions

Adsorbents	Langmuir			Freundlich		
	Q_e(mg g^{-1})	b(L mg^{-1})	R^2	K_F(mg g^{-1})	n(L mg^{-1})	R^2
(1) AC (IR:0.25)	24.52	0.31	0.998	41.54	3.23	0.9968
(2) AC (IR:0.5)	31.23	0.41	0.998	43.13	3.03	0.9947
(3) AC (IR:1.00)	34.52	0.47	0.996	45.82	3.85	0.9678

Batch Adsorption Kinetics

The present adsorption kinetics studies were carried out for arsenic removal using three adsorbents having different IR ratio of AC. The parameters of kinetic studies were shown in Table 7.5. From this study, it was observed that pseudo second order kinetics study were well fitted than pseudo first order reaction. From the pseudo second order kinetic reaction it was indicated that adsorption capacity of both adsorbent were dependent on available binding site. The plot of t/q_t Vs t (Figure 7.7) in pseudo second order kinetic modeling were represented. From the pseudo second order rate constant k_2 at different temperatures, the activation energy E_a (Activated carbon) was determined using the Arrhenius energy equation (Eq. 16). The comparative study of adsorption capacities, isotherm and kinetic models of various adsorbents which were already reported for arsenic removal with these three adsorbents in the present study, represented in the Table 7.5.

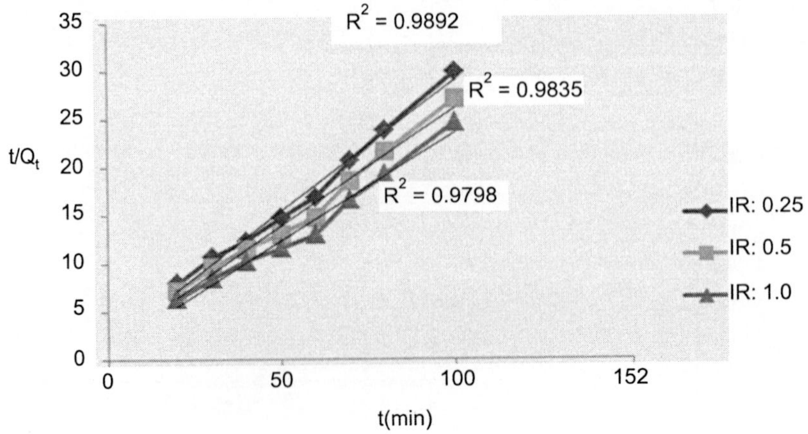

Fig. 7.7: Pseudo second order kinetic model for adsorption of arsenic by AC-Saw dust (IR:0.25,0.5,1.0)

Table 7.5: Comparison of Pseudo First Order and Pseudo Second Order Rate Constants for AC-Saw Dust (IR:0.25,0.5,1.00) at Optimized Conditions

Adsorbents	Pseudo first order kinetics			Pseudo second order kinetics		
	k_1(min)	q_e(mg g^{-1})	R^2	k_2(g mg^{-1})	q_e(mg g^{-1})	R^2
(1) AC (IR:0.25)	0.0033	19.21	0.9237	0.0821	36.72	0.9892
(2) AC (IR:0.5)	0.0011	22.11	0.9311	0.0782	29.79	0.9835
(3) AC (IR:1.00)	0.0009	25.54	0.9362	0.0652	23.49	0.9798

Response surface methodology for optimization of adsorption parameters

The determination of optimum conditions for arsenic adsorption by AC dependent on the three process variables, which were adsorbent dose, pH and contact time of the solution. The experimental ranges along with the levels of variables were given in Table 7.6. The percent removal of arsenic was the response of the system. Statistically the prediction of the optimum condition was obtained following the quadratic equation model given below (Eq. 17).

$$Y = \beta_0 + + ++ \varepsilon \qquad ...(17)$$

Here, Y = response (i.e. dependent variable), β_0 = constant coefficient, $\beta_i = \beta_{ii} = \beta_{ij}$ = coefficients of linear, quadratic and interaction effect, x_i and x_j = factors (independent variables)

And ε = error.

Percentage of arsenic removal efficiency was calculated with a standard RSM design (CCD)[19] and 20 experiments were carried out. The percent removal (%) of arsenic was determined by using the following equation (Eq. 18):

$$R(\%) = \frac{C - C_0}{C} \times 100 \qquad ...(18)$$

Where C_i is the initial arsenic concentration (mg L^{-1}) and C_0 is the final arsenic concentration in solution (mg L^{-1}).

Design Expert Version 11.1.6 (Stat Ease, USA) was applied for graphical analysis of the experimentally obtained data. The optimum values of the independent variables were obtained by solving the regression equation and by analyzing the contour plots. The coefficient of correlation and the quadratic model equation was used to predict the interaction effect of different factors within the specified range, which can be described mathematically.

Estimation of response surface for maximum arsenic removal

The results of the 20 experiments performed as per CCD analysis was shown in Table 7.6. The maximum arsenic removal was obtained 92.41% at 70 min contact time, at pH 2.00 and 1.5 gL^{-1} of adsorbent. The response variable which was expressed as a function of independent variables defined in quadratic model, developed by Design Expert software is expressed in the form of different numerical factors in equation (19) given below:

Table 7.6: Central Composite Design (CCD) Used for Optimizing Three Independent Variables Along with the Obtained Response

Sl.No.	A: Contact time min	B: Adsorbent dose g/L	C:pH	R1 %
1	45	1	5	78.45
2	45	1	5	78.45
3	45	1	5	78.45
4	45	1	5	78.45
5	45	1	5	78.45
6	45	1	5	78.45
7	45	1	10.04	76.28
8	45	1	0.04	88.78
9	45	1.84	5	70.34
10	45	0.16	5	66.78
11	87	1	5	79.43
12	3	1	5	52.43
13	70	1.5	8	80.31
14	20	1.5	8	65.48
15	70	0.5	8	67.37
16	20	0.5	8	62.57
17	70	1.5	2	92.4
18	20	1.5	2	71.29
19	70	0.5	2	89.45
20	20	0.5	2	70.86

Removal % of Arsenic (R1) = + 78.33 + 7.67*A+ 1.85*B – 5.12*C + 1.57* AB – 2.51*AC + 1.56*BC – 3.81*A^2 – 2.88*B^2 + 2.15 C^2 ...(19)

It is observed that A, B, C, AB, B^2, C^2 are significant model terms. The fitness of the model was verified by the correlation coefficient (R^2) between the experimental and model predicted values (Figure 7.8) of the response variable. Statistically, R^2 value of 0.9668 indicated that the model was statistically significant. Therefore, the model was applied to predict the percentage removal of arsenic in solution within the limits of the experimental factors.

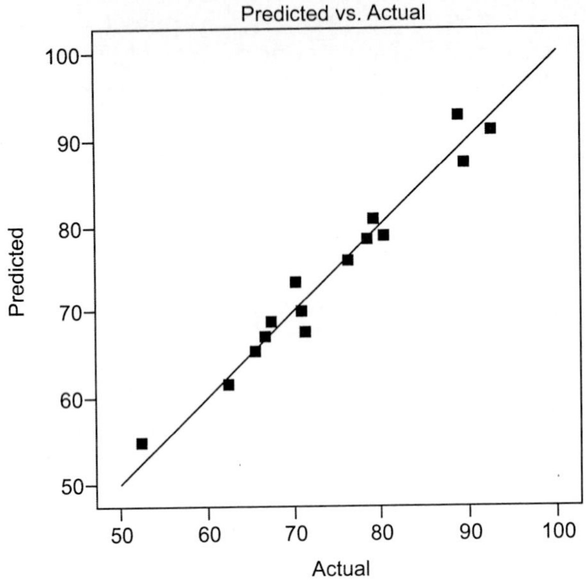

Fig. 7.8: Graphical Plot showing Predicted Response Vs Actual Response

Interaction Effect of Process Variables

Effect of variation in adsorbent dose and pH

The combined effect of adsorbent dose and pH for adsorption on arsenic removal was illustrated in the RSM plot of Figure 7.9. It was found that percentage of arsenic removal decreased on increasing pH the from 2.00 to 8.00 and also increased in the range of adsorbent dose from 0.33-1.5 gL^{-1}. The higher values of arsenic removal may be obtained by increase in adsorbent dose and also with decrease in pH. Due to increase in adsorbent dosage, the electrostatic force of attraction between the arsenic ions and adsorbent increased. From this given plot, maximum removal efficiency 92.41% was obtained at an 1.5 gL^{-1} adsorbent dose, at pH 2.00 and 70 min of contact time.

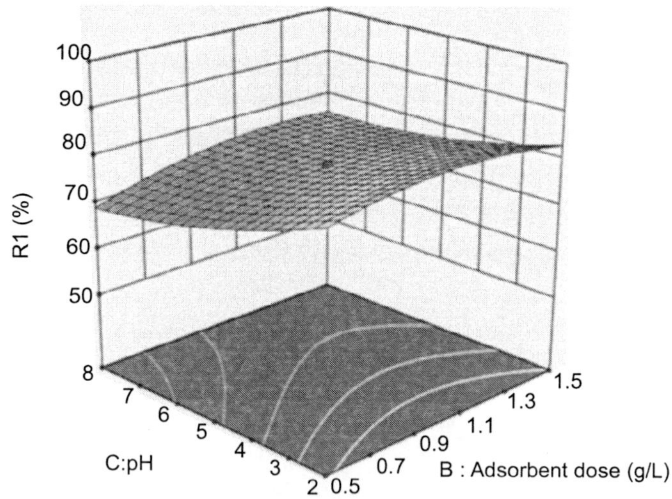

Fig. 7.9: Response surface plot showing the combined effect of absorbent dose and pH

Effect of variation in pH and contact time

The effect of different pH and contact time were required to remediate arsenic in solution using activated carbon. It was proved from Figure 7.10 that both the independent process variables play significant role on the % arsenic adsorption process. From this contour plot, maximal removal efficiency of 92.41% was achieved at pH 2.00 and 70 min of contact time, while the other variable was set at the middle value. As the contact time increased from 10-80 min, the 70 min of contact time uptake capacity increased at particular adsorbent dose which implied that the percentage of adsorption increased (due to higher attractive force between ions and adsorbent), consequently percentage efficiency of removal of arsenic ions increased.

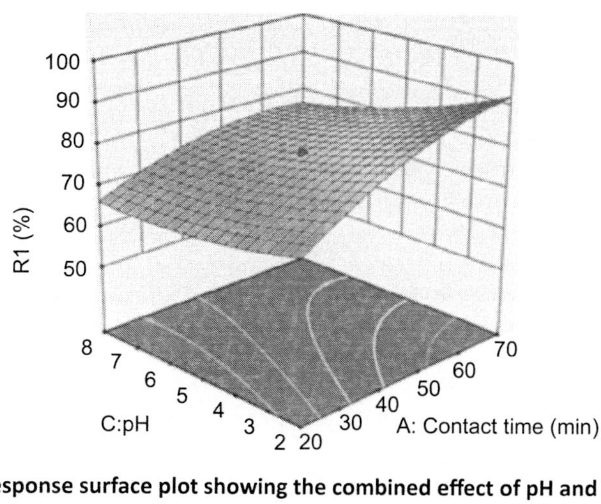

Fig. 7.10: Response surface plot showing the combined effect of pH and contact time

Effect of variation in adsorbent dose and contact time

The above plot of Figure 7.11 depicted that the interaction effects of the independent variables (contact time and adsorbent dose) in the above response. According to the contour plot of Figure 7.11, arsenic removal efficiency was increased with increasing dose of adsorbent and contact time. This trend was followed by maximum removal efficiency of 92.41%, obtained at 70 min contact time and adsorbent dose of 1.5 gL^{-1}.

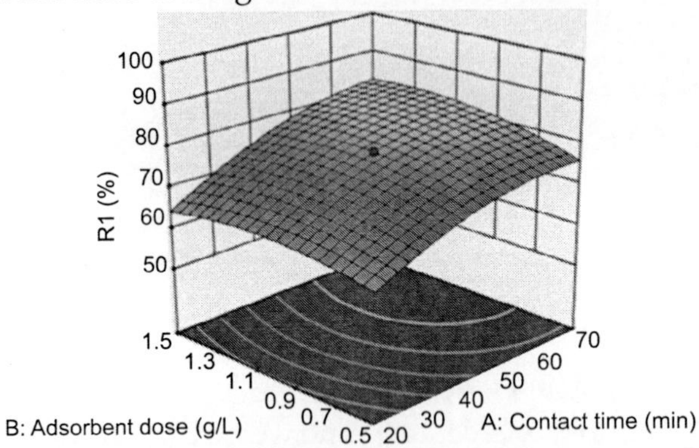

Fig. 7.11: Response surface plot showing the combined effect of absorbent dose and contact time

Conformational study

The optimized data are supported by numerical modeling[20], which are verified by confirmatory experiments (Figure 7.12) as suggested by the model (adsorbent dose 1.5 gL^{-1}; pH 2.00; contact time 70 minutes). These are found to be optimum condition for maximum percent fluoride removal and in that condition the maximum fluoride removal obtained as 92.41% and experimentally it is 92.46%. The difference between the removal efficiency in the two conditions being 0.05%. Here error data obtained after repeating the experiment.

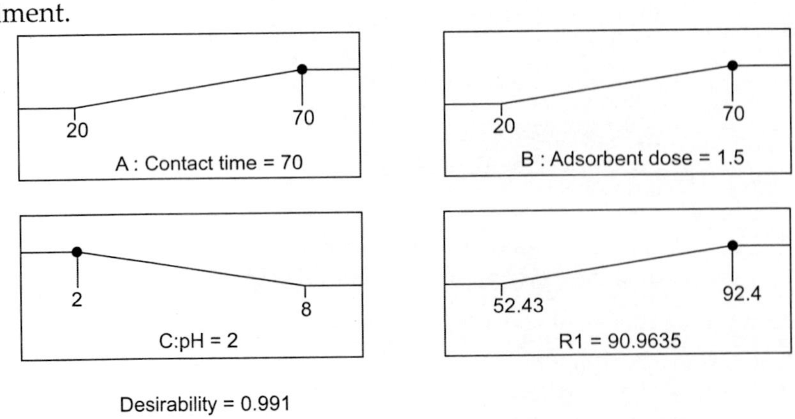

Fig. 7.12: Desirability Function

Regeneration study

The regeneration study of adsorbent in water treatment method was very important. As the activated carbon (IR:1.0) prepared from saw dust showed higher arsenic removal efficiency (92.4%) compared to other activated carbon (IR:0.25,0.5), so its desorption study was determined by 5 adsorption–desorption cycles. The present adsorption-desorption study was carried out with 100 ml of 50 mg·L^{-1} of synthetic arsenic solution at the starting of each cycle. The study was investigated with 1% sodium hydroxide as desorbing agent. The adsorption capacities of each cycle were 90.92%, 86.46%, 80.13%, 71.01%, and 62.53%. These experimental results (Figure 7.13) proved that activated carbon (IR:1.0) prepared from saw dust can be reused for arsenic removal in water.

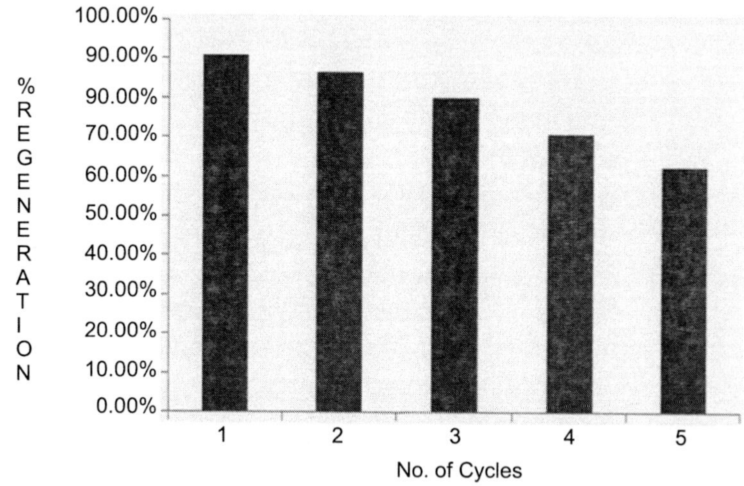

Fig. 7.13: % Regeneration study

Comparative Adsorption Capacity, Isotherm of Various Adsorbents with AC Synthesized in this Study

Adsorbent	Maximum adsorbent capacity (mg·g^{-1})	Reference
Hydrous Titanium Dioxide	8.3	[21]
Iron and Cesium mixed oxide	2.42	[22]
ZrO_2	9.2	[23]
Monoclinic Fe_2O_3/Graphene	2.904	[24]
Al doped Phenolic bead	20	[25]
Silver containing Yeast cell	0.975	[26]
Polymer Nanocomposite (Fe_3O_4)	2.83	[27]
Activated Carbon ((Saw dust, IR:1.0)	19.59 mg·g^{-1}	**Present Study**

Conclusion

The present work deals with the aim of studying arsenic adsorption process onto activated carbon prepared from saw dust in different impregnation ratio. The adsorption studies were carried out as a function of pH, contact time and dosage of adsorbent. The following conclusions may be inferred on the basis following experiment:

- It was proved that the adsorption equilibrium data were well fitted to the Langmuir adsorption model rather than Freundlich adsorption model at different pH for three adsorbents.
- The obtained experimental results showed good agreement with pseudo–second order kinetic modelin case of three adsorbents.
- Thermodynamic parameters such as change in Gibbs free energy (ΔG^0), enthalpy (ΔH^0), andentropy (ΔS^0) were determined from thermodynamic studies. Additionally, the nature of the adsorption process was spontaneous and endothermic.
- The desorption study was carried out using 1% NaOH as desorbing agent onto activated carbon (IR:1.0) in 5 cycles. The results showed that this adsorbent can be reused for further de-fluoridation .

As saw dust is very cheap and easily available and adsorbents were synthesized chemically from these materials which can be serve as effective adsorbent for removal of arsenic ion from solution. Additionally, from comparative study it was shown that this was better adsorbent for arsenic removal in water.

REFERENCES

[1] Viraraghavan T; Subramanian K.S; Aruldoss J.A. Arsenic in Drinking Water Problems and Solutions. Water Science Technology. 1999 *40*, 69-76.

[2] Khan A.H; Rasul S.B; Munir A; Habibuddowla M; Alauddin M; Newaz S.S; Hussan A. Appraisal of a Simple Arsenic Removal Method for Groundwater of Bangladesh. J. Environ. Sci. Health. 2000, *35*, 1021-1041.

[3] Kinniburgh D.G; Smedley P.L; Trafford J.M; Milne C.J; Hug S.M.I; Ahmed K.M; Burden S. The National Hydrochemical Survey. In: Kinniburgh D.G. and Smedley P.L. (Eds.), Arsenic Contamination of Groundwater in Bangladesh. Volume 2: Final Report. British Geological Survey Report, WC/00/19. British Geological Survey, UK (Chapter 6), 2001, *7*, 77-103.

[4] Smedley P.L; Nicolli H.B; Macdonald D.M.J; Barros A.J; Tullio J.O. Hydrogeochemistry of Arsenic and Other Inorganic Constituents in Ground Waters from La Pampa, Argentina. Applied Geochemistry. 2002, *17*, 259-284

[5] Jain C.K; Ali I. Arsenic: Occurrence, Toxicity and Speciation Techniques. Water Research. 2000, *34*, 4304-4312.

[6] Elizalde-Gonzalez M.P; Mattusch J; Wennrich R; Morgenstern P. Sorption on Natural Solids for Arsenic Removal. Chemical Engineering Journal. 2001, *81*, 187-195.

[7] Bajpai, S; Chaudhuri, M. Removal of Arsenic from Ground Water by Manganese Dioxide-Coated Sand. Journal of Environmental engineering. 1999, *126*, 782-787.

[8] Ramaswami A; Tawachsupa S; Isleyen M. Batch-mixed Iron Treatment of High Arsenic Waters. Water Research. 2001 *35*, 4474-4479.

[9] Berg M; Tran C.H; Nguyen C.T; Pham V.H; Schertenleib R; Giger W. Arsenic Contamination of Groundwater and Drinking Water in Vietnam: A Human Health Threat. Environmental Science and Technology. 2001, *35*,2621-2626.

[10] Ongley K.L; Armienta A.M; Heggeman K; Lathorop A.S; Mango H; Miller W; Pickelner S. Arsenic Removal from Contaminated Water by the Soyatal Formation, Zimapan Mining District, Mexicoóa Potential Low-cost Low-tech Remediation System. Geochemistry: Exploration, Environment, Analysis. 2001, *2*,0-9.

[11] Korngold E;Belayev N; Aronov L. Removal of Arsenic from Drinking Water by Anion Exchangers. Desalination. 2001, *141*, 81-84.

[12] Cheng R.C; Liang S. Enhanced Coagulation for Arsenic Removal, American Water Works Association. 1994, *86*, 79-90.

[13] Raji C; Anirudhan T.S. "Chromium (VI) Adsorption by Sawdust Carbon, Kinetics and Equilibrium," Indian Journal of Chemical Technology. 1997,*2*, 228-236.

[14] Su C.; PulsW.R.Arsenate and Arsenite Removal by Zerovalent Iron: Kinetics, Redox Transformation, and Implications for in situ Groundwater Remediation. Environ. Sci. Technol. 2001 *35*, 1487-1492.

[15] Shirzad Siboni M; Samarghandi M.R; AzizianS;Kim W.G; Lee S.M. "The Removal of Hexavalent Chromium from Aqueous Solutions using Modified Holly Sawdust: Equilibrium and Kinetics Studies", Environ. Eng. Res. 2011 *16*, 55-60.

[16] Evbuomwari B.O; Agbede A.M; Atuka M.M. A Comparative Study of the Physico-chemical Properties of Activated Carbon from oil Palm Waste, *International Journal of Science and Engineering Investigations*. 2013,*2*, 75-79.

[17] Jun T.Y;Arumugam S.D; Latip N.H.A; Abdulla A. M ;Latif P. A. Effect of Activation Temperature and Heating Duration on Physical Characteristics of Activated Carbon. Prepared from Agriculture Waste. 2010, *Environment Asia 3 (Special Issue)*,143-148.

[18] APHA, AWWA, WEF.Standard Methods for Examination of Water and Wastewater. 22nd ed. Washington: American Public Health Association. 2012, 1360pp ISBN978-087553-013-0.

[19] Roy, S; Manna, S; Sengupta, S; Ganguli, A; Goswami, S; Das, P. Comparative Assessment on Defluoridation of Waste Water Using Chemical and Bio-reduced Graphene Oxide Batch, Thermodynamic, Kinetics and Optimization using Response Surface Methodology and Artificial Neural Network. Process Saf. Environ. Protect. 2017, *111*, 221–231.

[20] Singh, K.P; Gupta, S; Singh, A.K; Sinha, S. Optimizing Adsorption of Crystal Violet Dye from Water by Magneticnanocomposite Using Response Surface Modeling Approach. J. Hazard. Mater. 2011. *186*, 1462–1473.

[21] Xu Z; Li Q; Gao S; Shang JK., As(III) Removal by Hydrous Titanium Dioxide Prepared from One-step Hydrolysis of Aqueous $TiCl_4$ Solution. Water Res. 2010, *44*, 5713–5721.

[22] Basu T; Ghosh UC. Nano-structured iron(III)-cerium(IV) Mixed Oxide: Synthesis, Characterization and Arsenic Sorption Kinetics in the Presence of Co-existing Ions

Aiming to Apply for High Arsenic Groundwater Treatment. Appl Surf Sci. 2013, *283*, 471–481.

[23] Cui H; Su Y; Li Q,;Gao S; Shang JK. Exceptional Arsenic (III, V) Removal Performance of Highly Porous, Nanostructured ZrO_2 Spheres for Foxed Bed Reactors and the Full-scale System Modeling. Water Res. 2013, *47*,6258–6268.

[24] Wang C;LuoH;ZhangZ;Wu ; Zhang J; Chen S. Removal of As(III) and As(V) from Aqueous Solutions Using Nanoscale Zero Valent Iron-reduced Graphite Oxide Modified Composites. J Hazard Mater 2014, *268*,124–131.

[25] Sharma A;Verma N; Sharma A; Deva D; Sankararamakrishnan N. Iron Doped Phenolic Resin Based Activated Carbon Micro and Nanoparticles by Milling: Synthesis, Characterization and Application in Arsenic Removal. ChemEng Sci. 2010,*65*,3591–3601.

[26] Selvakumar R; Arul Jothi N; Jayavignesh V; Karthikaiselvi K; Immanual Antony G; Sharmila PR; Kavitha S; Swaminathan K.As(V) removal Using Carbonized Yeast Cells Containing Silver Nanoparticles. Water Res. 2011 *45*,583–592.

[27] Vunain E; Mishra AK; Krause RW. Fabrication, Characterization and Application of Polymer Nanocomposites for Arsenic(III) Removal from Water. J Inorg Organomet Polym. 2013, *23*, 293–305.

[28] Kumar V; Talreja N; Deva D; Sankararamakrishnan N; Sharma A; Verma N. Development of bi-metal Doped Micro- and Nano Multifunctional Polymeric Adsorbents for the Removal of Fluoride and Arsenic(V) from Wastewater. Desalination. 2011, *282*, 27–38.

Technologies for Water and Wastewater Management **Pages 145-168**
Edited by: Dr. Vijender Singh & Dr. Pawan Kumar 'Bharti'
ISBN: 978-93-88854-53-5
Edition: 2020
Published by: Discovery Publishing House Pvt. Ltd., New Delhi (India)

8

Effect of Urban Wastewater on Growth and Development of Multipurpose Tree Species

Alok Kumar Patra[1], Ambraprava Mishra[2] & Ranjan Kumar Kar[3]

ABSTRACT

A field experiment was carried out at Instructional Farm of College of Forestry, Odisha University of Agriculture and Technology, Bhubaneswar during July 2017 to June 2018 to study the effect of urban wastewater on growth and development of six multipurpose tree species. The experiment was laid out in split plot design with 6 tree species (Acacia auriculiformis, Acacia mangium, Acacia nilotica, Gmelina arborea, Pongamia piñata and Cassia siamea) as main factor and 2 irrigation sources (potable water and urban wastewater) as sub factor replicated thrice. The tree species varied significantly in height, branches/plant, collar diameter, crown spread, primary and secondary root length and biomass production. Cassia siamea is fastest growing tree species among the six species tested. Plant height, collar diameter, secondary root length and biomass production were significantly influenced by wastewater irrigation. The nitrogen, phosphorus and potassium contents were comparatively more in leaves than stems and roots, irrespective of species. Nitrogen concentration in leaves, stems and roots were comparatively higher in Pongamia pinata, Acacia mangium and Gmelina arborea, respectively. Phosphorus content in leaves and stems were higher in Gmelina arborea and in roots it was with Acacia mangium. Similarly, K concentration in leaves, stems and roots were comparatively higher in Acacia auriculiformis, Acacia mangium and Gmelina arborea, respectively. The tree species varied significantly in N, P and K uptake by leaves, stems and roots. Cassia siamea removed the highest quantity of nutrients from the soil and Acacia auriculiformis removed the lowest. Source of

[1] Professor (Agronomy), All India Coordinated Research Project on Integrated Farming Systems, Odisha University of Agriculture and Technology, Bhubaneswar-751003, Odisha, India

[2] Junior Research Fellow, Odisha Biodiversity Board, Regional Plant Resource Centre Campus, Bhubaneswar-751015, Odisha, India

[3] Assistant Professor (Forestry Policy & Law), College of Forestry, Odisha University of Agriculture and Technology, Bhubaneswar-751003, Odisha, India

irrigation had no influence on nutrient removal by plant leaves and roots; however, it had a significant effect on nutrient removal by stems and the whole plant.

Key words: *Urban wastewater, Quality of irrigation water, Multipurpose tree species.*

Introduction

Wastewater irrigation is a traditional practice around the world. In Paris sewage farms existed as early as 1868. The use of sewage effluents for the irrigation of government farms in Egypt has been in implementation since 1915. A survey on wastewater use practices in developing countries carried out by the United Nations Development Programme and World Bank estimated that about 80% of the wastewater from urban areas in developing countries is currently used for permanent or seasonal irrigation (Cooper, 1991). However, the direct application of wastewater on agricultural land is limited by the extent of contamination with heavy metals, toxic organic chemicals and pathogens (Singh and Bhati, 2005; Ali *et al.*, 2012; Ali, 2013). Irrigation of forest species with wastewater for fuel and timber production is an approach which helps to overcome health hazards associated with sewage farming. Establishment of the green belts around the cities by forest trees under wastewater irrigation also helps revive the ecological balance and improves environmental conditions by self-treatment of wastewater through the application of forest irrigation (Hopmans, 1990: Ali *et al.*, 2011).

Land application using untreated municipal wastewater for biomass-production has many benefits (Idelovitch and Michael, 1984). Raw sewage used for irrigation in India over a 15-year period was reported to have improved the soil structure (Das and Kaul, 1992; Mathan, 1994), and increased soil nutrients and organic carbon content without increasing heavy metals to toxic levels (Gupta *et al.*, 1998). Rapid infiltration of sewage into sandy soils can result in improvement of its physical, chemical and microbiology quality. The soil and its associated ecosystem components act as physico-chemical and bio-reactors capable of treating or stabilizing pollutants of liquid and solid origin through degradation, adsorption and utilization by trees. The nutrients like nitrogen, phosphates and potassium of sewage along with the micronutrients as well as organic matter present in municipal wastewater could be added advantageously to add to the fertility of the soil, along with the irrigation potential of the water (Yudhistra Kumar and Vikram Reddy, 2010).

Treatment of urban wastewater is often energy consuming and cost-intensive and beyond the reach of many urban local bodies. An estimated 62,000 million litres per day (MLD) sewage is generated in urban areas in India, out of which less than 30% is being treated. In Odisha from 23 towns, about 600 MLD sewage is generated and only 50 MLD is treated. Irrigation potential can be increased with the urban wastewater as a source of irrigation water.

Disposal of wastewater and demand for fuel wood would be achieved by using urban wastewater as a source of irrigation to the urban forestry. On the other hand, nutrients like nitrogen, phosphates and potassium along with the micronutrients and organic matter present in city wastewater could enhance the fertility status of the soil. Thus, adoption of an appropriate wastewater management system wherein twin benefits of treatment and recycling can be achieved, and ecological development can be promoted.

Tree plantations can remove nutrients such as nitrogen and phosphates from land-applied wastewater for their growth without any harmful effect on the environment (Stewart *et al.*, 1990). Using municipal wastewater to grow trees in urban areas may help solve the dual problems of wastewater disposal and lack of fuel wood supply (Paliwal *et al.*, 1998; Singh and Bhati, 2003 & 2004; Yudhistra Kumar and Vikram Reddy, 2007). Thus, adoption of an appropriate wastewater management system wherein twin benefits of treatment and recycling and reuse can be achieved, and ecological development can be promoted. However, large scale use of municipal wastewater for the irrigation of tree-plantations is still low. Therefore, the present investigation was carried out to study the effect of urban wastewater on growth and development of multipurpose tree species with the following objectives.

Experimental Details and Methodology

The investigation was carried out at the Instructional Farm, Barmunda, Odisha University of Agriculture and Technology, Bhubaneswar during July 2017 to June 2018. The geographical location of the site was 20° 16′ 35.6″ North longitudes, 85° 47′ 25.9″ East latitude and an altitude is 25.9 meter above mean sea level. The study area falls in the sub-tropical zone. It is about 72 km away from the Bay of Bengal in the east.

Bhubaneswar has a warm and moist climate characterised by humid summer and mild winter. The normal rainfall of the place is 1493.7 mm with 113 rainy days in a year which is mostly received from the south-west monsoon. The monsoon sets on around mid June and recedes by mid-October. The rainfall received during the investigation period from July 2017 to June 2018 was 1793.6 mm in 104 rainy days. The mean maximum and minimum temperature during the experimentation ranged from 28.0 to 37.3 °C and 12.0 to 26.5 °C, respectively. The temperature begins to rise from the month of March and reaches its maximum in May. The mean minimum and maximum relative humidity in Bhubaneswar ranged between 55 to 91 per cent from July 2017 to June 2018. The maximum average bright sunshine hour (BSH) per day is 8.3 and minimum is 3.3 hours per days as averaged over 10 years. During investigation period the crop received the maximum BSH per day in April (8.4 hrs) while the minimum BSH per day in July (2.0 hrs). The normal average rate of evaporation varies from 8.7 to 7.5 mm per day.

The experimental field is fairly levelled and well drained. The physico-chemical status of soil of the study site was recorded from the profile 0-30 cm following the standard sample procedure. Soil is sandy loam texture. Soil samples were taken before conducting the experiment from a depth of 0-15 cm, taking all the possible precautions prescribed for soil sampling. The samples were brought to the laboratory, air dried and crushed to pass through 2.0 mm mesh sieve. The processed samples were subjected to appropriate mechanical and chemical analysis. The results thus obtained are presented in Table 8.1.

Table 8.1: Soil Physical and Chemical Properties of Experimental Site

Particulars	Value
Sand (%)	78.6
Silt (%)	10.2
Clay (%)	11.2
Textural class	Sandy loam
Bulk density	1.45 g/cm^3
Particle density	2.65 g/cm^3
Porosity (%)	41.9
*p*H	5.34
Electrical conductivity	0.197ds/m
Organic carbon (%)	0.72
Available N	203.4 kg/ha
Available P	19.8 kg/ha
Available K	180.2 kg/ha

The experiment was laid out in a split plot design with three replications. The experiment was consisted of 12 treatment combinations. The main plot treatments were six tree species and sub-plot treatments were irrigation from two sources. Thus, there were 36 plots, each plot measuring 16 m^2 (4 m × 4 m).

Main plot: Multipurpose tree species (S)

S_1 : *Acacia auriculiformis*

S_2 : *Acacia mangium*

S_3 : *Acacia nilotica*

S_4 : *Gmelina arborea*

S_5 : *Pongamia pinata*

S_6 : *Cassia siamea*

Sub plot: Source of irrigation water (I)

I_1 : Irrigation with potable water

I_2 : Irrigation with urban wastewater

The experimental land was ploughed after cleaning the weeds and unwanted shrubs thoroughly. Bunds were given to each individual plot with appropriate irrigation channels. Then pits with a dimension of 1 foot each in length, breadth and depth were opened at a spacing of 1 m × 1 m during first week of June before the onset of monsoon. One year old saplings of six species *Acacia* auriculiformis, *Acacia mangium, Acacia nilotica, Gmelina arborea, Pongamia pinata, Cassia siamea* were procured from College of Forestry and planted on 16th July 2017. In each plot 16 saplings were planted. At the time of planting chlorpyrifos dust was applied @ 20 g for each pit to protect the saplings from attack of white ants. In order to get accurate nutrient status of the soil interfacing with plant root system no amendment, manures or fertilizers was applied. As per the treatment schedules the plots were irrigated with groundwater and urban wastewater. Plots were given 23 flood irrigations with 5 cm water each time.

The first observation on growth parameters of saplings was recorded on the day of transplanting (16th July 2017). The subsequent filed observations were recorded at 60 days interval. Aerial biometric observations like plant height, number of branches/plant, collar diameter and crown width were recorded on all the six dates of observations. However, the destructive sampling was done only on 6th date observations (12th May 2018) and underground growth parameters like primary and secondary root length, and root fresh weight along with fresh weight of leaves and stems including tender branches were also recorded separately. Data on each parameter were recorded from 5 plants of each plot and were averaged for each treatment and each replication.

Root length was measured from the collar to the tip of the root using a measuring tape. In order to find out primary, secondary and tertiary roots, the developmental classification (Rose, 1983) was followed. The tap root developed through direct elongation of the radicle was considered as primary root. In some cases, when tap root appeared to be forked, the root showing minimum angle of deviation from the main root axis, maximum root diameter at the point of emergence or maximum penetration length was considered as primary root. The plant samples used for recording the fresh biomass of leaves, stem and roots were taken to laboratory and were oven dried in a hot air oven at 65 + 5 °C to constant weight and were used to determine the dry biomass of leaves, stem and roots of each sample plant. The dry biomass of each plant was also recorded.

Soil samples from 0 to15 cm soil depth were collected from each treatment at 360 days after transplanting of plants. The samples were air dried under shade, finely ground and passed through a 2 mm mesh sieve and finally 250 g of such soil were mixed thoroughly and composite samples were made for each treatment and filled in polythene bags with proper label for analysis of physico-chemical properties. Physico-chemical analysis of wastewater and potable water was also done (Jackson, 1973).

For determining the significance between the treatment means and to draw valid conclusion, statistical analysis was made. Data obtained from various observations were subjected to statistical analysis by adopting split-plot design method of *Analysis of Variance*. The significance of the treatment effect was judged with the help of 'F' test. The difference of the treatments mean was tested using *Critical Difference* at 5% level of probability (Gomez and Gomez, 1984). When the treatment difference is greater than or equal to the critical difference it is significant otherwise there is no significant difference between the treatment means.

Results and Discussion

Characteristics of urban wastewater

The water quality parameters such as *p*H, electrical conductivity, total dissolved solids, biological oxygen demand, chemical oxygen demand, nitrate nitrogen, chloride, sulphate, phosphate, sodium, potassium, calcium, magnesium, carbonates and bicarbonates of urban wastewater and potable water used for irrigation of saplings of six multipurpose tree species were analysed and

Table 8.2: Characteristics of Raw Sewage, Treated Sewage and that of Potable Water which was Used for Irrigation During Post-monsoon Period

Physico-chemical parameters	Potable water	Urban wastewater
Temperature (°C)	27.0	27.8
*p*H	6.5	7.0
Electrical conductivity (ds/m)	0.17	0.52
Total dissolved solids (mg/l)	294	482
Chemical oxygen demand (mg/l)	114	325
Bioligical oxygen demand (mg/l)	12	160
Chloride (mg/l)	92	188
Sulphate (mg/l)	18	29
Carbonates (mg/l)	0.48	2.16
Bicarbonates (mg/l)	76	132
Nitrates (mg/l)	10.6	30.2
Phosphates (mg/l)	0.1	1.5
Potassium (mg/l)	10	34
Ca (mg/l)	14	30
Mg (mg/l)	9	18
Sodium (mg/l)	28	108

the values are presented in Table 8.2. The average values of each of the above water quality parameters of urban wastewater were higher than that of the potable water.

Growth parameters

Plant height

The tree species varied significantly in height at all the stages. *Gmelina arborea* and *Cassia siamea* recorded the highest plant height (110 and 107 cm) at planting and these two species were at par with respect to height and were significantly higher than the other four species (42 - 96 cm). However, at 120 days of planting *Acacia mangium* attained the height that was at par with *Gmelina arborea* and *Cassia siamea* and these three species maintained significantly higher plant height till the last observation recorded at 300 days after planting (161, 153 and 154 cm, respectively). *Acacia nilotica* had the minimum plant height at planting (42 cm) and it continued till the last (92 cm). At 300 days after planting *Gmelina arborea* and *Acacia mangium* had recorded 75 and 67% higher plant height over *Acacia nilotica. Gmelina arborea, Cassia siamea* and *Acacia mangium* registered an increase of 46, 60 and 43% over their respective height at transplanting. Thus *Cassia siamea* is fastest growing tree species among the six species tested. There was no significant effect of source of irrigation on plant height at 60 and 240 days after transplanting, however at 120, 180 and 300 days after transplanting these were significant (Table 8.3). At 300 days after transplanting the increase in plant height due to urban wastewater irrigation was 13% higher over that of irrigation with potable water. Irrigation by potable water and wastewater registered an increase of 50 and 69% in plant height over their respective height at transplanting. The interaction effect between plant species and source of irrigation was not significant.

The significant increase in the sapling height and collar diameter in the treatment irrigated with urban wastewater was probably due to availability of increased organic matter, and both macro- and micro-nutrients, especially total and available N in the urban wastewater (Braatz and Kandiah, 1996). Omran *et al.* (1998) in corroboration to the present findings also reported increased shoot length in Navel Orange trees irrigated with sewage in Egypt. Similarly, increase in water and nutrient availability through effluent application influenced the growth of *Acacia nilotica* (Singh and Bhati, 2004), that of *Hardwickia binata* (Paliwal *et al.*, 1998) and *Eucalyptus grandis* (Stewart *et al.*, 1990). In India utilizing raw sewage for irrigation of plantations of *Eucalyptus tereticornis, Populus deltoides* and *Leucaena leucocephala* showed higher growth than that of the trees irrigated with well water; the eucalyptus being six percent taller after 48 months; the leucaena being 12 percent taller after 36 months; and the poplar being four percent taller after 24 months (Das and Kaul, 1992).

Table 8.3: Effect of Urban Wastewater on Height (cm) of Multipurpose Tree Species

Treatment	At transplanting	60 DAT	120 DAT	180 DAT	240 DAT	300 DAT
Tree species						
Acacia auriculiformis	83	101	119	121	126	135
Acacia mangium	96	114	135	137	145	154
Acacia nilotica	42	57	76	78	84	92
Gmelina arborea	110	127	148	150	155	161
Pongamia pinata	67	80	94	96	102	109
Cassia siamea	107	120	141	143	148	153
S. Em. (±)	3.0	4.7	5.2	6.5	9.6	7.1
CD ($P=0.05$)	9.5	14.7	16.4	20.4	30.2	22.3
Source of irrigation water						
Potable water	84	97	111	113	119	126
Wastewater	84	103	126	128	135	142
S. Em. (±)	2.1	3.2	3.5	4.4	6.5	4.8
CD ($P=0.05$)	NS	NS	11.1	13.9	NS	15.1

Branches/plant

The tree species varied significantly in branches/plant at all the stages starting from 60 days after transplanting. At the time of transplanting the saplings were not significant in branching behaviour. At 300 days after planting *Acacia nilotica* (7.8), *Acacia auriculiformis* (7.6), and *Cassia siamea* (6.2) had significantly higher number of branches than other three species. *Acacia mangium* recorded the lowest number of branches (3.2). There was no significant effect of source of irrigation on branches/plant at any stage (Table 8.4). The interaction effect between plant species and source of irrigation was also not significant with respect to branches per plant.

Table 8.4: Effect of Urban Wastewater on Branches/Plant of Multipurpose Tree Species

Treatment	At transplanting	60 DAT	120 DAT	180 DAT	240 DAT	300 DAT
Tree species						
Acacia auriculiformis	1.8	2.1	4.1	4.9	6.8	7.6
Acacia mangium	0.1	0.2	1.4	2.8	2.9	3.2
Acacia nilotica	2.4	2.7	5.5	6.0	6.7	7.8
Gmelina arborea	1.5	2.0	3.7	4.1	4.5	5.2
Pongamia pinata	1.4	1.8	3.8	4.3	4.7	5.9
Cassia siamea	1.5	1.9	4.0	4.7	5.5	6.2

S. Em. (±)	0.4	0.3	0.5	0.4	0.4	0.5
CD (*P=0.05*)	NS	0.9	1.6	1.2	1.3	1.6
Source of irrigation water						
Potable water	1.5	1.8	3.7	4.3	4.8	5.6
Wastewater	1.5	1.8	3.8	4.6	5.5	6.3
S. Em. (±)	0.1	0.2	0.3	0.3	0.2	0.3
CD (*P=0.05*)	NS	NS	NS	NS	NS	NS

Collar diameter

At transplanting the tree species did not vary in collar diameter. However, from 60 days after transplanting the tree species varied significantly in collar diameter at all the stages (Table 8.5). *Gmelina arborea* recorded the highest collar diameter at all stages starting from 60 days after transplanting which was closely followed by *Cassia siamea*. The lowest collar diameter was recorded with *Acacia nilotica* and this was at par with *Acacia auriculiformis, Pongamia pinata* and *Acacia mangium*. At 300 days after planting the collar diameter of *Gmelina arborea* (53.2 mm) and *Cassia siamea* (48.5 mm) were 76 and 60% higher over *Acacia nilotica* (30.3 mm).

There was no significant effect of source of irrigation on collar diameter up to 180 days after transplanting. However, at 240 and 300 days after transplanting the effects were significant (Table 8.5). At both 240 and 300 days after transplanting the increase in collar diameter due to urban wastewater irrigation (33.8 and 41 mm) was about 10% higher over that of irrigation with potable water (30.6 and 37.1 mm). Irrigation by potable water and wastewater registered 5-fold and 6-fold increase in collar diameter over their respective collar diameter at transplanting. The interaction between plant species and source of irrigation was not significant.

Table 8.5: Effect of Urban Wastewater on Collar Diameter (mm) of Multipurpose Tree Species

Treatment	At transplanting	60 DAT	120 DAT	180 DAT	240 DAT	300 DAT
Tree species						
Acacia auriculiformis	5.2	6.9	13.3	16.1	26.7	31.2
Acacia mangium	5.1	7.9	17.8	21.8	29.5	35.5
Acacia nilotica	4.8	8.7	12.6	17.2	24.2	30.3
Gmelina arborea	6.7	22.7	31.1	38.0	45.3	53.2
Pongamia pinata	5.4	7.9	13.1	18.9	26.5	35.4
Cassia siamea	9.2	21.8	29.0	34.0	41.2	48.5
S. Em. (±)	1.3	1.0	1.2	2.3	3.5	4.0
CD (*P=0.05*)	NS	3.0	3.8	7.3	11.0	12.5

Source of irrigation water						
Potable water	6.1	12.2	19.0	23.5	30.6	37.1
Wastewater	6.1	13.1	19.9	25.2	33.8	41.0
S. Em. (±)	0.8	0.3	0.4	0.7	0.9	1.0
CD (*P*=0.05)	NS	NS	NS	NS	2.8	3.2

Crown spread

The tree species varied significantly in crown spread at all the stages starting from 60 day after transplanting. *Gmelina arborea* recorded the highest crown spread at all the stages and it was closely followed by *Cassia siamea*. These two species recorded 167 and 147% higher crown spread over *Acacia mangium* which had significantly lowest crown spread (55 cm) at 300 days after transplanting. *Pongamia pinata* had also significantly higher crown spread over the other three species (Table 8.6). There was no significant effect of source of irrigation on crown spread at any stage. The interaction effect between plant species and source of irrigation was not significant with respect to crown spread.

Table 8.6: Effect of Urban Wastewater on Crown Spread (cm) of Multipurpose Tree Species

Treatment	60 DAT	120 DAT	180 DAT	240 DAT	300 DAT
Tree species					
Acacia auriculiformis	11	16	27	45	65
Acacia mangium	8	12	25	37	55
Acacia nilotica	14	25	48	62	67
Gmelina arborea	72	90	115	132	147
Pongamia pinata	22	45	70	97	112
Cassia siamea	85	96	108	122	136
S. Em. (±)	2.2	3.3	4.7	9.5	8.2
CD (*P*=0.05)	6.7	10.4	14.7	29.3	25.8
Source of irrigation water					
Potable water	36	47	63	80	95
Wastewater	35	48	68	85	99
S. Em. (±)	0.4	0.6	2.6	5.6	4.8
CD (*P*=0.05)	NS	NS	NS	NS	NS

Root growth

The tree species varied significantly in both primary and secondary root length. *Cassia siamea* recorded significantly higher primary and secondary root length than all 5 other species evaluated (Table 8.7). *Acacia mangium* had the shortest primary root length (42.3 cm) which was at par with that of *Acacia auriculiformis*. However, *Acacia auriculiformis* recorded the shortest secondary root length.

There was no significant effect of source of irrigation on primary root length; however, the secondary root length was significantly influenced by irrigation water. The increase in secondary root length due to urban wastewater irrigation was 30% higher over that of irrigation with potable water. The interaction effect between plant species and source of irrigation was not significant either on primary or secondary root length. These results are in harmony with those of Hopmans *et al.* (1990) on *Eucalyptus camaldulensis* and *Pinus radiata,* Gogate *et al.* (1995) on *Tectona grandis,* Hassan *et al.* (2002) on *Albizzia lebbek, Tectona distichum* and *Tectona speciosa* and Sebastiani *et al.* (2004) on poplar.

Table 8.7: Effect of Urban Wastewater on Root Length (cm) of Multipurpose Tree Species (at 300 DAT)

Treatment	Primary root	Secondary root
Tree species		
Acacia auriculiformis	43.0	23.8
Acacia mangium	42.3	26.0
Acacia nilotica	67.3	34.5
Gmelina arborea	68.8	35.5
Pongamia pinata	68.3	40.7
Cassia siamea	99.5	60.5
S. Em. (±)	4.1	2.3
CD (*P=0.05*)	12.5	7.3
Source of irrigation water		
Potable water	61.2	32.0
Wastewater	68.5	41.7
S. Em. (±)	2.8	1.3
CD (*P=0.05*)	NS	4.1

Biomass production

Fresh weight of leaves, stems with branches and roots were taken separately from each treatment and replication at 300 days after transplanting when destructive sampling was carried out and presented in Table 8.8. Similarly, dry weight of leaves, stems with branches and roots were taken and presented in Table 8.9. The tree species varied significantly in both fresh weight and dry weight of leaves, stems and leaves. *Cassia siamea* recorded significantly higher fresh weight of stems (1.32 kg/plant) and roots (0.36 kg/plant) than all 5 other species tested. *Acacia auriculiformis* recorded the lowest fresh weight of stem (0.3 kg/plant) and roots (0.05 kg/plant). However, *Gmelina arborea* produced the highest fresh weight of leaves (0.16 kg/plant) and *Acacia nilotica* recorded the least fresh weight of leaves (0.07 kg/plant). *Cassia siamea* and *Acacia auriculiformis* recorded the highest (1.81 kg/plant) and the lowest (0.46 kg/plant) total fresh weight, respectively. Many researchers have also reported that the tree species varied in growth parameters like plant height, branches/plant, collar diameter, root growth and biomass production (Hassan, 1996; Abbaas, 2002; Farooq *et al.*, 2006; Braatz and Kandiah, 2010; Hassan, 2011). There was no significant effect of source of irrigation on fresh weight of leaves and root; however, the fresh weight of stem and total fresh weight per plant were significantly influenced by irrigation water. The increase in fresh weight of stem and total plant fresh weight due to urban wastewater irrigation was 20 and 16% higher over that of irrigation with potable water. The interaction effect between plant species and source of irrigation was not significant.

Table 8.8: Effect of Urban Wastewater on Fresh Weight (g/plant) of Multipurpose Tree Species (at 300 DAT)

Treatment	Leaves	Stem	Roots	Total
Tree species				
Acacia auriculiformis	101	300	54	455
Acacia mangium	115	740	116	971
Acacia nilotica	71	403	91	564
Gmelina arborea	157	661	180	998
Pongamia pinata	107	448	119	674
Cassia siamea	129	1322	357	1808
S. Em. (±)	8.2	30.0	21.3	39.5
CD (*P=0.05*)	24.8	94.4	67.1	119.2
Source of irrigation water				
Potable water	109	588	147	844
Wastewater	117	703	159	979
S. Em. (±)	5.4	20.9	4.7	26.1
CD (*P=0.05*)	NS	64.4	NS	78.5

Cassia siamea produced significantly higher dry weight of stems (328 g/plant) and roots (68 g/plant) than all other species evaluated (Table 9). *Acacia auriculiformis* recorded the lowest dry weight of stem (72 g/plant) and roots (10 g/plant). However, *Gmelina arborea* produced the highest dry weight of leaves (28 g/plant) and *Acacia nilotica* recorded the least dry weight of leaves (14 g/plant). *Cassia siamea* and *Acacia auriculiformis* produced the highest (417 g/plant) and the lowest (103 g/plant) total dry matter, respectively. Total biomass production of other 4 species was in the range of 128 - 232 g/plant. There was no significant effect of source of irrigation on dry matter production contributed by leaves and roots; however, the contribution to dry matter production of stem was significantly influenced by irrigation water. The increase in dry weight of stem due to urban wastewater irrigation was 24.7% higher over that of irrigation with potable water. Total biomass production per plant was also influenced by irrigation water. The increase in total biomass production due to urban wastewater irrigation (229 g/plant) was 19.9% higher over that of irrigation with potable water (191 g/plant). The results are explained by many investigators, who found that urban wastewater had a stimulatory effect on vegetative growth of trees, provided the soil with plant nutrients and organic matter and improved the soil physical characteristics, that reflected on the growth by enhancing the cell elongation and division (Kaneker *et al.*, 1993 on *Acacia nilotica*; Hassan, 1996 on *Acacia saligna* and *Leucaena leucocephala*; Berbec *et al.*, 1999 on poplar; Abbaas, 2002 on *Casuarina glauca*, *Taxodium distichum* and *Populus nigra*; Singh and Bhati, 2003 on *Eucalyptus camaldulensis*; Singh and Bhati, 2005 on *Dalbergia sissoo*. The interaction effect between plant species and source of irrigation was not significant.

Table 8.9: Effect of Urban Wastewater on Biomass Production (g/plant) and Root: Shoot Ratio of Multipurpose Tree Species (at 300 DAT)

Treatment	Leaves	Stem	Roots	Total	Root: shoot ratio
Tree species					
Acacia auriculiformis	22	72	10	103	0.10
Acacia mangium	24	176	22	222	0.11
Acacia nilotica	14	97	18	128	0.16
Gmelina arborea	28	173	31	232	0.15
Pongamia pinata	19	112	26	157	0.19
Cassia siamea	21	328	68	417	0.20
S. Em. (±)	2.8	8.8	2.5	7.5	
CD ($P=0.05$)	8.6	26.9	7.7	22.7	
Source of irrigation water					
Potable water	21	142	28	191	0.17
Wastewater	22	177	29	229	0.15
S. Em. (±)	1.9	6.1	1.6	5.2	
CD ($P=0.05$)	NS	18.5	NS	15.8	

Root: shoot ratio

Cassia siamea and *Pongamia pinata* had higher root: shoot ratio of 0.20 and 0.19, respectively (Table 8.9). *Acacia nilotica* and *Gmelina arborea* recorded comparatively lower root: shoot ratio of 0.16 and 0.15. *Acacia auriculiformis* had the least root: shoot ratio (0.1). Higher root: shoot ratio was realised when the saplings were irrigated with pot water (0.17) as compared to that of urban wastewater (0.15).

Nutrient concentration and uptake by plants

Nitrogen

The nitrogen content was more in leaves as compared to stems and roots, irrespective of species. Nitrogen content in leaves varied from 0.934 to 1.015%, *Acacia nilotica* having the lowest and *Pongamia pinata* having the highest (Table 8.10). Similarly, nitrogen content in stems and roots varied from 0.454% (*Acacia auriculiformis*) to 0.519% (*Acacia mangium*) and 0.512% (*Pongamia pinata*) to 0.582% (*Gmelina arborea*), respectively. Much variation was not noticed in nitrogen content in plant parts owing to different source of irrigation water.

Table 8.10: Effect of Urban Wastewater on Nitrogen Concentration (%) in Plant Parts of Multipurpose Tree Species (at 300 DAT)

Treatment	Leaves	Stem	Roots
Tree species			
Acacia auriculiformis	1.001	0.454	0.522
Acacia mangium	1.007	0.519	0.568
Acacia nilotica	0.934	0.489	0.524
Gmelina arborea	0.977	0.518	0.582
Pongamia pinata	1.015	0.493	0.512
Cassia siamea	0.962	0.474	0.569
Source of irrigation water			
Potable water	0.982	0.489	0.547
Wastewater	0.983	0.493	0.545

The tree species varied significantly in nitrogen uptake by leaves, stems and roots (Table 8.11). *Gmelina arborea* recorded the highest nitrogen uptake by leaves (0.28 g/plant), however, it was at par with *Acacia mangium* (0.24 g/plant), *Acacia auriculiformis* (0.22 g/plant), *Cassia siamea* (0.2 g/plant) and *Pongamia pinata* (0.2 g/plant). *Acacia nilotica* recorded significantly lower nitrogen uptake by leaves (0.13 g/plant) as compared to all other species tested.

Cassia siamea recorded significantly higher nitrogen uptake by stems (1.55 g/plant) than all other species. *Acacia auriculiformis* recorded the lowest nitrogen uptake by stems (0.33 g/plant) which was at par with *Acacia nilotica* (0.47 g/plant). Similarly, *Cassia siamea* recorded significantly higher nitrogen uptake by roots (0.39 g/plant) than all other species evaluated. *Acacia auriculiformis* recorded the lowest nitrogen uptake by roots (0.05 g/plant) which was at par with *Acacia nilotica* (0.09 g/plant).

Cassia siamea removed the highest nitrogen (2.14 g/plant) from the soil, and it was significantly higher than any other species tested. *Gmelina arborea* removed the second highest nitrogen (1.35 g/plant), and it was par with *Acacia mangium* (1.28 g/plant). *Acacia auriculiformis* removed the lowest nitrogen (0.59 g/plant), which was at par with that of *Acacia nilotica* (0.7 g/plant).

Source of irrigation water had no influence on nitrogen removal by plant leaves and roots; however, it had a significant effect on nitrogen removal by stems (Table 8.10). Nitrogen removal by the whole plant was also influenced by the source of irrigation water. Stems and whole plant removed 24 and 19% higher nitrogen by providing irrigation with wastewater as compared to that of potable water. The interaction effect between plant species and source of irrigation was not significant with respect to nitrogen uptake by plant parts and the whole plant.

Table 8.11: Effect of Urban Wastewater on Nitrogen Uptake (g/plant) by Plant Parts of Multipurpose Tree Species (at 300 DAT)

Treatment	Leaves	Stems	Roots	Total
Tree species (S)				
Acacia auriculiformis	0.22	0.33	0.05	0.59
Acacia mangium	0.24	0.91	0.12	1.28
Acacia nilotica	0.13	0.47	0.09	0.70
Gmelina arborea	0.28	0.90	0.18	1.35
Pongamia pinata	0.20	0.55	0.13	0.88
Cassia siamea	0.20	1.55	0.39	2.14
S. Em. (±)	0.032	0.046	0.017	0.052
CD (*P=0.05*)	0.101	0.145	0.053	0.164
Source of irrigation water (I)				
Potable water	0.20	0.70	0.16	1.05
Wastewater	0.21	0.87	0.16	1.25
S. Em. (±)	0.021	0.030	0.011	0.034
CD (*P=0.05*)	NS	0.094	NS	0.106

Phosphorus

The phosphorus content was comparatively low in stems as compared to leaves and roots of the plant, irrespective of species. Phosphorus content in leaves varied from 0.07 to 0.076%, *Acacia mangium* having the lowest and *Gmelina arborea* having the highest (Table 8.11). Similarly, phosphorus content in stems and roots varied from 0.048% (*Cassia siamea*) to 0.073% (*Gmelina arborea*) and 0.063% (*Gmelina arborea*) to 0.077% (*Acacia mangium*), respectively. Much variation was not noticed in nitrogen content in plant parts owing to different source of irrigation water.

Table 8.12: Effect of Urban Wastewater on Phosphorus Concentration (%) in Plant Parts of Multipurpose Tree Species (at 300 DAT)

Treatment	Leaves	Stem	Roots
Tree species			
Acacia auriculiformis	0.073	0.051	0.068
Acacia mangium	0.070	0.051	0.077
Acacia nilotica	0.073	0.057	0.076
Gmelina arborea	0.076	0.073	0.063
Pongamia pinata	0.072	0.052	0.073
Cassia siamea	0.066	0.048	0.073
Source of irrigation water			
Potable water	0.072	0.056	0.071
Wastewater	0.071	0.055	0.072

The tree species varied significantly in phosphorus uptake by leaves, stems and roots (Table 8.12). *Gmelina arborea* recorded the highest phosphorus uptake by leaves (0.021 g/plant), however, it was at par with *Acacia mangium* (0.016 g/plant) and *Acacia auriculiformis* (0.016 g/plant). *Acacia nilotica* recorded significantly lower phosphorus uptake by leaves (0.01 g/plant).

Cassia siamea recorded significantly higher phosphorus uptake by stems (0.157 g/plant) than all other species. *Acacia auriculiformis* recorded the lowest phosphorus uptake by stems (0.036 g/plant) which was at par with *Acacia nilotica* (0.055 g/plant) and *Pongamia pinata* (0.058 g/plant). Similarly, *Cassia siamea* recorded significantly higher phosphorus uptake by roots (0.05 g/plant) than all other species evaluated. *Acacia auriculiformis* recorded the lowest phosphorus uptake by roots (0.007 g/plant).

Cassia siamea as a whole plant removed the highest phosphorus (0.221 g/plant) from soil, and it was closely followed by *Gmelina arborea* (0.166 g/plant) and *Acacia mangium* (0.124 g/plant). *Acacia auriculiformis* removed the lowest phosphorus (0.059 g/plant) from soil, which was at par with that of *Acacia nilotica* (0.078 g/plant) and *Pongamia pinata* (0.09 g/plant).

Source of irrigation water had no influence on phosphorus removal by plant leaves and roots; however, it had a significant effect on phosphorus removal from soil by stems (Table 8.12). Phosphorus removal by the whole plant was also influenced by the source of irrigation water. Stems and whole plant removed 23 and 18% higher phosphorus by providing irrigation with wastewater as compared to that of potable water. The interaction effect between plant species and source of irrigation was not significant with respect to phosphorus uptake by plant parts and the whole plant.

Table 8.13: Effect of Urban Wastewater on Phosphorus Uptake (g/plant) by Plant Parts of Multipurpose Tree Species (at 300 DAT)

Treatment	Leaves	Stem	Roots	Total
Tree species				
Acacia auriculiformis	0.016	0.036	0.007	0.059
Acacia mangium	0.016	0.090	0.017	0.124
Acacia nilotica	0.010	0.055	0.014	0.078
Gmelina arborea	0.021	0.125	0.019	0.166
Pongamia pinata	0.014	0.058	0.019	0.090
Cassia siamea	0.014	0.157	0.050	0.221
S. Em. (±)	0.002	0.008	0.002	0.025
CD (*P=0.05*)	0.006	0.025	0.006	0.079
Source of irrigation water				
Potable water	0.015	0.079	0.020	0.114
Wastewater	0.016	0.097	0.021	0.134
S. Em. (±)	0.001	0.005	0.001	0.016
CD (*P=0.05*)	NS	0.016	NS	0.051

Potassium

The potassium content was more in leaves as compared to stems and roots, irrespective of tree species. Potassium content in leaves varied from 0.935 to 1.028%, *Acacia nilotica* having the lowest and *Acacia auriculiformis* having the highest (Table 8.13). Similarly, potassium content in stems and roots varied from 0.317% (*Acacia nilotica*) to 0.397% (*Acacia mangium*) and 0.623% (*Acacia nilotica*) to 0.713% (*Gmelina arborea*), respectively. Irrigation by urban wastewater recorded comparatively higher potassium content in tree parts than that of potable water.

Table 8.14: Effect of Urban Wastewater on Potassium Concentration (%) in Plant Parts of Multipurpose Tree Species (at 300 DAT)

Treatment	Leaves	Stem	Roots
Tree species			
Acacia auriculiformis	1.028	0.335	0.663
Acacia mangium	0.962	0.397	0.697
Acacia nilotica	0.879	0.317	0.623
Gmelina arborea	0.952	0.361	0.713
Pongamia pinata	0.982	0.323	0.637
Cassia siamea	0.935	0.346	0.694
Source of irrigation water			
Potable water	0.950	0.336	0.668
Wastewater	0.962	0.357	0.675

The tree species varied significantly in potassium uptake by leaves, stems and roots (Table 8.14). *Gmelina arborea* recorded the highest potassium uptake by leaves (0.269 g/plant), however, it was at par with *Acacia mangium* (0.227 g/plant) and *Acacia auriculiformis* (0.222 g/plant). *Acacia nilotica* recorded significantly lower potassium uptake by leaves (0.122 g/plant) as compared to all other species tested.

Cassia siamea recorded significantly higher potassium uptake by stems (1.134 g/plant). The next highest potassium uptake by stems was recorded with *Acacia mangium* (0.698 g/plant) which was closely followed by *Gmelina arborea* (0.624 g/plant). *Acacia auriculiformis* recorded the lowest potassium uptake by stems (0.241 g/plant) which was at par with *Acacia nilotica* (0.306 g/plant). Similarly, *Cassia siamea* recorded significantly higher potassium uptake by roots (0.475 g/plant) than all other species evaluated. *Acacia auriculiformis* recorded the lowest potassium uptake by roots (0.065 g/plant).

Cassia siamea as a whole plant removed the highest potassium (1.805 g/plant) from soil, and it was significantly higher than any other species evaluated. *Gmelina arborea* removed the second highest potassium (1.114 g/plant), and it was par with that of *Acacia mangium* (1.078 g/plant). *Acacia auriculiformis* removed the lowest potassium (0.528 g/plant), which was at par with that of *Acacia nilotica* (0.54 g/plant).

Table 8.15: Effect of Urban Wastewater Potassium Uptake (g/plant) by Plant Parts of Multipurpose Tree Species (at 300 DAT)

Treatment	Leaves	Stem	Roots	Total
Tree species				
Acacia auriculiformis	0.222	0.241	0.065	0.528
Acacia mangium	0.227	0.698	0.152	1.078
Acacia nilotica	0.122	0.306	0.112	0.540
Gmelina arborea	0.269	0.624	0.221	1.114
Pongamia pinata	0.191	0.362	0.163	0.716
Cassia siamea	0.195	1.134	0.475	1.805
S. Em. (±)	0.022	0.036	0.012	0.042
CD (*P=0.05*)	0.069	0.113	0.038	0.132
Source of irrigation water				
Potable water	0.197	0.478	0.189	0.865
Wastewater	0.210	0.632	0.199	1.041
S. Em. (±)	0.014	0.023	0.008	0.027
CD (*P=0.05*)	NS	0.074	NS	0.086

Source of irrigation water had no influence on potassium removal by plant leaves and stems from soil; however, it had a significant effect on potassium removal by stems (Table 8.14). Potassium removal by the whole plant was also influenced by the source of irrigation water. Stems and whole plant removed 32 and 20% higher potassium by providing irrigation with urban wastewater as compared to that of potable water. The interaction effect between plant species and source of irrigation was not significant with respect to potassium uptake by plant parts and the whole plant.

The nitrogen, phosphorus and potassium contents were comparatively more in leaves than stems and roots, irrespective of species. Murage and Mwangi (2012) also reported that concentrations of N, P and K in leaves were much higher than those of shoots and roots. The results agree with the findings of Singh and Bhati (2005) who found that concentrations of N, P and K were greater in foliage compared to the other plant parts. Nitrogen concentration in leaves, stems and roots were comparatively higher in *Pongamia pinata, Acacia mangium* and *Gmelina arborea,* respectively. Phosphorus content in leaves and stems were higher in *Gmelina arborea* and in roots it was with *Acacia mangium*. Similarly, potassium concentration in leaves, stems and roots were comparatively higher in *Acacia auriculiformis, Acacia mangium* and *Gmelina arborea,* respectively. Several earlier researchers also confirmed the present findings the nutrient concentration in plant parts varied from species to species and it was higher in leaves than stems or roots (Ashiq *et al.*, 2018; Ge *et al.*, 2015 and He *et al.*, 2015). Plant species differ in their sensitivity or tolerance to salts (Ramoliya and Pandey, 2006; Masilamani *et al.*, 2009, Tewari *et al.*, 2006). This may affect the rate of uptake of nutrients by the root system of the plants and thus the concentration of different nutrients varies in plant parts according to the species variation even if they were grown under similar environment and management practices.

Cassia siamea removed the highest quantity of nitrogen, phosphorus and potassium from the soil. This was mainly due to high biomass production by *Cassia siamea. Acacia auriculiformis* removed the lowest quantity of nutrients from the soil owing to low biomass production by this species. Stewart *et al.* (1990) observed that accumulation of nutrients differed significantly between species. Similar results were also reported by Myers *et al.* (1996), Salem *et al.* (2000), Sopper (2003), Giselda Durigan *et al.* (2012) and He *et al.* (2015).

Source of irrigation water had no influence on nutrient removal by plant leaves and roots; however, it had a significant effect on nutrient removal by stems. Application of irrigation with urban wastewater removed 24, 23 and 32% higher nitrogen, phosphorus and potassium, respectively by plant stems as compared to that of potable water. The whole plant removed 19, 18 and 20% higher nitrogen, phosphorus and potassium, respectively by providing irrigation with wastewater as compared to that of potable water.

According to Farooq *et al.* (2006) wastewater individually increases the concentration of N, P and K in plants as compared to tap water. The increase of N, P and K in plant parts might be attributed to an increase in the occupancy root zone by applying sewage effluents that reflected on their uptake by roots (Murage and Mwangi, 2012). The urban wastewater provided the soil with plant nutrients and organic matter and improved the soil physical characteristics that reflected on the growth by enhancing the cell elongation and division (Kaneker *et al.*, 1993). Thus the urban wastewater had a stimulatory effect on growth of trees and produced higher biomass as compared to potable water. Similar results were also reported by Rattan *et al.* (2005) and Salehi *et al.* (2008).

Soil Chemical Properties After 300 Days of Transplanting

Composite soil samples were taken at 360 days after transplanting of saplings from each treatment analysed in laboratory for *p*H, organic carbon content and available nitrogen, phosphorus and potassium contents and the results are presented in Table 8.16.

The soil *p*H at 360 days after transplanting of saplings remained almost the same as the initial value of 5.34 recorded before the start of experiment in case of irrigation by potable water; however the *p*H value at the end of experimentation increased to 5.35 in case of irrigation by urban waste water.

The organic carbon content in soil ranged between 0.73 to 0.79% for different tree species at 360 days after transplanting as against initial value of 0.72%. The soil organic carbon content at 360 days after transplanting of saplings remained almost unchanged in case of irrigation by potable water; however soil organic carbon content at the end of experimentation increased to 0.78% in case of irrigation by urban waste water, the increase being 8.3%.

Table 8.16: Effect of Urban Wastewater on Soil Chemical Properties After 300 Days of Transplanting

Treatment	*p*H	Organic carbon (%)	Available N	Available P	Available K
Tree species					
Acacia auriculiformis	5.50	0.73	222	22	194
Acacia mangium	5.39	0.75	205	25	185
Acacia nilotica	5.42	0.76	233	22	201
Gmelina arborea	5.40	0.79	227	25	184
Pongamia pinata	5.50	0.77	215	25	192
Cassia siamea	5.47	0.74	212	22	191
Source of irrigation water					
Potable water	5.35	0.73	208	21	184
Wastewater	5.54	0.78	230	26	199
Initial value	***5.34***	***0.72***	***203***	***20***	***180***

Irrespective of species the available nitrogen, phosphorus and potassium content in the soil increased at 360 days after transplanting of saplings as compared to initial values recorded before the start of experiment. Only a small increase over the initial values in available nutrients in soil was recorded in case of irrigation by potable water (3 kg N, 1 kg P and 4 kg K/ha). However, irrigation to the saplings by urban wastewater increased available nutrients in soil by 27 kg N, 6 kg P and 9 kg K/ha over the respective initial values of 203, 20 and 180 kg/ha before the start of experiment.

Conclusion

Irrigation by urban wastewater favourably influenced the shoot and root growth of the multipurpose tree species as compared to the irrigation by potable water. Thus, irrigation potential can be increased by using the wastewater to establish the urban forests that would maintain the ecological balance and improve environmental conditions by self-treatment of wastewater with additional benefits of easy and cheap disposal of wastewater and meeting the demand for timber and fuel.

REFERENCES

Abbaas, M. M. 2002. Effect of Some Heavy Metals in the Irrigation Water on Growth and Chemical Constituents of Some Timber Trees. *Ph. D. Thesis*, Faculty of Agriculture, University of Cairo, Cairo, Egypt.

Ali, H. M., EL-Mahrouk, E. M., Hassan, F. A. and EL-Tarawy, M. A. 2011. Usage of Sewage Effluent in Irrigation of Some Woody Tree Seedlings. Part 3: *Swietenia mahagoni* (L.) Jacq. *Saudi Journal of Biological Sciences* 18(2): 201–207.

Ali, H. M., Khamis, M. H. and Hassan, F. A. 2012. Growth, Chemical Composition and Soil Properties of *Tipuana speciosa* (Benth.) Kuntze Seedlings Irrigated with Sewage Effluent. *Applied Water Science* 2(2): 101–108.

Ali, Hayssam. 2013. Performance of Forest Tree *Khaya senegalensis* (Desr.) A. Juss. Under Sewage Effluent Irrigation. *Ecological Engineering* 61(2): 117–126.

Ashiq, M. W., Bazrgar, A. B., Fei, H., Coleman, B., Vessey, K., Gordon, A., Sidders, D. Keddy, T. and Thevathasan, N. 2018. A Nutrient-based Sustainability Assessment of Purpose Grown Poplar and Switchgrass Biomass Production Systems Established on Marginal Lands in Canada. *Canadian Journal of Plant Science* 98: 255–266.

Berbec, S., Szewczuk, C., Sugier, D. 1999. The Effect of Irrigation with Municipal Sewage on the Catching and Growth Rate of Poplar Trees. *Folia Universitatis Agricultural* 77: 37–31.

Bhati, M. and Singh, G. 2003. Growth and Mineral Accumulation in *Eucalyptus camaldulensis* Seedlings Irrigated with Mixed Industrial Effluents. *Bioresource Technology* 88(3) : 221–228.

Braatz, S. and Kandiah, A. 1996. The Use of Municipal Wastewater for Forest and Tree Irrigation. *Unasylva* 47(185): 45–51.

Braatz, S. and Kandiah, A. 2010. Effects of the Utilization of Municipal Raw Sewage and Treated Effluents for Irrigation, A Comparative Study at Kalpakkam (India). *Journal of Environmental Sciences* 4(1): 21–31.

Cooper, R. C. 1991. Public Health Concerns in Wastewater Reuse. *Water Science and Technology* 24(9): 55–65.

Das, D. C. and Kaul, R. N. 1992. Greening Wastelands Through Waste Water. National Wastelands Development Board, Govt. of India, New Delhi.

Farooq, H., Siddiqui, M. T., Farooq, M., Qadir, E. and Hussain, Z., 2006. Growth, Nutrient Homeostasis and Heavy Metal Accumulation in *Azadirachta indica* and *Dalbergia sisso* Seedlings Raised from Wastewater. *International Journal of Agriculture and Biology* **8**: 504–507.

Ge, X., Tian, Y. and Tang, L. 2015. Nutrient Distribution Indicated Whole-tree Harvesting as a Possible Factor Restricting the Sustainable Productivity of a Poplar Plantation System in China. *PLoS One* 10(5): 1–14.

Giselda Durigan, G., Melo, A. C. G. and Brewer, J. S. 2012. The Root to Shoot Ratio of Trees from Open- and Closed-Canopy Cerrado (The Brazilian Savanna) in South-Eastern Brazil. *Plant Ecology and Diversity* 1(1): 1–11.

Gogate, M. G., Farooqui, U. M. and Joshi, V. S. 1995. Sewage Water as Potential for the Tree Growth: A Study on Teak (*Tectona grandis*) Plantation. *Indian Forester* 121(6): 472–481.

Gomez, K. A. and Gomez, A. A. 1984. *Statistical Procedure for Agricultural Research*, 2nd Edition. John Wiley & Sons, New York.

Gupta, A. P., Narwal R. P., Antil, R. S. 1998. Sewer Water Composition and Its Effect on Soil Properties. *Bioresource Technology* 65: 171–173.

Hassan, F. A. 1996. Effect of Sewage Effluent Irrigation on Growth, Specific Gravity and Fiber Length of *Acacia saligna* and *Leucaena leucocephala* Seedlings. *Journal of Agricultural Science Mansoura University* 21(11): 4093–4099.

Hassan, F. A. 2011. Usage of Sewage Effluent in Irrigation of Some Woody Tree Seedlings. Part 3: *Swietenia mahagoni* (L.) Jacq. *Journal of Biological Sciences* 18: 201–207.

Hassan, F. A., EL-Juhany, L. I., EL-Settawy, A. A. and Shehata, M. S. 2002. Effects of Irrigation with Sewage Effluent on the Growth of Some Forest Trees Species, Physical and Chemical Properties of the Soil. In: Proceeding of the Second Conference on Sustainable Agricultural Development, 8–10 May, 2002, Fayoum. pp. 300–311.

He, M., Zhang, K., Tan, H., H., Rui, Su, J., Wang, J., Huang, L., Zhang, Y. and Li, X. 2015. Nutrient Levels within Leaves, Stems, and Roots of the Xeric Species *Reaumuria soongorica* in Relation to Geographical, Climatic, and Soil Conditions. *Ecology and Evolution* 5(7): 1494–1503.

Hopmans, P. 1990. Nutrient Accumulation in Trees and Soil Following Irrigation with Municipal Effluent in Australia. *Environmental Pollution* 63(2): 155–177.

Hopmans, P., Stewart, H. T. L., Flinn, D. W. and Hillman, T. J. 1990. Growth, Biomass Production and Nutrient Accumulation by Seven Tree Species Irrigated with Municipal Effluent at Wodonga, Australia. *Forest Ecology Management* 30: 203–211.

Idelovitch, E. and Michael, M. 1984. A New Approach to an Old Method of Waste Water Reuses. *Journal of Water Pollution Control Federation* 56: 93–100.

Jackson, M. L. 1973. Soil Chemical Analysis. Prentice hall Pvt. Ltd., New Delhi. 326–338.

Kanekar, P.1993. Evaluation of *Acacia nilotica* (L.) del. and *Casuarina equisetifolia* Forst. For Tolerance and Growth on Microbially Treated Dyestuff Wastewater. *Environmental Pollution* 81(1): 47–50.

Masilamani, P., Saravanapandiyan P. and Annadurai K. 2009. Effect of Soil Alkalinity and Organic Matter on Germination and Growth of Eucalyptus Tereticornis. *Madras Agricultural Journal* 96: 100–105.

Mathan, K. K. 1994. Studies on the Influence of Long-term Municipal Sewage-effluent Irrigation on Soil Physical Properties. *Bioresource Technology* 48(3): 275–276.

Murage, H. and Mwangi, J. 2012. Effects of Wastewater Irrigation on Nutrient Accumulation on Selected Plants in Juja. *African Journal of Horticultural Sciences* 6: 17–26.

Myers, B. J., Theiveyanath, S. O., Brian, N. O. and Bond, W. J. 1996. Growth and Water Use of *Eucalyptus grandis* and *Pinus radiate* Plantations Irrigated with Effluent. *Tree Physiology* 16: 211–219.

Omran, M., Waly, T. M., Abd Elmaim, E. M. and El Nashir, B. M. B. 1998. Effect of Sewage Irrigation on Yield, Tree Components and Heavy Metals Accumulation in Naval Orange Trees. *Biological wastes* 23: 17–24.

Paliwal, K., Kurunlchamy, K. S. T. K. and Ananthavalli, M. 1998. Effect of Sewage Water Irrigation on Growth Parameter Biomass and Nutrient Accumulation in *Hardwickia binata* Under Nursery Condition. *Bioresource Technology* 68: 105–110.

Ramoliya, P.J. and Pandey A.N., 2006. Effect of Salinization of Soil on Emergence, Growth and Survival of Albizzia Lebbek Seedlings. *Tropical Ecology* 47: 27–36.

Rattan, R. K., Datta, S. P., Chhonkar, P. K., Suribabu, K. and Singh, A. K. 2005. Long-term Impact of Irrigation with Waste Water Effluents on Heavy Metal Content in Soils, Crops and Groundwater – A Case Study. *Agriculture, Ecosystems and Environment* 109: 310–322.

Rose, D. A. 1983. The Description of the Growth of Root Systems. *Plant and Soil* 75(3): 405–415.

Salehi A., Tabari, M., Mohammadi, J. and Ali-Arab, A. R. 2008. Effect of Irrigation with Municipal Effluent on Soil and Growth of *pinus eldarica* Medw. Trees. *Iranian Journal of Forest and Poplar Research* 16: 186–196.

Salem, M. M., El-Amir, S., Abdel-Aziz, S. M., Kandil, M. F. and Mansour, S. F. 2000. Effect of Irrigation with Sewage Water on Some Chemical Characteristics of Soils and Plant. *Egyptian Journal of Soil Science* 40: 49–59.

Sebastiani, L., Scebba, F. and Tognetti, R. 2004. Heavy Metal Accumulation and Growth Responses in Poplar Clones Eridano (*Populus deltoides × maximowiczii*) and I-214 (*P. deltoides × euramericana*) Exposed to Industrial Waste. *Environmental and Experimental Botany* 52(1): 79–88.

Singh, G. and Bhati, M. 2003. Growth, Biomass Production and Nutrient Composition of *Eucalyptus* Seedlings Irrigated with Municipal Effluents in a Loamy Sand Soil of Indian Desert. *Journal of Plant Nutrition* 26(12): 2469–2488.

Singh, G. and Bhati, M. 2004. Soil and Plant Mineral Composition and Productivityof *Acacia nilotica* (L.) under Irrigation with Municipal Effluent in an Arid Environment. *Environmental Conservation* 31(4): 331–338.

Singh, G. and Bhati, M. 2005. Growth of *Dalbergia sissoo* in Desert Regions of Western India Using Municipal Effluent and the Subsequent Changes in Soil and Plant Chemistry. *Bioresource Technology* 96: 1019–1028.

Sopper, E. W. 2003. Disposal of Municipal Wastewater Through Forest Irrigation. *Environmental Pollution* **76**(4): 263–284.

Stewart, H. T. L, Hopmans, P. W., Flinn, D. W. and Hillman, T. J. 1990. Growth, Biomass Production and Nutrient Accumulation by Seven Tree Species Irrigated with Municipal Effluent at Wodonga, Australia. *Forest Ecology and Management* **30**: 203–211.

Stewart, H. T. L., Hopmanns, P. W., Flinn, D. W. and Hillman, T. J. 1990. Nutrient Accumulation in Trees and Soil Following Irrigation with Municipal Effluent in Australia. *Environmental Pollution* 63(2): 155–177.

Tewari, P., Saxena, A. K. and Rao, O. P. 2006. Effect of Sodicity and Salinity on Seedling Growth of Two Early Succession Agroforestry Tree Species. *Tropical Ecology* 47: 125–132.

Yudhistra Kumar, A. and Vikram Reddy, M. 2007. Effects of Municipal Sewage Irrigation on the Growth of Tomato Plants on Sandy Soils at Kalpakkam, Tamil Nadu, India. *Nature Environment and Pollution Technology* 6(4): 549–556.

Yudhistra Kumar, A. and Vikram Reddy, M. 2010. Effects of Municipal Sewage on the Growth Performance of *Casuarina Equisetifolia* (Forst. & Forst.) on Sandy Soil of East Coast at Kalpakkam, (Tamil Nadu, India). *Applied Ecology and Environmental Research* 8(1): 77–85.

Index

A

Agricultural users, 65
Alcohol, 97
Ancient techniques of water harvesting, 9
Anitha, G., 16, 63, 97
Arsenic, 1234-144
Asian Development Bank, 30
Atmospheric water, 5

B

Bharti, Pawan Kumar, 1, 91

C

Capillary Water, 23
Central Ground Water Board (CGWB), 51, 52
Check dams, 10
Concept of ground water movement, monitoring and modeling, 91-96
  concept of ground water modeling, 95
  darcy and linear velocity/flow velocity, 93
  Darcy's Law, 92, 93
  groundwater flow pattern, 92
  groundwater monitoring techniques, 95
  industrialization, 91
  introduction, 91
  movement of ground water, 91, 92
  retardation factor, 94
  Richards Equation, 93
  urbanization, 91
Conserving water, 3
Contamination of groundwater, 91
Crop Farming, 97-122

D

Darcy velocity, 93
Dead Sea in Israel, 21
Deforestation, 10
Demand for water, 6
Demand of fresh water, 91
Demands for Various Sectors, 7
Distilleries, 97, 98

E

Earth today, 1
Earth's population, 1
Esakkimuthu, M., 16, 63, 97

F

Field studies, 13
Fresh water resources, 63

G

Geo-chemical reactions, 92
Government of India, 83
Great Salt Lake in Utah, 21
Groundwater, 5, 38, 48, 91-96
  investigations, 39
  modeling, 95
  monitoring, 94, 95

H

Hartebeespoort Dam, 28
Harvesting rainwater, 10
Hydrogeological Setting and Status of Water Table in Bonai Area, 38-62
  alluvium, 42
  aquifer systems, 48
  Bonai Granite, 42
  borehole data of the study area, 45
  consolidated formations, 47
  Darjing Group, 41
    of rocks, 41, 43
  Deogarh Group, 42
  depth to water table map, 56
  fracture zone, 49
  geologic methods, 40
  hydrogeological units, 46

introduction, 38
iron ore group, 41, 42
laterite, 42
literature, 39
lithologs, 40
lithostratigraphy, 40
methodology, 40
pumping
saprolitic zone, 49
saturated fractures and yield vis-a-vis lithological unit, 50
short term water level trends, 59
status of water table, 56
structure, 42
subsurface geology, 43
sundargarh district, 39-62
unconsolidated formations, 48
vertical electrical sounding (ves), 40
water table
contour map, 58
fluctuation map, 57
weathered mantle, 48
well inventory data of the study area, 53-56
well yields, 51
Hydrological cycle, 19

I

Industry, 3
Irrigation by urban wastewater, 165

J

jellyfish, 2

K

Kar, Ranjan Kumar, 145

L

Lake Urmia, 26
Leakage and pilferage, 4
Low-energy precision application (LEPA), 4

M

Mishra, Ambraprava, 145
Molasses, 97

N

National River Link project, 80
National Water Policy (NWP), 80
Natural resources, 2

O

Oxygen atom, 18

P

Patra, Alok Kumar, 145
Pumping Tests, 51, 52

R

Rainwater, 49
Richards, L.A., 93
River Brahmani, 59
Umgeni, 28
Zayandeh, 26
Roy, Swapnila, 123

S

Sahu, Pramod Chandra, 38
Salinization, 3
Shaw, Ashok Kumar, 123
Storage of water by construction, 2
Sugar mills, 97
Surface water pollution, 91

T

Tests, 52
Thermodynamics, Kinetics Study and Statistical Approach of Arsenic Removal in Waste Water, 123-144.
activated carbon, 123-144
adsorption kinetics, 128
adsorption thermodynamics, 129
batch adsorption isotherm, 134
– – kinetics, 135
– experiment, 128
boehm titration, 130
characterisationof activated carbon (saw dust), 130
conformational study, 140
determination of

ash content, 127
bulk density, 126
moisture content, 126
optimum contact time, 131
– dosage of adsorbent, 131
optimum ph, 131
pH, 127
dissolution of minerals, 124
effect of
adsorbent dose, 131
contact time, 132
pH, 133
variation in adsorbent dose and
contact time, 140
pH, 138
– – pH and contact time, 139
estimation of response surface for maximum arsenic removal, 137
experimental set up, 127
freundlich isotherm, 128
introduction, 124
Langmuir adsorption model, 142
Langmuir isotherm, 128
materials, 125
objective of the study, 125
physicochemical analysis, 126
– properties of adsorbents, 125
porosity determination, 126
preparation of adsorbents, 125
– – synthetic arsenic solution, 127
pseudo first order kinetics, 128
– second order kinetics, 129
regeneration study, 141
response surface methodology for optimization of adsorption parameters, 136
thermodynamic parameters, 142
– and kinetics study, 133-134
yield of carbon, 126
Third World war, 68
Total quantity of water, 6

U

Uncombined water, 22
United Nations Human Development Report, 16
Urban Wastewater and Development of Multipurpose Tree Species, 145-168
characteristics of urban wastewater, 150
experimental details and methodology, 147-150
growth parameters, 151
biomass production, 155-157
branches/plant, 152-153
collar diameter, 153-154
crown spread, 154
plant height, 151-152
root
shoot ratio, 157
– growth, 154
Instructional Farm, Barmunda, 147
introduction, 146-147
nutrient concentration and uptake by plants, 158
nitrogen, 158
phosphorus, 159
potassium, 161
soil physical and chemical properties of experimental site, 148
Utilization of Treated Water Effluent for Crop Farming, 97-122
application of TDE through fertigation, 100
available Nitrogen, 105
– Phosphorus, 106
Potassium, 106
biomethanated spent wash, 99
characteristics of raw spent wash, 98
crops farming, 110-111
millets, 111
pulses, 111
sugarcane, 110
sweet sorghum, 111
effect of TDE on
growth of rice and other crop, 109
soil properties, 101

effect on biological properties of soil, 108
physico-chemical Properties, 103
soil fertility, 104
electrical conductivity, 104
general characteristics and composition of TDE, 99
introduction, 97
methods of application, 100
micronutrients, 107
organic carbon, 105
physical properties of soil, 102
pre-plant application of treated distillery effluent, 100
rice growth with graded doses of NPK application, 111-112
secondary nutrients, 107
soil pH, 103

V

Vaal River Barrage, 28
Vrahat Sanhita, 2

W

Water conservation, 2
Water Crisis Management and Policy Interventions, 16-37
atmospheric water, 21
Australia, 28-29
biological classification of soil water, 24
available water, 24
field capacity, 24
hygroscopic coefficient, 24
moisture equivalent, 24
permanent wilting percentage, 24
superfluous water, 24
unavailable water, 24
capillary water, 23
change your daily habit, 34
China, 32
condensation, 20
distribution of fresh water, 19
ecological classification of soil water, 23
Egypt, 26-27
Ethiopia, 27
evaporation, 20
field capacity, 23
gravitational water, 23
groundwater, 21
how to conserve water, 34
hydrological cycle, 19
hygroscopic water, 23
importance of water, 19
India, 32
introduction, 16-17
Iran, 26
key policy interventions needed, 33
Morocco, 31
Niger, 29
Pakistan, 30
precipitation, 20
runoff, 21
soil water, 22
classification for water management, 22
reservoirs, 25
sources of water, 21
South Africa, 28
stored water, 21
structure and chemical formula of water, 17
surface water, 21
transpiration, 20
Turkmenistan, 30
Valuable Resource, 17
Water Availability in the World, 25
World Over Water Crisis Takes Many Shap, 25
Water crisis, 26
Water Effluent for Crop Farming, 97-122
Water of river, well, pond, 2
Water resources on earth, 1-15
distribution of water, 4
drip irrigation, 3

global supply and demand for water, 11
access to water, 11
total water demand, 11
– – supply, 11
initiatives, 1
interlinking of rivers, 14
negative impacts of river linking
possible solutions, 12
rivers, 8, 9, 10, 11
root zone of crops, 3
strategies, 2
water crisis of dimensions, 9
– demand & crisis, 6
– on earth, 1-4
– requirement for various sectors, 7-11
– scarcity, 1
Water Scarcity in Agriculture, 63-90
agricultural users, 65
alarming facts, 65-66
augmentation of water resources, 81
bangladesh city, 69
causes of water shortage, 63
challenges in water sector, 78
changes proposed in the national water policy, 80
agriculture sector, 80
domestic sector, 81
industrial sector, 81
control of water pollution, 83
current water usage, 74
desalination of sea water, 83
development of wastelands, 87
distribution of earth's water, 64
drivers of water usage, 78
efficient irrigation practices, 82-83
future water usage, 74
global water crisis, 72-73
groundwater pollution, 77
impact of watershed development, 85-86
increasing water storage capacity, 81-82
indian facts, 66-67
introduction, 63
livestock development, 87
national water policy (nwp), 80
over growth of population, 64
per capita water use, 73
present water availability, 67
priority areas for action, 84
river pollution, 76
sewage and industrial pollution, 77
success stories, 85
tree-based farming system, 86
water crisis, 72
– resources in india, 75
– scarcity and agriculture, 70
agricultural crisis, 71
environmental crisis, 71
increase in tensions, 71
rainfed agriculture, 70
water resources are becoming scarce, 71
– scarcity in agriculture, 84
– use efficiency in agriculture, 79
watershed development, 83
when plants most need water?, 67
world war for the water, 67
Water scarcity, 67
Water withdrawn from rivers, lakes and underground aquifers, 3
Waterlogging, 3
Water-saving farming techniques, 168
Watershed management, 9, 10
weathered residuum, 48
World Bank, 4
World Health Organization, 12, 13
World's available freshwater supply, 7

Z

Zurich, 13